D0919655

Library
The Missionary Training
Institute

MARK 16:15
MTI

Presented by

Christopherson
Memorial Fund
1961

THE LIBRARY OF HISTORY AND DOCTRINE

THE IMITATION OF GOD
IN CHRIST

THE LIBRARY OF HISTORY AND DOCTRINE

The aim of this international Library is to enable scholars to answer questions about the development of the Christian tradition which are important for an understanding of Christianity today

Editorial Committee

S. L. GREENSLADE, Regius Professor of Ecclesiastical History, Oxford (*Chairman*)
OWEN CHADWICK, Dixie Professor of Ecclesiastical History, Cambridge
G. W. H. LAMPE, Ely Professor of Divinity, Cambridge
JOHN T. MCNEILL, Auburn Professor Emeritus of Church History,
Union Theological Seminary, New York
Bishop STEPHEN NEILL, Editor of World Christian Books, Geneva
E. GORDON RUPP, Professor of Ecclesiastical History, Manchester
T. F. TORRANCE, Professor of Christian Dogmatics, Edinburgh

THE
IMITATION OF GOD
IN CHRIST

An Essay on the Biblical Basis
of Christian Spirituality

E. J. TINSLEY

Philadelphia
The Westminster Press

248.4
T49

29189

Library of Congress Catalog Card No. 60-11146

© SCM PRESS LTD 1960
PRINTED IN GREAT BRITAIN

CONTENTS

PREFACE

MODERN TRENDS in New Testament studies have been generally sceptical about the possibility of constructing a 'Life of Jesus' or analysing what used to be called the 'Messianic consciousness' of Jesus. The consequences of this for Christian ethics and spirituality have not always been made clear. The Christian religion is not centred on the Incarnation of the eternal Son of God in Jesus of Nazareth only as a unique historical event. For the believer the life and activity of the incarnate Lord Christ has paradigmatic significance both as to its form and content. Hence radical uncertainty about the pattern of the mission of Jesus tends to release Christian ethics from its traditional and distinctive control, the ideal of the imitation of Christ, and increasingly to blur the difference between Christian spirituality and an amorphous sense of 'spiritual values'. The place of the historical Christ in the life of the Christian is a subject where the sensitive interrelationship between critical study and piety can be most closely examined. This book is written to explore the possibility that the idea of the imitation of Christ not only exercised a powerful control on the formation of the primitive tradition about Jesus, but also had a firm basis in the mind and purpose of Jesus himself. This is a preliminary volume concerned with the biblical basis of the idea of the imitation of Christ, and is primarily an attempt to indicate the role which the historical revelation in Israel and in Christ play in the life of the Christian according to the New Testament. Since it is the imitation of Christ which has always been the distinguishing characteristic of Christian ethics, spirituality and worship, I intend in a forthcoming volume to study the practice and interpretation of this ideal in the patristic, medieval, Reformation and modern periods, and to draw some conclusions as to its significance for Christian doctrine, devotion, and evangelism.

Biblical quotations are taken from the Revised Standard Version in the majority of cases, but I have sometimes used the Revised Version or made my own translation to bring out more clearly the point I wished to make.

At an early stage in the planning of this book I was greatly encouraged and assisted by the late Professor William Manson. Professor S. H. Hooke gave me valuable help when I began work on the Old Testament section, and Professor Alan Richardson kindly read the whole of the book in typescript and made some useful suggestions. Throughout I have been fortunate to have the help and advice of my colleague the Reverend Patrick Thompson, and I wish to thank him and the Reverend William Richardson for reading and commenting on the typescript.

To my wife, Marjorie, I owe more than I can say, but I make this formal acknowledgment, hopelessly inadequate as it must be.

Department of Theology   E. J. TINSLEY
University of Hull

ABBREVIATIONS

ET	English translation
ExpT	*Expository Times*
JTS	*Journal of Theological Studies*
n.s.	new series
PG	Migne, *Patrologia Graeca*
PL	Migne, *Patrologia Latina*
SBT	Studies in Biblical Theology
ST	*Studia Theologica*, Lund
TWNT	*Theologisches Wörterbuch zum Neuen Testament*, ed. G. Kittel, Stuttgart, 1933 ff.

A person is a unity of a spiritual nature endowed with freedom of choice and so forming a whole which is independent of the world, for neither nature nor the State may invade this unity without permission. God Himself, who is and who acts from within, acts there in a particular way and with a supremely exquisite delicacy, a delicacy which shows the value He sets on it: He respects this freedom, in the heart of which nevertheless He lives; He solicits it, but He never compels.

Jacques Maritain, *True Humanism*

Another thing is that I am obsessed by the problem of mimicry, of mimesis—the outward adaptation of an organism to the colour of its environment. I think it throws an astonishing light on the relationship between the inward and outward world.

Boris Pasternak, *Dr Zhivago*

INTRODUCTION

The Form of the Christian Life

I

History, Mysticism and Biblical Spirituality

CHRISTIAN SPIRITUALITY has been, for some time now, a subject largely neglected by the professional theologian outside the Roman and Orthodox traditions. It is true that the Anglican Church has had a rich and worthy past in this field,[1] and there have been flowering periods in the history of the Free Churches, but on the whole the general attitude amongst the non-Roman Churches has been suspicious or hesitant, and this has led either to the complete neglect of the subject, or, through a lack of confidence, to an uncritical assimilation of Latin thought and practice.

There are a number of reasons for this attitude. In traditional Roman dogmatics Christian spirituality is divided into Ascetical and Mystical Theology. Many theologians of the Reformed traditions have feared that in Ascetical Theology there lies concealed a 'doctrine of works', and this fear, together with the suspicion that Mystical Theology inevitably leads, among other things, to a depreciation of ethics has been a powerful factor in the decline of the subject.

On the other hand, the nature of the spiritual life and the practice of prayer and meditation are occupying the attention of many who are not confessing Christians. The writings of Aldous Huxley and others[2] have revived an interest in mysticism, especially amongst intellectuals, and this makes the subject of Christian spirituality of special contemporary importance. The increasing vogue of Zen Buddhism in the United States may well be part of a reaction against a Christianity which in its excessive concern with moralistic edification has neglected the spiritual exercises of prayer and meditation.

It is important in this situation to try to make clear the unique and

---

[1] Cf. H. R. McAdoo, *The Structure of Caroline Moral Theology*, 1949, or Louis L. Martz, *The Poetry of Meditation*, 1954.
[2] Aldous Huxley, *The Perennial Philosophy*, 1946; Christopher Isherwood (ed.), *Vedanta for the Western World*, 1948.

distinctive features of Christian spirituality and ethics, especially since, externally, there is bound to be some overlapping between the morality of the Christian and the devout humanist. If the unique feature of the Christian religion is its indissoluble link with a series of historical events, it is natural to look for the distinctive characteristic of Christian ethics and piety in the relationship which they have to those events. To what extent is the historical revelation in the history of Israel and of Jesus determinative of the pattern of the Christian life both of the individual believer and of the Church? This question can best be studied in the context of the discussion as to whether a truly Christian mysticism is a possibility, because it is in mysticism that one finds most acutely focused the problem of the relation between historical events and spirituality.

MYSTICISM AND THE CHRISTIAN LIFE

For some men mysticism is the very essence of all true religion; for others it is its most dangerous aberration, if not downright blasphemy. There are Christian thinkers who suspect that in an antipathy to mysticism there lies a propensity to treat Christianity as a moralism. On the other hand, an attraction to mysticism is supposed to be the mark of those who sit loosely to the central affirmations of the Faith. It will therefore be useful at this point to give a brief outline of the traditional case against mysticism, as it will be found, for example, in the writings of Friedrich Heiler, Emil Brunner, and Reinhold Niebuhr.

1. There is the charge that mysticism is fundamentally disguised 'yoga': that it is a series of spiritual exercises whereby certain heightened states of consciousness are attained, these heightened states of awareness constituting true religious experience. Mysticism is a 'way', 'a continuous upward movement which leads finally to the goal which is God himself'.[1] In other words it is being asserted here that mysticism involves a denial of the doctrine of grace. This is one of the charges brought by Nygren in his *Agape and Eros*:

> Mysticism in the proper sense always belongs definitely to the Eros tradition; for mysticism is essentially an individualistic way by which the soul attains to salvation through an ascent to the divine. . . . Though we have to reckon here with important influence, at certain points, from the idea of Agape, the fact remains that both religious mysticism and philosophical idealism have their root ultimately in the idea of Eros.[2]

[1] E. Brunner, *The Mediator*, ET 1934, p. 126.
[2] *Op. cit.*, revised English edition, 1953, pp. 220 f.

This position is also taken by Friedrich Heiler:

> Mysticism shows a conscious intention; only in this way does it succeed in mortifying the natural and volitional life. It has devised refined methods of asceticism and meditation in order to induce or to facilitate the occurrences of mystical states.[1]

Emil Brunner makes the same point more starkly:

> [All types of mysticism] are forms of . . . assertion of the self over against God, assertions of an ultimate innermost possibility of self-defence, forms of self-assurance; the assertion that at least in the innermost depths of human personality continuity between God and man does exist . . . If grace is mentioned at all (in mysticism) it is grace which has been attained by man, grace which can infallibly be attained by following 'the way' of mystical practice; it is grace in which forgiveness plays no part, the *gratia infusa*, not the gracious word of mercy and pardon.[2]

2. A second and very frequent charge brought against mysticism is that it interprets sin negatively as lack of perfection or knowledge, or identifies it with man's finitude. Consequently, we are told, the mystics tend to by-pass the Christian doctrine of redemption, and to substitute a doctrine of enlightenment. Brunner, for example, cannot rid himself of the suspicion that all mysticism is 'gnostic' in its interpretation of sin:

> It would be going too far to say that the mystic absolutely denied the existence of evil. It is true that there are forms of mysticism where this happens quite obviously, where the moral struggle has been renounced both in theory and in practice, but such an attitude does not belong to the essence of mysticism. Mysticism admits the preliminary contradiction between God and the world of sense, between the state of union with God and that of being enmeshed in the toils of this earthly existence. At least it asserts that it does know this. But in its fundamental conception it denies it: the fact that the relation between man and God is continuous excludes it; 'at bottom' man is divine, indeed he is one with God. Thus here there is no real contradiction; here also is the conception that evil simply means that man is undeveloped. Here also evil simply means to be entangled in the things of sense, to be tied to the creature, to images, to illusions, to the 'surface of existence', but it is not opposition to the will of God; it simply means that man stands outside the sphere ruled by the will of God. The belief of the mystic is based upon the fact that ultimately the problem of evil is not taken seriously. Since evil is only 'superficiality', it is possible, by sinking down into the depths of one's being, to reach the divine Reality, and thus to become one with God.[3]

[1] *Prayer*, ET 1932, p. 145.   [2] *The Mediator*, pp. 230, 292 f.
[3] *Ibid.*, pp. 125 f.

This inadequate conception of sin, the critic of mysticism continues, leads necessarily to a drastic reinterpretation of the doctrine of redemption, because this is now not a decisive act of God in history but a process of liberation whereby a man learns to free himself from finitude and attachment to the senses. To quote Heiler again:

> Mysticism seeks salvation in liberation from the world and creaturely existence, from all 'non-being', and would in this way come to the only true being. Man should deny being and thus cast aside the veils of mortality and remove the difference between finite and infinite. Thus he becomes one with the Divine.[1]

3. One of the constants in the charge against mysticism is that it depends upon and fosters unrestrained emotionalism. Renan describes the mystic as '*roulant d'extase à extase*'. This is the root of the criticism of Herrmann in his *The Communion of the Christian with God*:

> The essence of mysticism lies herein: that its religious life exhausts itself in that long series of experiences just described. The influence of God upon the soul is sought and found solely in an inward experience of the individual, that is in an excitement of the emotions taken, with no further question, as evidence that the soul is possessed by God.[2]

4. Mysticism is further criticized for its loose hold on the meaning and implications of the Incarnation. In the mystical tradition, we are told, the Incarnation is of importance only for beginners in religion; the proficient will grow beyond the need for such a particular 'image'. So, for example, Herrmann: 'The mystic leaves Christ and Christ's kingdom altogether behind him when he enters that sphere of experience which seems to him to be the highest.'[3] This attitude arises, Herrmann goes on, from the mystic's denial of the relevance of the historical. This is an instance of the general suspicion that mysticism in all its forms is incompatible with biblical theology and religion and indisputably with the Old Testament. Since for the mystic history is not a realm of meaning, the Incarnation which took place in it cannot be of ultimate importance. Mysticism is in fact 'a piety which feels that which is historical in positive religions to be burdensome, and so rejects it'.[4] This is true for Heiler also:

> The static God with whom the mystic in his ecstasy becomes wholly one is outside time and space, without any vital relation to the world and history. The idea of a revelation of God in history is quite foreign to mysticism; it is a purely super-historical religion.[5]

---

[1] *Prayer*, p. 155.
[2] W. Herrmann, *The Communion of the Christian with God*, ET 1906, p. 23.
[3] *Ibid.*, p. 23.   [4] *Ibid.*, p. 27.   [5] *Prayer*, p. 149.

Under this heading also would come the suspicion that mysticism does not really accept the notion of personality in God, or regards this as an elementary crudity which must be outgrown.

5. Mysticism is regarded by many as, to use the phrase of Schweitzer, 'world- and life-denying'; it is passive, quietist, subjective, esoteric and anti-social. Heiler in fact defines mysticism as 'that form of intercourse with God in which the world and self are absolutely denied, in which human personality is dissolved, disappears and is absorbed in the infinite unity of Godhead';[1] and he continues:

> Thorough-going mysticism is indifferent to all values of civilized life; it can live only in isolation from civilised activities and occupations. It does not tolerate contact with the world and matter; like moral action, work is, for it, simply ascetic discipline . . . Therefore all great mystics preach contempt of the world and flight from it.[2]

6. Next there is the feeling with some critics that mysticism is incompatible with traditional Christian eschatology; that it is 'realized eschatology' realized absolutely; that it identifies the consummated union with God which is the destiny of the believer with the 'mystical experience' in this human life. Furthermore, and this is perhaps the criticism of mysticism most frequently made, it is not compatible with the Christian belief in the resurrection of the body, if we mean by this that the life after death is fully personal communion with God in its perfection. The mystics use language which suggests that they think of eternal life not in terms of a truly personal relationship, but as an 'absorption' into ultimate Being in a completely depersonalized way.

7. Lastly, and this is a point to which Heiler gives special attention, mysticism is seriously defective in its conception of the nature and practice of prayer. Prayer is regarded, says Heiler, only as a means to an end, which is union with God. There is no place here for the I-Thou relationship which is essential to Christian prayer. In mysticism, Heiler asserts, 'Prayer is only a silent, emotionless sinking into the immeasurable flood of the One, the Divine.'[3] Mystical prayer is concerned only with meditation and contemplation (ecstasy), and it neglects the elements of petition (especially for forgiveness of sins) and intercession.

These are some of the main heads in the indictment of mysticism. There are many more. Heiler has in fact set out these charges against mysticism on one side, and on the other he puts the characteristics of what he calls 'prophetical piety', and this is done in such a neat point-for-point way as

---

[1] *Ibid.*, p. 136. [2] *Ibid.*, p. 165. [3] *Ibid.*, p. 175.

B

to suggest that 'prophetical piety' is on every issue what 'mystical piety' ought to be, but is not. 'Prophetical piety' is based on a doctrine of grace, is thoroughly biblical in its conception of sin and redemption, sets little store by the emotions, is firmly grounded in the Incarnation and the historical revelation, is world- and life-affirming, is male and active (in contrast with mysticism which is female and passive!), is thoroughly social, ethical, and practises petitionary prayer—and so on. Heiler's attempt to codify in this way 'prophetical' and 'mystical' piety is an oversimplification of a very complex matter. I do not propose to take all these heads and try and prove from the mystics themselves that the charges are all mistaken, but it is not at all self-evident that these two types of spirituality are as absolutely incompatible as Heiler would have us believe.

The traditional argument against mysticism ignores, for example, the stress in the mature mystics on the necessity of grace. Julian of Norwich, an undoubted mystic, can write as follows of the 'homeliness' of God's dealings with man:

> This marvellous homeliness may no man fully see in this time of life, save he have it of special shewing of our Lord, or of great plenty of grace inwardly given of the Holy Ghost . . . The continual seeking of the soul pleaseth God full greatly: for it may do no more than seek, suffer and trust. And this is wrought in the soul that hath it, by the Holy Ghost; and the clearness of finding is of His special grace, when it is His will.[1]

Or one could take these words of Paul Tillich which make the same point:

> Classical mysticism denies the possibility of self-salvation at the last stage of ecstasy. In spite of all the preparations, the ecstatic reunion with the ultimate cannot be forced when this point has been reached. It must be given, yet might not be given at all. This decisive limit to the self-saving methods of mysticism should curb the often very summary and unrefined criticism of the great mystics by Protestant theologians, Ritschlian as well as neo-orthodox.[2]

What we have in the writing of the mystics is a *retrospective* analysis of their life of prayer, closely akin as a mental process to the 'emotion recollected in tranquillity' which Wordsworth and others have believed lies behind the writing of poetry. This is certainly what many of the mystics think (and say) is happening. In the preface to her *Life* St Teresa states her purpose in writing as 'to write about my way of prayer and the favours which God has granted me'. Suso says in the preface to his *Little Book*

---

[1] *Revelations of Divine Love* (ed. G. Warrack, 1901), pp. 17, 24.
[2] *Systematic Theology*, Vol. II, 1957, p. 97.

of Eternal Wisdom that he is writing a 'form of instruction . . . for devotional prayers'. St Teresa, again, in the preface to the *Interior Castle* says that she wishes 'to write something on the subject of prayer . . . to enlighten them on certain doubtful matters of prayer'.

Nor can we sustain the argument that in all mysticism there is necessarily an inadequate doctrine of sin and redemption. This is not true even of such suspect mystics as Suso and Jacob Boehme. In the *Little Book of Eternal Wisdom* Suso speaks of 'meditating on the lovable sufferings [of our Lord] on which all salvation rests',[1] or again:

> Thou hast by thy wounds and pangs conciliated and healed the breach which all creatures together could not amend.[2]
> [The Lord speaks:] Then with cheerfulness the believer should consider the infinite goodness of my Atonement, for the least little drop of my precious blood, which flowed on all hands copiously from my loving body, could atone for the sins of a thousand worlds; and yet every man receives satisfaction for his sins in the same measure as he resembles me in his imitation of my passion.[3]

This is not the kind of language which suggests a belittling of the redemptive death of the Lord Christ, nor is this from Julian of Norwich:

> We know in our Faith, and believe by the teaching and preaching of Holy Church, that the blessed Trinity made mankind to His image and to His likeness. In the same manner-wise we know that when man fell so deep and so wretchedly by sin, there was none other help to restore man but through Him that made man. And He that made man for love, by the same love He would restore man to the same bliss, and overpassing; and like as we were like-made to the Trinity in our first making, our Maker would that we should be like Jesus Christ, Our Saviour, in heaven without end, by the virtue of our again-making.[4]

Furthermore, I cannot think it possible to maintain the charge of 'unrestrained emotionalism' against mysticism after, say, a reading of St John of the Cross. The word 'arid' would come first to the mind here, rather than 'emotional'. And is this charge true of Meister Eckhart, *The Cloud of Unknowing*, or Walter Hilton?

Equally indefensible is the assertion that in mysticism there is bound to be a loose hold on the Incarnation. Two passages, out of very many, must suffice here:

> *The Servant :* But, Lord, there is a great wonder in my heart. Beloved Lord, I seek thy Divinity everywhere, but thou dost only reveal thy humanity. I seek thy sweetness, thou dost put forward thy bitterness . . .

[1] *Little Book of Eternal Wisdom* (ed. James M. Clark, 1953), p. 43.
[2] *Ibid.*, p. 62.   [3] *Ibid.*, p. 104.   [4] *Revelations of Divine Love*, p. 23.

Eternal Wisdom: No one can attain to divine heights or to unusual sweetness, unless he be first drawn through the example of my human bitterness. The higher one climbs without passing through my humanity, the deeper one falls. My humanity is the way by which one must go, my sufferings are the gate through which one must pass, if one would attain what thou seekest.[1]

Then had I a proffer in my reason, as if it had been friendly said to me: Look up to Heaven to His Father. And then saw I well, with the faith that I felt, that there was nothing betwixt the Cross and Heaven that might have harmed me. Either me behoved to look up or else to answer. I answered inwardly with all the might of my soul, and said: Nay; I may not: for thou art my Heaven. This I said for that I would not. For I would liever have been in that pain till Doomsday than to come to Heaven otherwise than by Him. For I wist well that He that bound me so sore, He should unbind me when that He would. Thus was I learned to choose Jesus to my Heaven, whom I saw only in pain at that time: meliked no other Heaven than Jesus, which shall be my bliss when I come there.[2]

It is my belief, which I hope to substantiate in a later book, that the mysticism which is distinctively and uniquely Christian is always firmly grounded in the doctrines of the Incarnation and Atonement, and is thereby safeguarded from deviating into mysticism of a neo-Platonic kind. The essential feature of such a Christian mysticism is the conception of the Christian life as the imitation of Christ.

The traditional Protestant polemic against mysticism springs from an arbitrary definition of it. That given by Heiler is typical:

Mysticism is that form of intercourse with God in which the world and self are absolutely denied, in which human personality is dissolved, disappears and is absorbed in the infinite unity of the Godhead.[3]

If this definition of mysticism is accepted, then it is clearly incompatible with Christianity. But a good deal of confusion has arisen from taking the lyrical phrases of some of the mystics about being 'lost in God' as literal metaphysical statements. Mystics are of poetic temperament and use words poetically. Consequently it is misleading to erect a metaphysics on the basis of the poetic metaphorical language of the mystics, just as no one would think of erecting a logical scheme on phrases about being 'lost in a book', 'absorbed in a book' or 'forgetting oneself'. It might make for clarification if there were a return to the early patristic use of μυστικός, where the primary reference is either to the Scriptures or the Sacraments. To this we must now turn.

---

[1] *Little Book of Eternal Wisdom*, pp. 51 f.
[2] *Revelations of Divine Love*, p. 42.   [3] *Prayer*, p. 136.

MYSTICISM AS MYSTERY

Mysticism is now generally taken to mean a particular kind of 'spiritual' experience, an intense awareness of the Being of God which may be accompanied by all kinds of extraordinary phenomena. This may be so now, but mysticism has not always meant this, and in any case the mystics themselves have stressed again and again that the experiences and their accompaniments are not of central importance, are to be treated with great reserve and caution, and are certainly not to be induced or clung to. Recent patristic studies, particularly those of Père Bouyer,[1] have opened up a new approach which makes the issues involved much clearer.

Bouyer starts from the fact that μυστικός and μυστήριον are etymologically associated and inquires into the relation between mystery and mysticism in the Bible and early Christian usage. In the Bible itself 'mystery' is used for two things: (*a*) the 'plan' of God, his eternal purpose in history and sovereignty over it because hidden in his secret counsel; (*b*) the means or process by which (*a*) is in part made known, the medium of the revelation, the 'sign'. St Paul speaks of Christ as the mystery of God, meaning not only that he is (*b*), the means by which the secret of God has become an 'open' one but that he *is* what he reveals (*a*). He is that special kind of symbol which is designated 'sign'. 'God was in Christ . . .' Mystery is at one and the same time 'sign' and reality; in 'mystery' the sign and what is signified constitute one reality. Mystery is simultaneously the human sign and the divine reality which it reveals and bestows. The 'sign' and that which it signifies must be taken together in faith. Without faith the mystery is opaque; it is nothing more than a human reality. The attitude which the mystery demands includes reverence, concentration, worship, imaginative and not primarily intellectual curiosity.

The 'mystic' is technically one who is initiated into the mysteries; mysticism is that which concerns the mysteries. Fr Plé defines 'mysticism' as an 'experience which comes to us through mystery'.[2] In this sense, mysticism means taking the 'mystery', the 'sign', with the profoundest seriousness, the perception of a veiled reality, a piercing the divine incognito. In Christian tradition it means taking the visible, the historical, the incarnate, as sacramental and not a '*skandalon*'.

This mysticism would seem to me to be alone compatible with the divine pedagogy revealed in the mission of Jesus. Mysticism as mystery

---

[1] In *Mystery and Mysticism*, a symposium, ET 1956, pp. 18 ff. and 119 ff.
[2] In *Mystery and Mysticism*, p. 12.

would rule out all those mysticisms which seek to deny or ignore the created, the historical, and the visible. 'Since God has chosen to make use of intermediaries,' says Fr Plé, 'which can be perceived by our senses, that is, mysteries, in order to make himself manifest, how can we pretend to find any other means of access to the Inaccessible ?'[1] This is a mysticism which accepts and acts upon the implications and consequences of the Christian doctrines of Creation, Incarnation and Redemption and sees that 'it is folly to attempt the finding or the making of any shorter way to God than that of the closest contact with His own condescensions'.[2]

There is a distinctive Christian mysticism clearly differentiated from what may be called 'natural mysticism'. 'Christian mysticism proceeds from revealed mysteries, that is the specification that clearly differentiates it from natural mysticism.'[3] One could say, in fact, that Christian mysticism provides the meditative prayer of revealed religion, and 'natural' mysticism that of natural religion.

The real home of this Christian mysticism is, as Père Bouyer has shown, the Bible and the Liturgy. In the early Church μυστικός is used in two main contexts: the Bible and the Sacraments. The 'mystical' sense of Scripture shows how much more there is to it than meets the literal (or historical) eye. To discern the mystical meaning of Scripture means perceiving the nature of the fulfilment which there is in Christ. In the Eucharist the mystical meaning to be discerned is that the sign and the things signified are to be taken together as one reality. The mystical nature of worship is an insight which has been characteristic of the Orthodox Church more perhaps than of the Church in the West. The Orthodox have never lost hold of the fact that in the Liturgy time past and time future are realized in time present. This is what Bulgakov calls the 'religious realism' of the Orthodox Church. The Orthodox Liturgy, he writes, 'is not only the commemoration, in artistic forms, of evangelical or other events concerning the Church. It is also the actualization of these facts, their re-enactment on the earth.'[4]

Mysticism as mystery stresses the profound significance of the particular. There is no 'scandal of particularity' in mysticism of this kind. The particular place has sacramental significance, and past, present and future are experienced in a manner more nearly simultaneous than successive. This kind of mysticism has perhaps never been more satisfactorily articu-

---

[1] *Ibid.*, p. 13.
[2] F. von Hügel, *The Mystical Element of Religion*[2], 1923, Vol. II, p. 266.
[3] A. Plé in *Mystery and Mysticism*, p. 17.
[4] S. Bulgakov, *The Orthodox Church*, ET 1935, p. 150.

lated than in T. S. Eliot's *Four Quartets*. In 'Little Gidding' particularly he is concerned with the sacramental significance of place and time:

> . . . A people without history
> Is not redeemed from time, for history is a pattern
> Of timeless moments. So, while the light fails
> On a winter's afternoon, in a secluded chapel
> History is now and England.
>
> Here the intersection of the timeless moment
> Is England and nowhere. Never and always.[1]

This acute awareness of the transcendence of the successive within temporality and of the sacramental significance of time is a feature of mysticism. There is nothing unbiblical about it. As will be pointed out later, the Hebrews were not concerned with time and history as merely successive. They were concerned with the past only in so far as it could be experienced as a present reality, and this they believed to be possible in worship and personal relationships. Again, in the New Testament the basic tenses 'Christ was', 'Christ is', 'Christ is to come' are certainly there, but blended in the experience of present Christian existence.

The following pages are written in the conviction that Christian spirituality can contain within itself a genuine mysticism which enhances rather than weakens its attachment to a particular historical revelation, and that this mysticism is centred on the idea of the imitation of Christ. Unfortunately the phrase 'imitation of Christ' has several limitations. To many it will suggest first Thomas à Kempis' great work, and there would be misgivings about accepting that as a completely satisfactory reflection of New Testament spirituality. For others the word 'imitation' implies something spurious or artificial, and the 'imitation of Christ' would suggest a manner of life which lacked spontaneity or creativeness. Or it might suggest some endeavour after a literal mimicry of Christ. German scholars have shown themselves specially hesitant about the use of the term 'imitation of Christ'. They have distinguished between the 'following of Christ' (*Nachfolge Christi*), which they hold has a basis in the New Testament, and the 'imitation of Christ' (*imitatio Christi*), which they believe has not.[2] Bosse suggests, for instance, that the 'imitation of Christ' so stresses the '*Christus vor uns*' as to neglect the '*Christus für uns*' upon which it alone depends for its possibility. This insistence that the imitation

---

[1] *Four Quartets*, Faber and Faber, 1944, pp. 43, 37.
[2] Cf. F. Bosse, *Prolegomena zu einer Geschichte des Begriffes 'Nachfolge Christi'*, Berlin, 1895.

of Christ is alone possible because of the prevenient redeeming work of Christ is, as we shall see, one of the main features of the New Testament teaching on the subject. Furthermore, 'following' is closely associated in biblical thought with *mimesis*, and there is a distinctively Christian concept of the mode of the 'imitation of Christ' which it is important to make clear.

PART ONE

The Idea of the Imitation of God
in the Old Testament and Judaism

2

'Mimesis' in the Ancient World

ONE OF THE CONSTANTS in the religion of the ancient world, determining to a large extent its liturgy, ethics and spirituality, was the idea of the imitation of God. Knowledge of God was held to result in or require a real likeness to him, and religion in some way to render life an imitation of the life of God himself.

Men engage in the activity of worship before they formulate the nature and implications of it in theology. Christ was worshipped as Lord, for example, before there was a Christology. Consequently it is in the great cultic practices of the ancient world that we find the idea of the imitation of God first expressed.

This liturgical expression of the *imitatio Dei* had its own characteristic features. It was a duty, even a necessity, laid upon all members of the community for the preservation of social and individual life and well-being. Amongst the philosophers and moralists, on the other hand, the imitation of God tended to be regarded as a possibility only for some members of the community, an ideal of a very limited realization.

In many of the rituals of the ancient world the king played the chief role, since he was the most important mediator between God and man. In Egyptian religion the king was a god, and for the ritual drama in which he took part we ought to use the term μέθεξις rather than μίμησις,[1] because the god was not so much the object of the process, as, in the king, the subject of it. To some extent the same is true of Babylonian religion. There, says Professor Mowinckel, 'the king is not a god, as in Egypt; but he has been endowed with a divine vocation and with a superhuman power and quality, which in some respects puts him on the same plane as the gods.'[2]

In ancient Persian religion, life was regarded as primarily a means of becoming identified with the great struggle in which the god Ahura Mazda is engaged against the evil power. This identification was brought about through *mimesis*, and the idea of the imitation of God determined

[1] Cf. Jane Harrison, *Themis*, 1912, p. 125.   [2] *He that Cometh*, ET 1956, p. 48.

the ethics of the old Persian religion. The highest virtue was to participate in Ahura's struggle, and this could be attained even by tilling the soil, since the whole process of agriculture was one aspect of the contest with the evil god. In fact the whole task of civilization was viewed as the way in which a man imitated and identified himself with the conflict of his god, and so culture, morality and worship were all means of 'following' the fighting god.[1]

The idea of the imitation of God is unmistakably present in the mystery religions. Here again the essence of the ritual practice of the Hellenistic mysteries was the belief that the initiate mimed, and thereby really participated in, the life and death of the saviour god.[2] The initiate in the Orphic mysteries had to go through the motions of the 'passion' of the god as a means of sharing in his resurrection, and in the Eleusinian mysteries the initiated lived through afresh the tribulations of Demeter. In Mithraism the conflicts of Mithra were the prototypes for the daily life of his followers. The idea of actual identity with the god was applied to the individual initiate so that, in the mystery religions, the worshipper became, so to speak, *homoousios* with the deity.

When we turn to ancient philosophy we can more properlyuse the term *mimesis* of the way in which the imitation of God was there interpreted; the wise thinker became, not *homoousios* but *homoiousios* with God.[3] The idea of the *imitatio Dei* in Plato may have been one of the things which he took up from Pythagoras. Burnet says that we may attribute to Pythagoras the doctrine that the end of man is likeness to God.[4] It is the desire of God, said Plato, that the soul should become as like himself as possible. The qualities of the imitator of God, according to Plato, were wisdom, temperance, justice and courage, together with the bodily virtues of health, beauty, strength, wealth and piety.[5] On this view the so-called 'moral virtues' played the part assigned by Christian scholasticism to the 'theological virtues', faith, hope, and charity. The moral and intellectual *ascesis* of the imitation of God resulted in a true unworldliness: 'We ought to fly away from earth to heaven as quickly as possible; and to fly away is to become like God, as far as is possible; and to become like him is to become holy, just and wise' (*Theaetetus* 176 A f.).[6] The practice of the

---

[1] Cf. G. van der Leeuw, *Religion in Essence and Manifestation*, ET 1938, pp. 484 f.
[2] Cf. S. Angus, *The Mystery Religions and Christianity*, 1925, p. 106, and S. H. Hooke's essay 'The Way of the Initiate' in *The Siege Perilous*, 1956.
[3] Cf. H. Merki, '*ΟΜΟΙΩΣΙΣ ΘΕΩ*, Fribourg, 1952.
[4] Cf. the article 'Pythagoras and Pythagoreanism' in *Encyclopaedia of Religion and Ethics*, Vol. X, p. 526.
[5] Cf. G. G. Rutenber, *The Doctrine of the Imitation of God in Plato*, 1947.
[6] Speaking of popular Greek religion A. J. Festugière describes this flight to the gods

imitation of God reached its highest form, for Plato, in the contemplation of the *apatheia* of the Deity. This severely intellectual form of the imitation of God could only appeal to very few. For most men, as we shall see, some visible exemplar is necessary. Even when Greek art had provided a visible model, the Hellenic conception of the imitation of God remained a pose to be held, a state of mind to be attained. The imitation of God in the Christian tradition could never be that; there it was always dynamically conceived as the imitation of a true life-history, which in the life of the Church, through the action of the Holy Spirit, had a contemporaneous existence with that of the believer.

The imitation of God was also the ethical ideal of the Stoics. A good man, says Seneca, 'differs only in point of time from God, whose disciple and imitator he is'; i.e., man may hope to become for a while such as God always is. God is the exemplar for man, and the conduct of man must be an imitation of him, the divine attributes most frequently stressed being benevolence and loving-kindness:

> We are next to learn what the gods are; for such as they are found to be such must he who would please and obey them to the utmost of his power endeavour to be. If the deity is faithful, he too must be faithful; if free, beneficent and exalted, he must be beneficent and exalted likewise, and in all his words and actions behave as an imitator of God.[1]

Philo occupies an interesting and important position in the development of the idea of the imitation of God. He sought to blend the themes of the Book of Deuteronomy, the classic Old Testament statement of the Hebraic conception of the *imitatio Dei*, with Platonic thought. In the *De Migratione Abrahami* XXIII (131) he interprets the imitation of God in Old Testament fashion as a walking after the law of the Lord: 'The aim, then, according to the most holy Moses, is to follow God, as he says in another place, "You shall walk after the Lord your God"', and he directly cites Deut. 13.5. On the other hand, in the *De Fuga* XV (77 f.) he interprets the imitation of God along the lines of Plato's 'flight from the world' in the *Theaetetus*. Or again, he takes up from the Old Testament the command to rest on the sabbath day as a *mimesis* of God's rest from the work of creation on the seventh day, but he interprets it Platonically by specifying that the rest is to be given over to philosophy and contemplation. For Philo, also, the office of kingship and the practice of

as 'a desire of escape, . . . the homesickness for heaven, . . . the aspiration to lose oneself, to pass from this world into the unsounded depths of divine peace', *Personal Religion among the Greeks*, 1954, p. 21.
[1] Epictetus, *Discourses* II 14.

government must be mimetic reproductions, in human terms, of the creative and providential functions of God. In one passage he states that the imitation of God takes the form of the imitation of the Logos: from birth the Logos has imitated the Way of the Father, and therefore men have in the Logos the perfect model.[1] This is of special interest, as we shall see, in connection with the presentation in the Fourth Gospel of the Son's imitation of the Father.

In the cultic practices of ancient religion the imitation of God was really a type of sympathetic magic; the ritual action ensured that the god performed the action symbolized. In ancient philosophy and ethics the imitation of God was the ideal for the cultured intellectual *élite*. In neither case was the conception of the imitation of God controlled by any historical event. This was to be the distinctive feature of the *imitatio Dei* in both the Old and the New Testaments. There we find the conviction that God has revealed the pattern of the human imitation of himself in a particular series of events; these constitute the 'Way of the Lord'. The association of the image of the 'Way' with the imitation of God is not of course unique. Imitation of the 'Way' is a basic feature of Chinese Taoism (Tao=the 'Way'), and the same image appears also in the Eightfold 'Way' of the Buddha. Here however it is only 'under the patronage of' or 'in the spirit of' Heaven or the Buddha, not a point-by-point reliving *more humano* of the *gesta Dei* or *gesta Christi* as in the Hebrew and Christian traditions.

[1] *De Conf. Ling.* xiv (63).

3

The 'Way' of Israel in
Old Testament History and Imagery

THE ORIGIN of the Old Testament is the conviction that a certain series
of events in the history of Israel was unique and decisive, and constituted
a special revelation of God to mankind. In these events God had spoken;
they were his 'Word' to Israel and through Israel to the world. The kernel
of this 'saving history', the part of it which determined the shape of all
subsequent reflection, was the trek undertaken by some of the Hebrew
tribes, under the leadership of Moses, which took them on a journey from
Egypt to Palestine during the thirteenth century BC. The interpretation
which came to be put upon this journey was such that the Exodus from
Egypt, the law-giving at Sinai, the crossing of Jordan, the temple on Zion
were seen as the formative phases in God's creation[1] of his people Israel,
and, as we shall be discussing later, the life of the people of God had
necessarily to retain (through 'remembering' and 'meditation') an intimate
organic relation to this vital formative period of their history, because in
it the essential shape of life had been clearly indicated by God himself.[2]
In this sequence of history God had shown that he is always *prevenient*:
life is a journey where he goes before men as guide[3] and as example;[4]
and that he is always *provident*: he accompanies them as their companion[5]
and instructor,[6] and, as it turns out in the end, he is himself the route.

This is the stretch of the nation's history which provides the main

---

[1] 'I am the Lord, your Holy One, the Creator of Israel, your King', Isa. 43.15. Notice
that the heathen divine king or earthly god is replaced by the Hebraic heavenly King.
[2] As E. Jacob points out in his *Theology of the Old Testament* (ET 1958), p. 191, this
forms the framework of the salvation history used by St Paul at Pisidian Antioch (Acts 13);
cf. Rom. 9.4–6.
[3] 'And the Lord went before them . . . to lead them along the way', Ex. 13.21.
G. Östborn in *Tōrā in the Old Testament*, Lund, 1945, pp. 4–22, claims that the ety-
mology of הוֹרָה points to the belief that God is pre-eminently the one who 'shows the
way'.
[4] 'O that my people would listen to me, that Israel would walk in my ways!' Ps. 81.13.
[5] 'And your ears shall hear a word behind you saying, "This is the way, walk in it"',
Isa. 30.21. Cf. Lev. 26.12.
[6] For Torah as 'instruction in the Way' see below.

clauses in Israel's credal 'recital',[1] the Hebrew statement of belief always taking the form of a rehearsal of this cardinal 'walk with God'. Perhaps the very earliest credal affirmation of the Old Testament[2] is the triumphant shout of Miriam:

> Sing to the Lord for he has triumphed gloriously,
> The horse and his rider he has thrown into the sea.[3]

This was later expanded and turned into the personal confession of the 'Song of Moses' which celebrates the victorious progress from the Exodus to Zion:

> I will sing to the Lord, for he has triumphed gloriously;
>   the horse and his rider he has thrown into the sea.
> The Lord is my strength and my song,
>   and he has become my salvation;
> this is my God, and I will praise him,
>   my father's God, and I will exalt him.
> The Lord is a man of war;
>   the Lord is his name.
>
> Pharaoh's chariots and his host he cast into the sea;
>   and his picked officers are sunk in the Red Sea.
> The floods cover them;
>   they went down into the depths like a stone.
> Thy right hand, O Lord, glorious in power,
>   thy right hand, O Lord, shatters the enemy.
> In the greatness of thy majesty thou overthrowest thy adversaries;
>   thou sendest forth thy fury, it consumes them like stubble.
> At the blast of thy nostrils the waters piled up,
>   the floods stood up in a heap;
>   the deeps congealed in the heart of the sea.
>
> The enemy said, 'I will pursue, I will overtake,
>   I will divide the spoil, my desire shall have its fill of them.
>   I will draw my sword, my hand shall destroy them.'
> Thou didst blow with thy wind, the sea covered them;
>   they sank as lead in the mighty waters.
>
> Who is like thee, O Lord, among the gods?
>   Who is like thee, majestic in holiness, terrible in glorious deeds, doing
>   wonders?
> Thou didst stretch out thy right hand, the earth swallowed them.

---

[1] Cf. G. E. Wright, *God Who Acts* (SBT 8), 1952, for biblical theology as 'recital'.
[2] The New Testament begins from another triumph shout: 'The Lord is risen! Jesus is Lord!'
[3] Ex. 15.21.

Thou hast led in thy stedfast love the people whom thou hast redeemed,
    thou hast guided them by thy strength to thy holy abode.
The peoples have heard, they tremble;
    pangs have seized on the inhabitants of Philistia.
Now are the chiefs of Edom dismayed;
    the leaders of Moab, trembling seizes them;
    all the inhabitants of Canaan have melted away.
Terror and dread fall upon them;
    because of the greatness of thy arm, they are as still as stone,
    till thy people, O Lord, pass by,
    till the people pass by whom thou hast purchased.
Thou wilt bring them in, and plant them on thy own mountain,
    the place, O Lord, which thou hast made for thy abode,
    the sanctuary, O Lord, which thy hands have established.
The Lord will reign for ever and ever.[1]

The impact of this basic journey on the liturgy, ethics, and spirituality
of Israel was never more clearly displayed than in the continuing creative
role played by the imagery of 'the Way', which, because it is the most
inclusive image in both the Old and the New Testaments, could easily
and legitimately be made the basis of a unifying treatment of biblical
theology. The Hebrews were never able to speak of their 'religion' apart
from reference to this course of decisive events which had thrown up the
images[2] which became the key terms in the Old Testament religious
vocabulary: Torah is, as we shall see, literally the *signpost along the Way*;
sin is *turning aside from the Way*, leaving the main track as if it were ultimately possible to escape from God; repentance is *turning back into the
Way*, turning round to face him from whom one is seeking to flee, and the
other fundamental Old Testament terms like knowledge, Covenant, election, Messiah, father-son, are all associated with the imagery of the 'Way'.

The Hebrew word translated 'way' (*derek*) is derived from a root *darak*
meaning 'to tread, march', and its first use is of a road, a path, a way in the
literal sense. It is used with this meaning in Gen. 48.7, and of course very
frequently elsewhere. Quite early it came to be used in a metaphorical
sense of a 'way of life', particularly the way of life as taught by Yahweh:

You shalt teach them the statutes and the decisions, and make them
know the way (*derek*) in which they must walk and what they must do.[3]

---

[1] Ex. 15.1–18. For other Old Testament credal recitals using the Exodus-to-Zion
framework cf. Deut. 6.20–24; Josh. 24.2–13; Ps. 77.12 ff.; 78, 99, 136; Jer. 32.17 f.
[2] 'The memory of Israel preserved the otherwise unimportant story because the irrup-
tion of the spirit transfigured the pragmatic event into a drama of the soul and the acts
of the drama into symbols of divine liberation', E. Voegelin, *Order and History*, Vol. I
Israel and Revelation, 1956, p. 113.
[3] Ex. 18.20; cf. I Kings 8.36.

In the Book of Deuteronomy there is continual oscillation between *derek* meaning the actual historical way which Israel has traversed from Red Sea to Promised Land, and *derek* meaning the 'way of life' to which the people are consequently summoned.[1] As Östborn puts it, 'The significance of Deuteronomy is not confined to its character as a basis for instruction in "the law". Deuteronomy is, at the same time, a "showing the way".'[2]

The part played by *derek* and its cognate imagery in the book of Deuteronomy is an instructive example of the interaction, in the religion of Israel, between historical events and religious imagery, and of the distinctive character which the idea of the *imitatio Dei* there assumed. Israel was summoned to 'walk in all the way' of Yahweh (*halak bekol derek Y.*), to follow Yahweh (*halak 'ahere Y.*). Even when used metaphorically, *derek* was not completely detached from its setting in history. On the contrary its meaning as the *derek Adhonai* depended upon the extent to which, through cultic mime and ethical obedience, the original *derek* was made one's own, participated in, and experienced anew as a present reality. Deut. 8.1 f. is a good example of the ambiguity which arises from the Deuteronomic style of writing where there is reference both to the historical past and to the existential present:

> All the commandment which I command you this day (*hayyom*) you shall be careful to do, that you may live and multiply, and go in and possess the land which the Lord swore to give to your fathers. And you shall remember (*zakar*) all the way (*derek*) which the Lord your God has led you these forty years in the wilderness, that he might humble you, testing you to know what was in your heart, whether you would keep his commandments or not.

Of this passage Michaelis writes: 'The way here means not simply the actual road, nor even perhaps the wandering as such, but the wilderness journey both in its entirety and in detail as evidence of God's dealings with Israel.'[3] The singular *derek* is used of the whole of the historical journeying conceived as a sequence wherein Yahweh established a significant pattern of relationships which were henceforth normative for all Israel. The plural *derakhim* is usually accompanied by a number of parallel clauses: to fear Yahweh thy God, to love him, to keep the commandments of Yahweh, to cleave unto him. Journeying, travel,

---

[1] There is a similar alternation in the New Testament Gospels between ὁδός meaning first, the actual particular journey Jesus made, and, second, the 'way of life' his historical journeying has made possible.

[2] G. Östborn, *Torā in the Old Testament*, p. 64.

[3] Article on ὁδός, *TWNT* V, p. 49.

directedness is, in fact, the vehicle or form of the revelation. It is the unpredictable and in one sense unrepeatable episodes along the road which make up its content. One is reminded of the relation between ῥήματα and λόγος in the Fourth Gospel.

The continuing dominance of the imagery of the 'Way', with its suggestion of movement and advance, meant that for the Hebrew mind the contemplation of God must take not the static form of thinking about the being and perfection of God, but the dynamic form of conforming one's conduct to what he had shown himself to be during the journey to the Promised Land.[1]

The 'Way' in the Old Testament means not only direction, the path leading to a goal, but it is also used in the sense of 'manner', 'style'.[2] The 'way God wants you to behave' is logically dependent on 'the way God shows himself to behave', and both condition 'the way to find out how God behaves' (which includes what he requires, rewards, promises, etc.). The 'Way of God', that is to say, included both the *content* of the revelation (e.g. the Torah) and the *method* of it, and therefore, as we shall be considering later, the form and manner of the proclamation of the Gospel of God, in both the Old and the New Testaments, could not be divorced from its content.

The 'imitation of God' was expressed in the imagery of the 'Way' but, as with everything else in the Old Testament, it was controlled by the interpretation given by the Hebrews to their own history. This gives the Old Testament treatment of the idea of the *imitatio Dei* its own distinctive features. The Old Testament expression for the 'imitation of God' is 'to *walk* in the way of the Lord' or 'to *walk* after God'. The call of Israel is to '*follow* after' God in the Way of Torah, the Way of Sonship, and the Way of Knowledge, and it is interesting to note that this threefold 'Way' is associated in varying degrees with the three dominant figures in Old Testament history: the prophet (Torah), the king (Sonship) and the priest (Knowledge).

1. *The Way of Torah*

It is clear that although in the passages cited above from Deuteronomy *derek* is used to mean 'way of life', the image of the 'Way' is never detached from the historical journey once taken. In biblical religion this historical journey must be constantly referred to, indeed, as we shall see,

---

[1] For 'contemplation' and 'meditation' in the Old Testament, cf. J. Pedersen, *Israel* I–II, 1926, pp. 126 ff.

[2] This, of course, is not peculiar to Hebrew. Cf. 'the Driffield *way* to Scarborough' and the Yorkshire *way* of speaking of 'any road' (=in any event).

it must be lived over again in some real sense, if the Lord's 'Way' for Israel is to be truly seen and appropriated.

The experience of the historical journeying had brought with it the conviction that God was setting before Israel not only the object of the journey, but the manner of behaviour during it. *En route* God was instructing his people in his 'Way'; he was giving them Torah.[1] Gunnar Östborn in his book *Tōrā in the Old Testament* has pointed out the close association in Hebrew thought between *torah* and *derek*.[2] He contends convincingly that the primary meaning of the verb *horah* was 'to point with the finger', 'to indicate', and so the first meaning of *torah* would be 'a certain gesture, a movement of the hands or fingers and simultaneously or subsequently, the statement accompanying or expressing the purpose of such a gesture'.[3] *Torah* then means 'an indication of the way', a 'direction', a 'signpost'. An interesting early instance of this use of the word occurs in relation to the primitive tree cult. When we find the epithet used of certain trees, it may well be, that in the first instance, the trees were 'finger-pointers' in a literal sense. They were signposts. 'It is undeniable', writes Östborn, 'that the terebinth in Gen. 12.6 had some sort of connection with a real path. It constituted a point to aim at in the course of Abraham's journey to Shechem, and travellers may perhaps have looked upon it as a "path-shower" to Shechem, or the sacred place at Shechem.'[4] Similarly there seems to have been a connection with an actual path in Deut. 11.30: 'Here', writes Östborn, 'the terebinth serves as a kind of landmark, from which the position of Mount Ebal and Mount Gerizim may be determined (cf. Judg. 9.37).'[5]

That '*torah*' retained this directional meaning is shown by the fact that it is synonymous in the Old Testament with 'walking in the way'. The great rosary on the Torah, Psalm 119, begins:

> Blessed are they that are perfect in the way (*derek*)
> Who walk in the law of the Lord (*torah*) (RV).

The phrase 'to walk in the *torah*' occurs quite frequently[6] as a parallel to 'walking in the way', and the likelihood that this kind of imagery has been determined by the nature of the historical events is suggested by the fact that it is peculiar to the Old Testament.[7] The vocation of Israel

---

[1] For God as the imparter of Torah cf. G. Östborn, *Tōrā in the Old Testament*, ch. II.
[2] The logic of imagery would *a priori* have led us to associate *torah* and *derek* because both share a basic suggestion of 'direction'.
[3] *Op. cit.*, p. 9.   [4] *Ibid.*, p. 29.   [5] *Ibid.*, p. 29 n. 5.
[6] Cf. Ex. 16.4; Dan. 9.10; Neh. 10.29.
[7] Cf. G. Bertram's article on πατέω, *TWNT* V, p. 941.

and of the individual was to 'follow after' the Lord in the path which he had indicated:

> And now, Israel, what does the Lord your God require of you, but to fear the Lord your God, to walk in all his ways . . . (Deut. 10.12).

> He has showed you, O man, what is good;
>   and what does the Lord require of you
> but to do justice, and to love kindness,
>   and to walk humbly with your God (Micah 6.8).

The same association of obedience to the Torah and journeying is found in Deuteronomy:

> You shall be careful to do therefore as the Lord your God has commanded you: you shall not turn aside to the right hand or to the left.[1]

This 'Way' was not one that Israel had chosen or preferred; it was part of the covenant terms to which assent had been given, it was the Covenant Way.

A comparison of the expressions which are used in parallel with 'walking in the way', 'walking after the Lord', makes clear the nature of Israel's covenantal discipleship. It was, first, obedience: 'to keep the commandments';[2] then reverence: 'to fear the Lord';[3] then love: 'to love the Lord and to cleave to him';[4] then 'perfection': 'to be perfect in the way';[5] and finally knowledge: 'to know the Lord'.[6] We shall return to these demands when we consider Israel as the *imitator Dei*.

Israel's vocation to walk in the 'Way' of the Lord was embodied in the three exemplifying figures of the Old Testament: the king, the priest and the prophet. These three functionaries manifest activities, as E. Jacob says, which are performed in their perfection by God himself.[7] These three figures, together with the 'wise man', were concrete exemplars of how the imitation of God could be undertaken; they were annunciatory 'signs' of essential features of the vocation of Israel.

The *king* was regarded as the imparter of *torah* to Israel,[8] and in this he imitated the giving of the Torah to him by Yahweh himself. The king's covenant with the people was further a kind of *mimesis* of the covenant between Yahweh (*the* King) and Israel, and obedience to the king's *torah*

---

[1] Deut. 5.32 (cf. 17.11, 20; 28.14).
[2] Cf. Deut. 8.6; 10.12 f.; 28.9; I Kings 11.33; II Chron. 17.3; Neh. 10.29; Jer. 9.13; Ezek. 11.20; Dan. 9.10.
[3] Cf. Deut. 8.6; 10.12; Ps. 128; Jer. 44.10.   [4] Cf. Deut. 10.12; 11.22.
[5] Cf. Gen. 17.1; I Kings 8.61; Ps. 101.6; 119.1; Prov. 11.20.
[6] See below: 'The Way of Knowledge'.
[7] E. Jacob, *Theology of the Old Testament*, p. 233.
[8] Cf. G. Östborn, *Tōrā in the Old Testament*, ch. III.

was the means whereby obedience to the law of Yahweh was wrought. In fact so intimate was the relation of the king to Yahweh that as Östborn argues, he can be said to have embodied the covenant in his person. 'And so the king personifies the divine will, "the law", which has a binding power both for him and his people (cf. I Sam. 12.14).'[1] This character of the king as 'law incarnate' was probably made specially clear, as Östborn suggests, at his coronation when he was handed the *torah*. This feature of Hebrew kingship is not far removed from the later Hellenistic idea expressed in the phrase νόμος ἔμψυχος.

The *priest* is the figure most commonly associated with *torah* in the Old Testament. He came to appropriate almost entirely this function which had originally been confined to the king. The transmission of *torah* was primarily a priestly function and the priests were castigated when they failed in this their fundamental task.[2]

The *prophet* was also concerned with *torah*, either to recall the people to the Mosaic *torah* which they were forgetting or neglecting, or to point to contemporary events and situations in which God was giving *torah* anew.

2. *The Way of Sonship*

One of the indelible features of the first historical 'saving' journey was Israel's conviction that in it God was encountered in a personal manner. Consequently the 'Way' became an image in the Old Testament for an intensely intimate personal relationship between Israel and God. The 'Way' of Israel was discovered to be the 'Way' of sonship. The course of the journey from the Exodus to Zion[3] was a revelation of Yahweh as Father to Israel and of the fact that he had dealt with his 'son' in true paternal fashion: '. . . in the wilderness . . . you have seen how the Lord your God bore you, as a man bears his son, in all the way that you went' (Deut. 1.31).

Before we examine further this association of the 'Way' with sonship we need to remember that in Hebrew thought the father-son relationship had a much deeper significance than physical kinship.[4] It was essentially

---

[1] *Ibid.*, p. 77.   [2] Micah 3.11; II Chron. 15.3; Jer. 18.18; Ezek. 7.26; Zeph. 3.4.
[3] Cf. also Hos. 11.1, 3; Jer. 31.9 ff.; Isa. 1.2; Deut. 32.6; Isa. 63.16; 64.8.
[4] 'With the Hebrews . . . the two terms [father and son], and especially "son", are used when a physical relationship is out of the question, and where the son is so called because he is the representative, the manifestation, the embodiment of him, or of that, of which he is said to be the son. We can talk of a son of peace, of worthlessness (Belial) or of consolation. And we should probably understand in this sense the phrase "sons of God" (*Bene Elohim*) if it does not carry us back to the realms of mythology.' W. F. Lofthouse, 'Fatherhood and Sonship in the Fourth Gospel', *ExpT* 43, 1931/32, p. 443.

a moral and spiritual relationship; true fatherhood being revealed only where there was the obedient son. It was the father's task to show his son the way in which he should walk and to guide him along it,[1] and it was the son's duty to 'walk after' his father, to 'imitate'[2] his ways:

> His [Samuel's] sons did not walk in his ways, but turned aside after gain; they took bribes and perverted justice (I Sam. 8.3).

> But they [the Rechabites] answered, 'We will drink no wine, for Jonadab the son of Rechab, our father, commanded us, "You shall not drink wine, neither you nor your sons for ever." . . . We have obeyed the voice of Jonadab the son of Rechab, our father, in all that he commanded us, to drink no wine all our days' (Jer. 35.6, 8).

> A son honours his father, and a servant his master (Mal. 1.6).

This is perhaps most frequently illustrated in the Wisdom literature where there is particular emphasis on the 'doxological' duty of the son, which is performed through obedience: 'My son, keep your father's commandment' (Prov. 6.20). The son's obedience to his father is one of the ways, perhaps the chief way, of 'loving' the Lord: 'Solomon loved the Lord, walking in the statutes of David his father' (I Kings 3.3).

In the Old Testament sonship to God was the vocation to which Israel was called:

> Israel is my first-born son (Ex. 4.22).

> I am a father to Israel, and Ephraim is my first-born (Jer. 31.9).

> Is not he your father, who created you,
> who made you and established you? (Deut. 32.6).

> When Israel was a child, I loved him,
> and out of Egypt I called my son (Hos. 11.1).

> You are the sons of the Lord your God (Deut. 14.1).

This meant that, as Covenant People, Israel had agreed to walk in obedience to the Father of Israel; the way of sonship to which Israel was called was another way of expressing the way of Torah. The sonship of Israel was focused and exemplified in the king who was the living embodiment of it for each generation of Hebrews. At his enthronement the king was solemnly declared to be 'son' of Yahweh, pledged to follow his Lord in obedience.[3]

---

[1] The father 'blesses' the son, and this includes both a 'charge' and an endowment (of strength) to fulfil it, e.g. Gen. 28.1, 6; I Kings 2.1.

[2] 'By obedient submission to the father's will, the son becomes a perfect reproduction of his father at every point', R. H. Fuller, *The Mission and Achievement of Jesus* (SBT 12), 1954, p. 84.   [3] Ps. 110.

3. *The Way of Knowledge*

The 'Way' of Israel was also the 'Way' of Knowledge.[1] We have seen that the kernel of Israel's 'salvation-history' had brought with it the recognition that God's relationship to Israel was of a unique, intimate, and personal character. The distinctive feature of Old Testament *gnosis* is that it reflects the influence of this historical encounter, and constantly points back to it as its essential source of reference.

'Knowledge' in Hebrew thought has its own characteristic features. It is closer to sympathetic understanding and intuitive perception than to analysis or argumentation. It is a 'knowledge' which is experientially, intuitionally, and not logically verifiable.[2] The Hebrew language is unique in using the verb 'to know' (*yada'*) of sexual relationship, and this personal, intimate, and reciprocal association remained in the Hebrew conception of the knowledge of God.

The 'knowledge' which man has depends upon the 'knowledge' which God has of man; it is a *mimesis* of God's 'knowledge'. In the beginning there is God's knowledge of man. God knows a man in pursuing after him: 'O Lord, thou hast searched me and known me!' (Ps. 139.1); and what is involved in God's knowledge of man had been shown in his 'knowledge' of Israel during the basic stage of the revelation in history, during 'the Way' from the Red Sea to Zion. This constant reference to historical happenings marks off the Hebrew conception of the knowledge of God from the non-historical, predominantly intellectual, interpretation of classical Greek philosophy. The historical journey of Israel from Egypt was the norm for any consideration of the meaning of the knowledge of God in both its subjective and objective sense; this was certainly a period when the Lord 'knew' Israel:

Hear this word that the Lord has spoken against you, O people of Israel, against the whole family which I brought up out of the land of Egypt:

'You only have I known
of all the families of the earth;
therefore I will punish you,
for all your iniquities' (Amos 3.1 f.).

I am the Lord your God
from the land of Egypt;
you know no God but me,
and beside me there is no saviour.

[1] Cf. S. Mowinckel, *Die Erkenntnis Gottes bei dem Alttestamentlichen Profeten*, Oslo, 1941; G. Botterweck, *Gott erkennen*, Bonn, 1951.
[2] 'The word *da'ath* denotes a knowledge gained by living communion, by actual experience', H. Schultz, *Old Testament Theology*, ET 1892, Vol. II, pp. 118 ff.

> It was I who knew you in the wilderness,
>   in the land of drought (Hos. 13.4 f.).

The Lord your God knows your going through this great wilderness; these forty years the Lord your God has been with you (Deut. 2.7).

On the day when I chose Israel, I swore to the seed of the house of Jacob, making myself known to them in the land of Egypt, I swore to them, saying, I am the Lord your God (Ezek. 20.5).

That God 'knew' Israel meant that he had 'chosen' Israel,[1] liberated him, providentially[2] cared for him, and given 'signs'[3] of his presence and activity. It is only because God 'knew' Israel in this sense that Israel could walk in the 'Way of the Lord' at all. God's 'knowledge' of Israel was like his 'knowledge' of Abraham; it was an act of grace making possible the response of following in the 'Way':

> For I have known him [Abraham], to the end that he may command his children and his household after him, that they may keep the way of the Lord, to do justice and judgement.[4]

The vocation of Israel was to walk in this 'Way' of knowledge, to 'know' the Lord. This is what the covenant obligation involved, and the nation was castigated by the prophets for 'not knowing' the Lord:

> Hear the word of the Lord, O people of Israel;
>   for the Lord has a controversy with the inhabitants of the land.
> There is no faithfulness or kindness,
>   and no knowledge of God in the land.
> My people are destroyed for lack of knowledge;
>   because you have rejected knowledge,
>   I reject you from being a priest to me (Hos. 4.1, 6).

'Knowledge' of the Lord should be in fact Israel's true glory:

> Let him who glories glory in this, that he understands and knows me, that I am the Lord who practises kindness, justice, and righteousness in the earth (Jer. 9.24).

As with the 'Way' of Torah and the 'Way' of sonship, the 'Way' of knowledge meant first reverence and obedience. There is, in fact, an intimate connection in the Old Testament between *da'ath* and *torah*.[5] Israel's obedient 'knowledge' of God was the way in which God's gracious

---

[1] God's 'knowledge' of his prophet meant that he had chosen him, cf. Jer. 1.5.
[2] Cf. the Pharaoh who 'did not know' Joseph, Ex. 1.8.   [3] Cf. Ex. 16.12.
[4] Gen. 18.19; cf. Gen. 28.20.   [5] Cf. Hos. 4.6 and Mal. 2.7.

knowledge of Israel would be imitated. To 'know' God was therefore, first, to 'call upon the name of the Lord':

> Pour out thy anger on the nations
>   that do not know thee
> and on the kingdoms
>   that do not call on thy name![1]

> Have they no knowledge, all the evildoers
>   who eat up my people as they eat bread,
>   and do not call upon the Lord? (Ps. 14.4).

> Because he cleaves to me in love, I will deliver him;
> I will protect him, because he knows my name (Ps. 91.14).

'Knowledge' is used as a general term for obedience in Jer. 2.8:

> The priests did not say, 'Where is the Lord?'
> Those who handle the law did not know me.

The call to the 'Way' of knowledge meant, secondly, that Israel must recognize the 'signs of the times'. Israel must 'see and know'.[2] Along the 'Way' in which Israel had to go the Lord would give 'signs' of his presence and purpose, and his people must be alert to recognize them. The implication is that these signs were always of such a character that Israel ought to have recognized them, and, further, this knowledge which was demanded of Israel was not an endowment which only a few possessed, but was potentially within the reach of all. Recognition of the 'signs' of God's saving purpose was not, in fact, absolutely dissimilar from a natural faculty like a 'homing instinct':

> The ox knows its owner,
>   and the ass its master's crib;
> but Israel does not know,
>   my people does not understand (Isa. 1.3).

> Even the stork in the heavens
>   knows her times;
> and the turtle dove, swallow, and crane
>   keep the time of their coming;
> but my people know not
>   the ordinance of the Lord.[3]

When we consider in more detail the vocation of Israel as *imitator Dei* we shall see that the chief temptation of the people of God was to seek

---

[1] Ps. 79.6; cf. Jer. 10.25.   [2] Cf. Isa. 41.20.
[3] Jer. 8.7; the same parallel between the 'signs' in nature and the 'signs' in history was drawn by Jesus, cf. Luke 12.55 f.

for 'signs' of their own choosing, rather than to accept in humility and obedience those which the Lord was in fact giving.[1]

Thirdly, the 'Way' of knowledge meant that Israel must act justly and with compassion:

> He [Josiah] judged the cause of the poor and needy:
>   then it was well.
> Is not this to know me?
>   says the Lord (Jer. 22.16).

In caring for the underprivileged and helpless Israel would be imitating Yahweh's providential care for the poor and outcast, exemplified in his treatment of Israel.

Again, the three primary figures of the king, the priest, and the prophet are all associated with knowledge.

The *king* was charged to 'know' Yahweh. Jeremiah compared Jehoiakim unfavourably with his father Josiah in this respect:

> He judged the cause of the poor and needy;
>   then it was well.
> Is not this to know me?
>   says the Lord (Jer. 22.16).

The king did not receive his office in order to exalt himself, to act arrogantly, to emulate the grandeur of great despots, or to oppress his fellow-countrymen (his 'neighbours'), but in order to prove by his actions that he 'knew Yahweh'.[2]

The prescribed path for the *priest* was also the 'Way' of knowledge, and he was castigated for departing from it.[3] Like the prophet he was summoned to 'know' the Lord, but whereas the prophet's *da'ath* was direct, that of the priest was mediated (through divination, precedent, tradition, etc.).[4] He was particularly concerned with the guidance for the 'Way' to be derived from sacrifice.

The *prophet* was the possessor of a special knowledge of God[5] because he had been taken into the counsels of God. He was the exemplary 'knower', and 'Would that all the Lord's people were prophets!' (Num. 11.29). It is worth noting also that Torah, Sonship, Knowledge: Prophet,

---

[1] Why are signs needed where God himself is present and active? Because the presence of the true God is always in principle disputable (the presence of false gods, idols, is always easily verifiable).

[2] S. Mowinckel, *He that Cometh*, p. 92. 'The authentic Israelite ideal of Kingship . . . culminates in the knowledge of Yahweh', *ibid.*, p. 93.

[3] I Sam. 2.12; Hos. 4.6; Mal. 2.7.

[4] Cf. E. Jacob, *Theology of the Old Testament*, p. 248 n. 1.

[5] S. Mowinckel, *Die Erkenntnis Gottes bei den Altestamentlichen Profeten*, p. 9.

King, Priest are all functions of the community, which is itself the true object of God's direction, adoption, and self-communication.

4. *Sin, Repentance, Redemption and Restoration*

The imagery of the 'Way', the journey, also dominates and controls the Old Testament conception of sin, repentance, redemption and restoration.

Sin in Old Testament thought was usually conceived as a wandering off the right 'way', a turning aside to 'walk after' other gods. This was not a casual innocuous straying from the right course, but a deliberate attempt to escape from it, a falling out on the march, a determined *flight from God*,[1] desertion. Sin for the Hebrew meant a loss of the freedom and unselfconsciousness which a man has when he has 'peace' with God, and an attempt to flee from the Presence, as if this were an ultimate possibility:

> And they heard the voice of the Lord God walking in the garden in the cool of the day, and the man and his wife hid themselves from the presence of the Lord God among the trees of the garden (Gen. 3.8).

> Behold, thou hast driven me this day away from the ground; and from thy face I shall be hidden; and I shall be a fugitive and a wanderer on the earth (Gen. 4.14).

Once begun, the momentum of the flight from God increased. Israel was dispersed in a scattered and disunited stampede:

> My sheep were scattered, they wandered over all the mountains and on every high hill; my sheep were scattered over all the face of the earth (Ezek. 34.6).

Repentance (*shub*) meant pausing in the flight, turning round and back into the 'Way' which had been left behind:

> 'Return (*shub*), faithless Israel, says the Lord.
>   I will not look on you in anger,
>   for I am merciful,'
>   says the Lord;
>   'I will not be angry for ever.'
>   Only acknowledge your guilt,
>   that you have rebelled against the Lord your God
>   and scattered your favours among strangers under every green tree;
>   and that you have not obeyed my voice,'
>   says the Lord (Jer. 3.11–13).

[1] It is interesting to compare, in passing, the image of flight as used in Plato and in the Old Testament. In Plato, as we have seen, it is an image for a good and noble thing, indeed for salvation. In the Old Testament flight is an image for sin. The motive of flight from the world, where it occurs in biblical thought, is conditioned by eschatology

'It may be that their supplication will come before the Lord, and that every one will turn (*yashub*) from his evil way' (Jer. 36.7). It was the particular function of the prophet to recall Israel to the 'Way':[1]

> I have sent to you all my servants the prophets, sending them persistently, saying, 'Turn now every one of you from his evil way, and amend your doings, and do not go after (*halak 'ahere*) other gods to serve them' (Jer. 35.15).

> Yet the Lord warned Israel and Judah by every prophet and every seer, saying, 'Turn from your evil ways and keep my commandments and my statutes, in accordance with all the law which I commanded your fathers, and which I sent to you by my servants the prophets' (II Kings 17.13).

The imagery of the 'Way' also dominates Hebrew thought about the purposes of God for the future. The historical journey of Israel was the portion of history which gave the meaning to all history, past, present, and future. This journey was the significant form and norm to which all the actions of God in history, whether with Israel in particular or with the nations in general, would bear clear and intimate relation. This was the initial and regulative phase of God's saving purpose, and God's steadfast intention to redeem would be displayed in events which could not help but repeat the phases of the archetypal journey from Egypt to Jerusalem. It is this first formative journey which has determined the structure of the prophetic oracles of Deutero-Isaiah and Ezekiel.

Deutero-Isaiah begins by urging his hearers to see in their present circumstances the start of a new, and not merely metaphorical, Exodus, beginning with the moment when God hears the cry of suffering from his people:

> Comfort, comfort my people,
>   says your God.
> Speak tenderly to Jerusalem,
>   and cry to her
>   that her warfare is ended,
>   that her iniquity is pardoned,
>   that she has received from the Lord's hand
>   double for all her sins (Isa. 40.1 f.).

> For a long time I have held my peace,
>   I have kept still and restrained myself:
> now will I cry out like a woman in travail,
>   I will gasp and pant (Isa. 42.14).

and not by metaphysics. The exhortation to flee from the world is given not because the world is incurably bad, but because the time is critically short.

[1] Cf. G. Östborn, *Tōrā in the Old Testament*, ch. VI.

Once again there will be a journey through the wilderness to Zion and the Promised Land with the Lord as guide:

> In the wilderness prepare the way of the Lord,
> make straight in the desert a highway for our God (Isa. 40.3).

> Awake, awake, put on strength,
> O arm of the Lord;
> awake as in the days of old,
> the generations of long ago.
> Was it not thou that didst cut Rahab in pieces,
> that didst pierce the dragon?
> Was it not thou that didst dry up the sea,
> the waters of the great deep;
> that didst make the depths of the sea a way
> for the redeemed to pass over?
> And the ransomed of the Lord shall return,
> and come with singing to Zion (Isa. 51.9–11).

> Thus says the Lord,
> who makes a way in the sea,
> a path in the mighty waters,
> who brings forth chariot and horse,
> army and warrior . . .
> I will make a way in the wilderness
> and rivers in the desert (Isa. 43.16–19).

The first Exodus was a hasty flight, the new one about to be realized is an ordered triumphal progress:

> For you shall not go out in haste,
> and you shall not go in flight,
> for the Lord will go before you,
> and the God of Israel will be your
> rear guard (Isa. 52.12),

and with this newly liberated Israel a New Covenant will be made.[1]

In a similar way, Ezekiel sees the restoration of Israel to involve first a real return to the desert to learn again the essential basis of the relationship between Yahweh and his people:

> And I will bring you into the wilderness of the peoples, and there I will enter into judgment with you face to face. As I entered into judgment with your fathers in the wilderness of the land of Egypt, so I will enter into judgment with you, says the Lord God (Ezek. 20.35 f.).

Ezekiel sees himself occupying something like the position of Moses, as one who must warn his people and point to the coming of a new guide, a

---

[1] Isa. 54.

new David, and the whole book comes to a climax in the vision of a new
Jerusalem with a new temple on Zion. *Gerusalemme consolata* is of course
the *scopus* of Deutero- (and Trito-) Isaiah too: 'Arise, shine, for thy light
is come.'

Deutero-Isaiah and Ezekiel show the influence of the imagery of the
'Way' in shaping the structure of a whole book, but there is ample evidence of the central place which the kernel of the nation's history occupied
in the prophetic mind generally. The prophet pointed back to the Exodus
period as the cardinal place of revelation, and prophetic eschatology reflected the conviction that there would be some kind of going over again
of the wilderness experience:

> Therefore, behold, I will allure her,
>   and bring her into the wilderness,
>   and speak tenderly to her . . .
> And there she shall answer as in the days of her youth,
>   as at the time when she came out of the land of Egypt (Hos. 2.14 ff.).

The Age to Come would see the realization of the 'Way of Knowledge'.
The 'earth shall be full of the knowledge of the Lord, as the waters cover
the sea' (Isa. 11.9; cf. Hab. 2.14); then 'you shall know that I am in the
midst of Israel, and that I, Yahweh, am your God' (Joel 2.27). True
knowledge was one of the gifts which Yahweh as bridegroom of Israel
would give to his bride 'in that day':

> I will betroth you to me in faithfulness,
>   and you shall know the Lord (Hos. 2.20).

'I will give them a heart to know that I am the Lord; and they shall be
my people, and I will be their God, for they shall return to me with their
whole heart' (Jer. 24.7). This was to be the feature of the New Covenant:
'No longer shall each man teach his neighbour and each his brother,
saying, "Know the Lord", for they shall all know me, from the least of
them to the greatest, says the Lord' (Jer. 31.34). In the Age to Come Israel
would be the true 'disciple' of the Lord: 'And all thy children shall be
disciples of the Lord; and great shall be the peace of thy children'
(Isa. 54.13); and he would give shepherds after his own heart 'who will
feed you with knowledge and understanding' (Jer. 3.15). There are some
passages which indicate the belief that the true knowledge of God was to
be the possession of the Messiah. He would be one who truly 'knows' God,
and truly 'knows' Israel: 'And the spirit of the Lord shall rest upon him,
the spirit of wisdom and understanding, the spirit of counsel and might,

the spirit of knowledge and the fear of the Lord' (Isa. 11.2). Deutero-
Isaiah's 'Servant of the Lord' was to be endowed with 'saving' knowledge:

> By his knowledge shall the righteous one, my servant, make many to
> be accounted righteous (Isa. 53.11).

Finally, because the Age to Come would bring God's decisive act of
forgiveness of sin, it was to be marked by the 'ingathering' of Israel scattered in its flight from the 'Way of the Lord':

> The wilderness and the dry land shall be glad,
>   the desert shall rejoice and blossom; . . .
> And a highway shall be there,
>   and it shall be called the Holy Way; . . .
> And the ransomed of the Lord shall return,
>   and come to Zion with singing,
>   with everlasting joy upon their heads;
>   they shall obtain joy and gladness,
>   and sorrow and sighing shall flee away (Isa. 35.1 ff.).

> And it shall be said,
>   Build up, build up, prepare the way,
>   remove every obstruction from my people's way (Isa. 57.14).

> I remember the devotion of your youth,
>   your love as a bride,
>   how you followed me in the wilderness,
>   in a land not sown (Jer. 2.2 f.).

The Age to Come would be marked by the actualization of the 'Way of
Torah'. In the 'latter days' Yahweh himself would teach the people his
torah,[1] either directly or through the Messianic King. This would involve
giving them the 'way': 'I will give them one heart and one way' (Jer. 32.39).
W. D. Davies has shown,[2] from an examination of the relevant material
in the Old Testament, the Apocrypha and Pseudepigrapha, and in the
rabbinical sources, that obedience to the Torah was expected to be a
dominant feature of the Messianic Age. Jer. 31.31 ff. indicates, says
Davies, 'that Torah, new in some sense and yet not divorced utterly from
the old Torah, i.e. an external Torah, is part of Jeremiah's hope for "the
latter days" '.[3] Again, the author of the 'Servant-poems' of Deutero-
Isaiah sees the 'Servant' as a teacher of Torah.[4] In Isa. 2.1–5 there is
expressed the belief that the Torah of the future Jerusalem would be in
line with the Torah of Sinai.[5]

---

[1] Isa. 2.3; Micah 4.2.
[2] In *Torah in the Messianic Age and/or the Age to Come*, Philadelphia, 1952.
[3] *Ibid.*, p. 28.   [4] Isa. 42. 1–4.   [5] Davies, *op. cit.*, p. 37.

In the Age to Come also the 'Way of Sonship' was to be realized. The coming Davidic King would be a true realization of Israel's sonship to Yahweh:

> I will be his father, and he shall be my son (II Sam. 7.14).

> He shall cry unto me, 'Thou art my father,
>   my God, and the rock of my salvation.'
> I will also make him my first-born (Ps. 89.26 f.).

The Lord your God will . . . have compassion upon you, and will gather you again from all the peoples where the Lord your God has scattered you (Deut. 30.3).

I will gather the remnant of my flock out of all the countries where I have driven them, and I will bring them back to their fold (Jer. 23.3).

This ingathering was to be one of the works of the 'Servant' in Deutero-Isaiah:

> And now the Lord says,
>   who formed me from the womb to be his servant,
>   to bring Jacob back to him,
>   and that Israel might be gathered to him . . . (Isa. 49.5).

This final ingathering seals the communal reference of all God's dealings with men in Israel.

D

4

Israel as 'Imitator Dei'

You shall be holy, for I the Lord your God am holy.
LEVITICUS 19.2

IT IS CLEAR from the foregoing that the experiences of the Hebrew people during that part of their history which took them from the Red Sea to the Promised Land forced upon them the conviction that this episode was no mere transitory series of occurrences but contained within itself something which would never be outdated. The Lord had shown them that 'religion' was essentially a journey which he invited men to undertake. The revelatory history had not only occurred; it had thrown up images of perennial significance. The way ahead had been indicated by the Lord himself and Israel was committed by the Covenant to 'follow after' him in this 'Way'. This is the form which the 'imitation of God' takes in the Old Testament, and we must now consider in detail what it involved both for the nation and for the individual.

It is often said, and rightly, that the distinctive feature of Hebrew religion is that it is rooted in history. This does not mean, however, simply that the Hebrews had a 'sense of history', and certainly not that they had the antiquarian's interest in 'the historical'. The Hebrews were profoundly aware of the *present* reality in their lives of the past 'saving events'. Hebrew piety was to live the present as though it were the privileged stretch of the remembered past, so that it was actualized and realized afresh again and again. If by history we mean the record of *past* events, then certainly in this sense the Hebrews were not interested in history or attached to it. As L. Koehler has put it: 'History presupposes the past, and what is past is what has lost its reality. In this sense the Hebrew mind hardly knows the past or history . . . What happened once is not a "once" but a "now" . . . Past and present are one single act of God . . . It is hardly comprehensible to us to-day that the Hebrew still experienced after centuries what had once happened. For the Hebrew mind this release from the past and from history was a living reality which creates life. It may well be because of this that the names of those who compiled the writings of the Old Testament are almost all unknown, and that we know practically nothing even about the great prophets. What do they matter to a mind which does not ask about the past?'[1] The historical 'Way of the Lord' was followed by Israel, 'imitated', and known as a present reality through liturgy, social and personal relationships, and in the interior life of the individual believer.

1. *Imitation of the 'Way' in Liturgy*

The powerful influence of the imagery of the 'Way' is impressively demonstrated in the manner in which the three great Hebrew festivals of Passover, Weeks, and Tabernacles became 'historified'. These festivals were originally agricultural celebrations, but so strong was the impression of journey from the Exodus to Zion that they became more and more the occasions when the key phases of this initial redemption-history were lived over again by being dramatically mimed in the context of corporate worship, with the king himself taking part. It is exceedingly probable that the way in which these events have been written up in the Book of Exodus has been determined by the fact that they were continually dramatized at these festivals.[2] The Exodus was not simply an event of past history; each year, especially in such a festival as the Passover, it was experienced as a contemporary reality, and increasingly, as we can see in the prophets, it came to have eschatological significance.[3] It looked forward to the great Exodus to come, indeed it was a proleptic experience of it. As we now have it in the Book of Exodus, the whole narrative of the primary events has become what Pedersen calls a 'cultic glorification'.[4]

The Passover came to be a pilgrimage feast, and it seems probable that the pilgrimage procession up to and around Jerusalem assumed such prominence and importance because this was the means whereby the journey of the children of Israel was mimed, with the entrance of the procession into the temple on Zion as the climax. As Pedersen has shown, the time references in the account of the events in Ex. 1–15 indicate the manner in which the Passover festival was constructed as a liturgical miming of the main stages of the saving events which the participants experienced as living present realities.[5] It was a festival which

---

[1] L. Koehler, *Hebrew Man*, ET 1956, pp. 139 f. Cf. E. Jacob, *Theology of the Old Testament*, p. 213: '. . . faith, in Israel, while having an historical foundation, does not bind itself to the historical events themselves, but to the objective realities created by those events.'
[2] Cf. J. Pedersen, *Israel* III–IV, 1940, pp. 376–465.
[3] Cf. E. Jacob, *Theology of the Old Testament*, p. 326.
[4] *Op. cit.*, p. 731.   [5] *Ibid.*, p. 411.

began in the evening, continued through the night, and reached its climax the following day. The 'holy night' (Ex. 12.42) began on the evening of the fourteenth of the first month (Abib) when the animal was killed (Ex. 12.6). At midnight came Yahweh's striking down of the first-born (Ex. 12.29). During the night the people fled, and Pharaoh pursued them, but the result was certain, even though at first the Egyptians were allowed to pursue. As morning dawned Yahweh looked out over the Egyptians through the pillar of fire. The pursuit was now at its height (Ex. 14.24). But Yahweh intervened and the waters closed over the Egyptians (Ex. 14.27). Then came the victory song and dance (Ex. 15). The miming of this primary journey in which the king probably took part involved the pilgrims actually dressing as those about to leave in a hurry (Ex. 12.11). It is even possible that the architectural setting of worship in the temple in Jerusalem was influenced by the Exodus-to-Zion theme. The darkness ('araphel) in the temple where the Lord willed to dwell recalled the darkness ('araphel) which enveloped Moses on Mount Sinai.[1] The ark (with the two tables of stone) recalled the law-giving at Sinai and the wilderness period, while the place of sacrifice was entered as the goal of Israel's journey—the rock of Zion itself.

The realization of the contemporary actuality of these events through participation in the Passover ritual is indicated in the 'rubrics' given in the Mishnah for the celebration of this feast. One of the children asks the head of the family: 'Why is this night different from all other nights?' Then follows an exposition of Deut. 26.5–9, which includes the comment: 'In every age a man is bound to regard himself as if *he* went forth out of Egypt, as it is written, "And thou shalt tell thy son in that day, saying, It is because of what the Lord did for *me* when I came out of Egypt"' (Ex. 13.8). It is an occasion, according to Rabbi Gamaliel, when the worshipper gave praise and thanks to 'him who wrought all these wonders for our fathers and for us. He brought us out from bondage to freedom, from sorrow to gladness, and from mourning to a festival-day, and from darkness to great light, and from servitude to redemption; so let us say before him the Hallelujah.'[2] As W. D. Davies has pointed out,[3] the significant thing about this language is the blurring of the distinction between those who were involved in the original historical events and those participating in the present celebration of the Passover. 'The external facts have to become living, present realities: the realization of one's own per-

---

[1] Cf. E. Jacob, *Theology of the Old Testament*, p. 259.
[2] Pesahim 10.4 f. (*The Mishnah*, tr. H. Danby, 1933, pp. 150 f.).
[3] In *Paul and Rabbinic Judaism*, 1948, pp. 102 ff.

sonal participation, as it were, in these external acts of history *ipso facto* makes one a member of the nation.'[1] This easy transition from the past event to present existence, made clear by the change from third-personal pronoun to first, is frequently found in the Old Testament itself. In the 'farewell discourse' of Joshua, for example, we find:

> I brought *your fathers* out of Egypt, and *you* came to the sea; and the Egyptians pursued *your fathers* with chariots and horsemen to the Red Sea. And when *they* cried to the Lord, he put darkness between *you* and the Egyptians, and made the sea come upon *them* and cover *them*; and *your* eyes saw what I did to Egypt; and *you* lived in the wilderness a long time (Josh. 24.6 f.)

In present existence there can be experience of that which was, and foretaste of that which is to come. 'Was', 'is', 'is to come' are the three basic tenses of the Old Testament—and of the New.[2]

The cultic mime as a means whereby the past crucial events were made contemporary would explain many of the features of the Book of Deuteronomy.

Von Rad has suggested that the structure of Deuteronomy—paraenesis, commandments, the making of a covenant, blessing and cursing—points to 'the course of a great cultic celebration',[3] which he identifies as the old festival of the renewal of the covenant at Shechem. The shape of the book certainly reflects some festival where through imitative mime the Yahweh who was, the Yahweh of the great saving acts, is known as the Yahweh who is now, the Yahweh whose present *dabhar* is known in the recited *debharim*.

The cultic origin of Deuteronomy is explicitly indicated in 31.9 ff.: 'At the end of every seven years, at the set time of the year of release, at the feast of booths, when all Israel comes to appear before Yahweh your God at the place he will choose, you shall read this law before all Israel in their hearing.' Originally an agricultural festival of thanksgiving, by the time of Deuteronomy Tabernacles had become historicized as a pilgrimage feast, a *mimesis* of Yahweh's actions on the Exodus journey. This is clearly stated in the Holiness Code:

> You shall dwell in booths for seven days; all that are native in Israel shall dwell in booths: that your generations may know that I made the children of Israel dwell in booths when I brought them out of the land of Egypt (Lev. 23.42 f.).

---

[1] *Ibid.*, p. 104.   [2] Cf. Rev. 1.4, 8; 4.8.
[3] *Studies in Deuteronomy*, ET (SBT 9) 1953, p. 14.

It is remarkable that while Deuteronomy explicitly attaches the *anamnesis* motif to the other two great festivals of Passover and Weeks, it omits any reference of this kind in connection with Tabernacles. The description of the festival in 16.13–15 suggests simply a harvest thanksgiving. There is no association with the primary history. This is especially remarkable in view of the reference in this passage to the stranger (*ger*), the orphan and the widow, relations with whom are elsewhere in Deuteronomy always the media by which Yahweh's 'Way' with Israel is imitated. Either Deuteronomy represents a stage when the mimetic symbolism of the tents was still attached exclusively to the Passover rites (16.7), or, possibly, since the whole Book of Deuteronomy has the feast of Tabernacles in mind, and is an extended *mimesis* of the journeying and law-giving, a mere isolated rubric was pointless.

This makes clear the significance of the very frequent repetition of *hayyom* in Deuteronomy.

> The Lord our God made a covenant with us in Horeb. The Lord made not this covenant with our fathers, but with *us*, even *us*, who are all of us here alive *this day* (Deut. 5.2 f.).

> You shalt keep his statutes, and his commandments, which I command you *this day* (Deut. 4.40).

> These words which I command you *this day*, shall be upon your heart (Deut. 6.6).

> *This day* the Lord your God commands you to do these statutes and ordinances; you shall therefore be careful to do them with all your heart and with all your soul. You have declared *this day* concerning the Lord that he is your God, and that you will walk in his ways, and keep his statutes and his commandments and his ordinances, and will obey his voice; and the Lord has declared *this day* concerning you that you are a people for his own possession (Deut. 26.16–18).[1]

Hayyom points to a present occasion, say the feast of Tabernacles, wherein through the recital of the history and law of Israel with whatever cultic and dramatic *mimesis* went with it, the presentness of the past was experienced anew. As Voegelin puts it: 'The *hayom* of Deuteronomy in fact symbolizes a peculiar time experience of "To-day and always to-day", in which the transcendent-eternal presence of God with his people has become a world-immanent, permanent presence of his revealed word.'[2]

Israel's first duty, as *imitator Dei*, was to 'remember' the 'Way of the Lord', and the cultic mime in liturgy was the primary manner in which

---

[1] Cf. also 4.4; 8.1, 11; 10.13; 30.2, 8; Ps. 95. 7 f.; 2.7.
[2] *Israel and Revelation*, p. 374.

this was done. Again and again in Deuteronomy there are exhortations to 'remember' the way in which the Lord led Israel from the Red Sea to Jordan:

> You shall remember all the way which the Lord your God has led you these forty years in the wilderness, that he might humble you, testing you to know what was in your heart, whether you would keep his commandments, or not (Deut. 8.2).

In Hebrew thought, as Pedersen has emphasized, 'remembering' meant much more than merely recalling to the memory. It was more than mental recollection:[1] 'When the soul remembers something, it does not mean that it has an objective memory image of some thing, or event, but that this image is called forth in the soul and assists in determining its direction, its action. To remember the works of Yahweh and to seek him, i.e. to let one's acts be determined by his will, is in reality the same.'[2] Consequently, to 'remember' the 'Way' from the Red Sea onwards is to act *now* on the basis of the relationship between God and Israel there revealed, and in so doing to appropriate it, and know it to be most real.[3]

All this shows that we have in the Old Testament something which may fairly be called liturgical mysticism. We noted in the Introduction the common assumption that the Old Testament has no place for mysticism. Certainly if we understand by that term the notions that time and history are of no relevance whatsoever in the religious life, that matter and the body are ultimately unredeemable, and that the destiny of man is to be dissolved into Godhead, and that this may be attained through some 'technique' of spirituality, then of course there need be no discussion. Nothing could be more alien to the outlook of the Old Testament than that. But to experience in the symbol the presence of that which is symbolized, to be profoundly aware of living continuity with past events through liturgical action, to know worship as 'mystery', this is the primary reference, as Père Bouyer has shown,[4] of the early Christian use of the

---

[1] Cf. also A. Bentzen, *King and Messiah*, ET 1955, p. 12: ' "To remember" the saving facts of religion means to the Ancient World that these facts are tangibly experienced, that the members of the congregation, to use an expression from Kierkegaard, "become contemporary" with the fundamental act of salvation in the history of the world.'

[2] J. Pedersen, *Israel* I–II, pp. 106 f.

[3] 'It is possible that the cult included (cf. especially Ps. 66.5) dramatic representations of the great events of the past such as the Exodus from Egypt and the crossing of the Jordan; but, whether by gesture or simply by word, the recalling of these events had as its object the overcoming of chronological and spatial distance and the real introduction of the onlookers into the presence of God who not only acted there and then, but who still acts *hic et nunc*', E. Jacob, *Theology of the Old Testament*, p. 267.

[4] Cf. his essay 'Mysticism' in *Mystery and Mysticism*, pp. 119 ff.

term μυστικός. There is therefore possible a distinctive biblical mysticism which, far from being 'non-historical', is, through liturgy, as securely rooted in the historical revelation as any so-called 'prophetical' piety. In the Old Testament the *anamnesis* of these events is realized in the Passover and other festivals. In the New Testament the *anamnesis* of these events is realized through Eucharistic union and communion with him in whose life they have been embodied.

2. *Imitation of the 'Way' in Life*

The conviction that Israel's special vocation was to walk in the 'Way of the Lord' has determined not only the shape of Old Testament liturgical practice, but also the structure of Old Testament 'ethics'. The imitation of God, for Israel, took quite concrete form in the situations and relationships which the course of life threw up. There Israel must reproduce the 'ways' which God had adopted towards his people in the course of the revelatory history. The 'way' of Israel was to be an extended mime of the Lord's relations with Israel as they had been revealed in the sacred history. Israel's life must bear the marks of an *imitator Dei*; Israel was elect to the imitation of God. As H. H. Rowley has put it: 'If the first message of the election was that Israel was called to receive the revelation of God, it became increasingly clear that she was called to reflect the character of the God who was revealed to her.'[1] The prophetic call to Israel is a summons to return to the vocation of an *imitator Dei*: 'Yahweh asks of men that they shall reflect his own character, so far as it can be reflected within the limitations of human life. . . . When the prophets denounced harshness and oppression and called for compassion for the unfortunate they were calling men to reflect the character which was uniquely expressed in God's deliverance of his people.'[2] This meant for Israel, as we have seen, walking in the 'Way' of Torah, sonship, and knowledge, and we need now to consider more fully what this involved.

Israel must follow in the track of the Lord. He was always ahead of Israel, ready with tokens and indications of where the next part of the journey lay. He gave 'signs' to Israel, and Israel as his faithful follower had to be alert to recognize and act upon them.

In the Old Testament the words used for 'miracle' can be divided into two main groups. There are first those words which emphasize the obviously portentous and prodigious character of certain events, that which makes them 'miraculous' in the modern sense. These words are

[1] H. H. Rowley, *The Biblical Doctrine of Election*, 1950, p. 56.
[2] H. H. Rowley, *The Unity of the Bible*, 1953, p. 25.

niphla'ah, norah, nebulah. They suggest the quality of certain events to compel astonishment, awe, fear. For these the New Testament word is τέρας. Then, second, there are those words which mark how certain events tacitly suggest, without imposing, some inner meaning. They are suggestive gestures rather than unquestionable pronouncements. The words used here are *'oth* and *mopheth*. Their New Testament equivalent is σημεῖον. At certain key points in Israel's history events happened which were called 'signs and wonders'. The 'wonder' element made no more demands on a person than the use of his eyes or ears, but to perceive these events as 'signs' made severe moral and spiritual demands. Only to the humble and the obedient were these events self-authenticating 'signs'. Pride and self-concern led to 'hardening' of the heart which could not get beyond the 'wonder' element, and remained confined in its own stupor or fear, as in the case of Pharaoh.

God, as Lord of the covenant, had promised to be with his people, and his presence was indicated by 'signs', but they were not of such a character that their recognition was inevitable. Israel was again and again rebuked for not recognizing them, because this was not a matter of some excusable moral defect, but of a wilful moral turpitude for which the people were accountable:

> And the Lord said to Moses, How long will this people despise me? and how long will they not believe in me, in spite of all the signs (*'othoth*) which I have wrought among them? (Num. 14.11).

They were always willing to derive comfort in a self-regarding way from events which contained the 'miraculous' in the modern sense, while wilfully ignoring the moral demands which these events, as 'signs' and not mere 'wonders', made upon them. The 'sign' was a trial or 'temptation' of faith; only in faith would it be seen as a 'sign' making demands, and not merely a 'wonder' giving satisfaction.[1] Israel's call to be ready to seize on the 'signs' which the Lord would give was being continually disobeyed because she was 'hard-hearted' and 'stiff-necked', too readily accepting 'wonders' as deserved confirmations of a permanent status, rather than significant indications of the task of the moment. In the Old Testament, 'sign' and 'temptation' are closely associated. They are two aspects of the one event. In certain events God tests the fidelity of his Israel, and these

---

[1] Cf. E. Jacob, *Theology of the Old Testament*, p. 224: 'For the Old Testament the essential mark of a miracle does not lie in its "miraculous" character, but in the power of revelation that it contains . . . The crossing of the Red Sea only became a miracle by a concatenation of circumstances, firstly the presence of the Israelites at that particular moment, and still more that of Moses who gives to these circumstances a religious interpretation.'

events are experienced by Israel as 'temptations'. To 'tempt' God, in the Old Testament, is to seek for more and more satisfying 'proofs' of one's own, rather than to accept in trust and act upon those which God in fact gives, but in his own way. This was Israel's temptation at Massah, to demand a token of certainty acceptable to herself:

> And he called the name of the place Massah, and Meribah, because of the striving of the children of Israel, and because they tempted the Lord saying, Is the Lord among us or not? (Ex. 17.7).

Equally important for an understanding of the close relation between 'temptation' and 'sign' is Deut. 13.1–3:

> If a prophet arises in the midst of you, or a dreamer of dreams, and gives you a sign or a wonder, and the sign or wonder which he tells you comes to pass, and if he says, 'Let us go after other gods', which you have not known, 'and let us serve them', you shall not listen to the words of that prophet or to that dreamer of dreams; for the Lord your God is testing you, to know whether you love the Lord your God with all your heart and with all your soul.

The 'sign' is, in other words, a possible 'stumbling-block'.[1] It may be received and interpreted as a 'sign' of merited approval, and not a gratuitous confirmation of a vocation. The 'sign' which easily and immediately satisfies may do so only by way of a trial of obedience, a 'temptation' to turn aside from the stern realities which walking in the 'Way' of the Lord involves. True obedience is the criterion by which a man may recognize the 'signs', whether they be of God or not. This is an important point to which we shall return in our discussion of the New Testament.

The 'signs' of God, because they are the gestures of a God who acts in a personal manner, never thrust their meaning on men in an arbitrary way. As true 'signs' they are equivocal. This is particularly true of the 'signs' given through symbolic actions of the prophet. Isaiah believed that he and his children round him were called to be a 'sign' for the times: 'Behold, I and the children whom the Lord hath given me are for signs and for wonders in Israel from the Lord of hosts, which dwelleth in mount Zion' (Isa. 8.18). For those who obeyed and therefore believed (obedience and belief being practically synonymous in the Old Testament) the prophet and those around him would be a 'sign' of perfect trust and waiting upon the Lord, but not for others who might see there only visionary escapism or the like. In a similar way, Ezekiel was requested to perform certain actions which God would constitute 'signs' to the house

---

[1] Isa. 8.15.

of Israel (4.1 ff.; 12.6). He was to say, 'I am a sign for you' (12.11). 'Thus shall Ezekiel be to you a sign; according to all that he has done shall you do. When this comes, then you will know that I am the Lord God' (24.24). The 'sign' is a revelatory event, a source of 'knowledge' for those who do not cause themselves to 'stumble' through pride, arrogance, or self-sufficiency. It was these hindrances which prevented the 'nations' from recognizing in the life and work of the 'Servant' of Deutero-Isaiah a 'sign' of God's redemptive purpose for the world through Israel; it was only when they looked again that they recognized the significance of what had been taking place in front of their eyes:

> Surely he has borne our griefs
> and carried our sorrows;
> yet we esteemed him stricken,
> smitten by God, and afflicted.
> But he was wounded for our transgressions,
> he was bruised for our iniquities;
> upon him was the chastisement that made us whole,
> and with his stripes we are healed (Isa. 53.4–6).

Israel, then, as *imitator Dei* must act upon the tokens which God gives in the situations and relationships which are encountered during the historical process. In Israel there must be reproduced the 'ways' which God has adopted towards Israel. The 'Way' of Israel was to be an extended mime of Yahweh's relations with Israel as history had revealed them. The exemplar had been given in history, and the 'imitation' must be wrought out in the same medium.

Israel's love of God, for example, was to be an imitation of God's love of Israel. Not only in liturgy but in ordinary life there was to be a mimetic tribute to the kind of love shown by God during the basic period of the journey from Red Sea to Zion:

> The Lord set his heart upon your fathers and chose their descendants after them, you above all peoples, as at this day . . . For Yahweh your God is God of gods and Lord of lords, the great, the mighty, and the terrible God, who is not partial and takes no bribe. He executes justice for the fatherless and the widow, and loves the sojourner, giving him food and clothing. Love the sojourner therefore; *for you were sojourners in the land of Egypt.* You shall fear the Lord your God; you shall serve him and cleave to him, and by his name you shall swear . . . You shall *therefore* love the Lord your God, and keep his charge, his statutes, his ordinances, and his commandments always (Deut. 10.15 ff.).

Specially relevant here are those roots which are used both for divine and for human activity. The words *'emeth* and *'amunah*, for example, are used both for the 'truth' and reliability of God, and for the 'faith' of man. Israel's response of 'faith', therefore, is a mimetic response to God's 'faith' in Israel. God's 'faith' means his steadfast purpose, his fidelity to his covenant, and Israel's 'faith' is an imitation of this 'faithfulness'.[1] Israel is to walk in the 'Way', confident that the God who has made the covenant promises will fulfil them, and that this walking in faith will be accompanied by ability to recognize in her history the 'signs' that this is so.

Hesedh is another of the words used for both the activity of God and of man. Man's *hesedh* towards his neighbour is the means whereby he imitates, in terms of a personal relationship, the *hesedh* of God:[2]

> And the king said, 'Is there not still some one of the house of Saul, that I may show the kindness of God (*hesedh 'Elohim*) to him?' (II Sam. 9.3).

> If I am still alive show me the loyal love of the Lord (*hesedh Adhonai*), that I may not die (I Sam. 20.14).

As Jacob points out, the expression *'asah hesedh we 'emeth* is used of both God and man, and if the ideal of the Israelite is to be *hasidh*, this makes him an imitator of the Lord who is himself perfect *hesedh*.[3] Jacob makes the further interesting suggestion that the Levitical formula 'I am the Lord' points to the possibility that the idea of the *imitatio Dei* lay behind the legislation, and that the culmination of this in 'Thou shalt love thy neighbour as thyself' was seeking to reproduce on the human plane the method of God 'who by creating man in his image and clothing him in a dignity like to his own, loved him as himself'.[4]

The 'righteousness' (*mishpat*) of Israel is an imitation of the 'righteousness' (*zedek*) of God.[5] As Norman Snaith has pointed out, the 'righteousness' of God means his particular care for the 'poor and outcast, the widow and the orphan'.[6] This was shown during the historic 'Way' from Egypt to Canaan, and the 'righteousness' of the nation and of the individual was to be an *anamnesis*, and thereby a proclamation of the 'righteousness' of God:

> You shall not pervert the justice due to the sojourner or to the father-less, or take a widow's garment in pledge; but you shall remember that you were a slave in Egypt and the Lord your God redeemed you from there; therefore I command you to do this. . . . When you gather the

---

[1] Cf. S. H. Hooke, *The Kingdom of God in the Experience of Jesus*, 1949, p. 126.
[2] E. Jacob, *Theology of the Old Testament*, p. 174. [3] *Ibid.*, p. 174.
[4] *Ibid.*, p. 175. Cf. H. H. Rowley, *Unity of the Bible*, p. 79: 'God made man in his own image, and his essential law for man is that he shall reflect the image of God and become like him in character.'
[5] Cf. P. Ramsey, *Basic Christian Ethics*, 1953, p. 5.
[6] *Distinctive Ideas of the Old Testament*, 1944, p. 69.

grapes of your vineyard, you shall not glean it afterward; it shall be for the sojourner, the fatherless, and the widow. You shall remember that you were a slave in the land of Egypt; therefore I command you to do this (Deut. 24.17 f., 21 f.).

It has been suggested above that the status and role of the king, the priest and the prophet indicate the need for the *imitatio Dei* mission of Israel to be seen in terms of a visible human exemplar. One can already detect a move in the Old Testament towards the idea of a person who embodies in his life and work the vocation of Israel to 'walk' in the 'Way' of the Lord. This is particularly noticeable in relation to the figure of the king who comes to be regarded as representing Israel in such a unique and intimate way as to be, in some sense, Israel himself. All three, however, king, priest and prophet, were dedicated to order their lives in such a fashion as to be suitable models for the people to imitate. Israel's *imitatio Dei* meant, in its perfection, a mission of kingship, priesthood, and prophecy,[1] and in the Old Testament one can trace a tendency for these three functions to coalesce in one figure who in a quite special way represents the people. In the tradition, for example, Moses appears as the ideal *imitator Dei* in whom the duties of king, priest and prophet are all fulfilled,[2] and consequently there develops the belief that Moses will appear again as the one best suited to usher in the Messianic Age. It is just possible that the Book of Deuteronomy represents an important stage in the history of this idea of a personal exemplar. It is interesting, in this respect, to compare Deuteronomy with the Book of the Covenant. Deuteronomy seems to have the same kind of relationship to the Book of the Covenant as the Fourth Gospel bears to the Synoptic tradition. Voegelin has suggested that the Deuteronomic treatment of the material in the Book of the Covenant reveals a desire to personalize the *imitatio Dei* motif in the form of an *imitatio Mosis*. 'An effective *imitatio Mosis*', he writes, 'required a paradigmatic prophet and lawgiver who could be imitated.'[3] In the Book of the Covenant, to quote Voegelin further, 'no Moses is interposed as a speaker between the author and the events narrated', whereas in Deuteronomy Moses and his work are in the foreground of the symbolism, and this he attributes to the prophetic revolt in the crisis of the ninth century. Certainly there is in Deuteronomy a blurring of the distinction between Yahweh the Lawgiver and Moses the Lawgiver,[4] and

---

[1] Israel is anointed, like the king, cf. Ps. 28.8; 84.9; 89.38, 51; Hab. 3.13. For Israel as priest cf. Ex. 19.6; Isa. 61.6; Hos. 4.6; and for Israel as prophet Num. 11.29 and the *Ebed Yahweh* songs of Deutero-Isaiah.

[2] For Moses as king, priest and prophet cf. G. Östborn, *Tōrā in the Old Testament*, and E. Jacob, *Theology of the Old Testament*, pp. 233–54.

[3] *Israel and Revelation*, p. 384.   [4] Cf. 17.3; 28.20; 29.5.

to turn away from Moses is tantamount to turning away from Yahweh.[1] If Moses in Deuteronomy is a prototype *imitator Dei* then the undoubted influence of the Book of Deuteronomy on the central figure of the New Testament, which will be discussed in the following chapter, takes on new and special interest.

Quite naturally, the three ideal *imitatores Dei*, the king, the priest and the prophet, were regarded in Old Testament eschatological expectation as 'signs' of that which was to come, and consequently contributed features to the figure of him who was to be *the* 'sign': the Messiah.[2] Royal, priestly and prophetic characteristics coalesce in the complex imagery which surrounds the Old Testament figure of the Messiah. The growth of the idea of the Messiah as future King in Old Testament and Jewish literature has been set out in full in a number of recent studies,[3] and there is no need to repeat the discussion here. The Messianic Age was expected to take the form of a recapitulation of the basic saving history, and the Messiah would accomplish perfectly and finally that which the kings of Israel and Judah, even the best of them, had failed to effect. During the Maccabean period, as one might expect, it was the idea of a priestly Messiah which became predominant, and where two Messiahs were expected, as in the *Testaments of the Twelve Patriarchs* or at Qumran, it was the priestly Messiah, the 'Messiah of Aaron', who took precedence. There was also a Messianism which stressed particularly the prophetical character of the person and work of the future deliverer.[4]

A particularly important personal delineation of the 'Way' of Israel as *imitatio Dei* is given in the biography of the 'Servant' in the Servant-poems of Deutero-Isaiah. The life of the Servant has significant form; as Mowinckel puts it, 'The Servant's life is his real work.'[5] Bentzen speaks of the Servant-poems as 'expressions of an idea of the "imitation of Christ" in Israel'.[6] Here again the figures of the king, priest and prophet coalesce. Like a prophet, the Servant is predestined[7] and 'called'[8] of God for a special task, that of establishing *mishpat* in Israel.[9] As we have noted previously, *mishpat* is parallel to *torah*, and so the Servant is commissioned as king[10] to walk in the *torah* of the Lord. Indeed, if the Scandinavian

---

[1] The same words *sur* and *'ahere* are used of each.

[2] For the 'anointing' of the King cf. I Sam. 9.16; 16.3; I Kings 1.34; of the prophet cf. I Kings 19.16; and of the priest Ex. 28.41.

[3] Cf. S. Mowinckel, *He that Cometh*; A. Bentzen, *King and Messiah*; H. Ringgren, *The Messiah in the Old Testament* (SBT 18), 1956.

[4] Passages like Deut. 18.15 and Mal. 4.5 were influential in the development of this idea.   [5] *He that Cometh*, p. 230.

[6] *Introduction to the Old Testament*[2], 1952, Vol. II, p. 113.

[7] Isa. 49.1.   [8] Isa. 42.1.   [9] Isa. 42.4.

[10] Cf. C. R. North, *The Suffering Servant in Deutero-Isaiah*, 1948, p. 91.

'myth and ritual' school is right, the Servant-songs reflect aspects of the cultic festival when, for example, the king underwent a voluntary humiliation. The priestly function of the Servant is seen in his sacrificial giving of himself as a sin-offering (*'asham*)[1] and also in the fact that he acts as intercessor.[2]

The Servant figure in Second Isaiah possibly represents a significant stage in the development of the belief that Israel was called to walk in the way of martyrdom. E. Stauffer has a very interesting Appendix I to his *New Testament Theology*[3] where he gives a list of passages to illustrate the principal elements in what he calls 'the old biblical theology of martyrdom'. As might be expected, this theology of martyrdom received special stimulus from the Maccabean wars, but there are sufficient passages to show that a high doctrine of martyrdom is rooted in the Old Testament. The Servant-poems may already be expressing the idea, which was to be given prominence in later Judaism, that the sufferings and death of the martyr are much more than a display of heroism and devotion. They have atoning power. If this is so, it is interesting to note that in both the Old and the New Testaments it is the martyr who is held to be the imitator of God *par excellence*. Furthermore, Jesus may have interpreted the Servant-sequences in Isaiah in this way and taken them to be a representation of Israel's martyr destiny under God, and this would certainly have influenced his conception of the Way of the Son of Man, and particularly the atoning, redemptive significance he attached to it.

The idea of the *imitatio Dei* occupies an important place in rabbinic Judaism.[4] That human life is meant to be an *imitatio Dei* was believed to be the consequence of God's having created man in his own image and likeness. This was interpreted in rabbinic tradition to mean that the destiny of man is to be like God. A midrash, for example, interprets 'And you are this day as the stars for multitude (*larob*)' by taking the word *rb* in its sense of 'Lord', 'Master', and goes on: 'To-day you are like the stars, but in the world to come, you are destined to be like your God.'[5] The *imitatio Dei* consisted of 'walking' in 'the Way', 'cleaving' to God, and this was particularized as imitating the attributes (*middoth*) of God. The whole Torah from Genesis to Deuteronomy was interpreted as a divine summons to Israel to imitate God.[6] The model for human behaviour was God's manner with Israel, particularly with the patriarchs. God's actions

---

[1] Isa. 53.10.   [2] Isa. 53.12.   [3] ET 1955, pp. 331–4.
[4] Cf. I. Abrahams, *Studies in Pharisaism and the Gospels*, Series II, 1924, pp. 138 f.; Martin Buber, *Mamre: Essays on Religion*, ET 1946; A. Marmorstein, *Studies in Jewish Theology*, 1950; G. F. Moore, *Judaism*, Vol. II, 1927, pp. 109 ff.
[5] Debarim Rabba, *passim*.   [6] I. Abrahams, *op. cit.*, p. 146.

in clothing the nakedness of Adam and his wife, visiting the sick Abraham in the grove at Mamre (there was a tradition that Abraham came here after his circumcision), comforting the mourning Isaac, burying the dead Moses, constituted his *middoth*—visible patterns of behaviour for imitation.[1] Just as in Philo the patriarchs Abraham, Isaac and Jacob are a νόμος ἔμψυχος for imitation, so in rabbinic Judaism there is traceable a move towards the idea of individual human exemplars of the *imitatio Dei*. This development, like the personification in the Servant-poems, suggests that there is a basic human need for the concrete human model, and perhaps also it is the result of a partial overlaying of the liturgical tradition by the study of a canonized literature—a development parallel to that which Christian spirituality began to show in the fourth century—the 'fathers' playing in Judaism the part to be played in Christianity first by the martyrs, then by the saints in general.

[1] Sotah 14a.

PART TWO

The Imitation of God in the New Testament

5

Jesus' Mission to be Himself the 'Way'

THE CHRISTIAN RELIGION was first known as 'the Way'.[1] Already by the time the Acts of the Apostles was written this had become a technical term for the belief and practices of the early Church. The concept of the 'Way' is deeply rooted, as we have seen, in the Old Testament, but it is very probable that there is more to the early Christian use of ὁδός than merely the taking up of a term common in pre-Christian Israel.[2] There are suggestions in the New Testament that the 'Way' was specially associated in the minds of the early Christians with Jesus himself, and we shall later suggest reasons for believing that the imagery of the 'Way' did in fact occupy an important place in his mind. The Johannine logion, 'I am the way, the truth and the life', is evidence of the early Christian belief that 'the Way' is Jesus himself, his life, his actions and his teaching. The same belief is expressed in the Epistle to the Hebrews where Jesus is presented as himself 'the new and living way', and also, as Riesenfeld[3] has indicated, by St Paul, who introduces the thirteenth chapter of I Corinthians, behind which, as we shall suggest subsequently, there stands the life of the Lord Christ himself, as 'a still more excellent way (ὁδός)'. Furthermore, the vocabulary of the New Testament is dominated by terms associated with the imagery of the 'Way', and we have to ask whether the early Christians inevitably turned to language of this kind because of certain features of the Lord's mission which were indelibly fixed in their minds. As followers of 'the Way' they imitated him who was himself the 'Way', leading in front.

The mission of Jesus was given him by the Father, and this is a point stressed in different ways in all four Gospels. The Father showed him the

---

[1] Acts 9.2; 16.17; 18.25 f.; 19.9, 23; 22.4; 24.14, 22.

[2] The Qumranists used *derek* as a designation of their way of life. S. V. McCasland ('The Way', *Journal of Biblical Literature* 77, 1958, pp. 222–30) thinks that the Christians derived the idiom ultimately from Qumran, and that the agent of the transmission was John the Baptist. As I have indicated throughout, it seems more likely that the term was of basic significance to Jesus himself, and that primitive Christian allusions point to his unique use of it.

[3] H. Riesenfeld, 'La voie de charité', *ST* 1, 1948, pp. 146–57.

'Way' in which he must walk, and Jesus committed himself to this task. As Stauffer has put it, 'The "must" of divine predestination covered every step that Jesus took.'[1] 'I must go on my way today and tomorrow and the day following' (Luke 13.33); Jesus must be 'up to Jerusalem' as soon as possible. There was no time to lose. This note of urgency is specially brought out, as we shall see, in the Fourth Gospel. The 'Way' in which Jesus must go had Jerusalem as its destination, and the compulsion to get to Jerusalem is particularly a theme of St Luke: 'When the days drew near for him to be received up, he set his face to go to Jerusalem' (Luke 9.51). Other Lucan evidence that Jesus felt himself under constraint to finish a certain journey in a certain time is found in the following passages: 'I have a baptism to be baptized with; and how I am constrained until it is accomplished' (12.50); 'I must preach the good news of the kingdom of God to the other cities also; for I was sent for this purpose' (4.43). Again, Jesus *must* enter the house of Zacchaeus (Luke 19.5), even though it caused offence. If the Father has given indication that salvation comes to this house this day through him, then he must go.

More precisely, Jesus must go this 'Way' because thereby 'Scripture will be fulfilled'. The early Christians felt themselves obliged to interpret Jesus as the fulfilment of Scripture because he had himself first done it for them, not only in teaching but, and perhaps primarily, in his actions.[2] The early Christian preachers and interpreters of Jesus were simply underlining a fact which was central to the mission of Jesus himself. Old Testament piety was rooted in certain actions whereby the significant events of the 'salvation-history' were made contemporaneous.[3] This was particularly true of the Passover festival, and it may well have been that Jesus, acting under the compulsion of the Spirit, believed that he must allow himself to be used by the Father for the actualization in his own life of the 'Way of Israel', that he must be himself Israel in the flesh, and his 'Way' a recapitulation of the events 'remembered' at Passover. Certainly the divine imperative lies on the 'Son of Man': 'For the Son of man goes as it is written of him.'[4] This means, at least, that the 'Way' of the 'Son of Man' (to death?) has been indicated in Old Testament writings, and that in his own life there is taking place a reproduction of that 'Way'.

---

[1] *New Testament Theology*, p. 26.

[2] Cf. C. H. Dodd, *History and the Gospel*, 1938, pp. 61 f.: 'There has been some principle of selection at work by which certain sides of the messianic idea are held to be fulfilled, and others are set aside. What was that principle of selection? Surely the simplest explanation is that a true historical memory controlled the selection of prophecies. Those were held to have been fulfilled which were in general consonant with the memory of what Jesus had been, had said, had done and had suffered.'   [3] Cf. p. 50 above.

[4] Mark 14.21. Luke 22.22 has 'For the Son of man goes as it has been determined'.

It is written of the Son of man, that he should suffer many things and be treated with contempt (Mark 9.12).

It is very likely that here Jesus was alluding to the Servant-poems of Deutero-Isaiah, where he believed there had been set out what was now being fulfilled in his own time.

Day after day I was with you in the temple teaching, and you did not seize me. But let the scriptures be fulfilled! (Mark 14.49).

The arrest indicated that all was going according to the forewritten plan. One more stage had been reached along the Father's way into which the Spirit was guiding Jesus.

This 'Way' along which Jesus must go to 'fulfil Scripture' is further alluded to as the 'Way of the Son of Man'. The implication is that as 'Son of Man' Jesus *must* (not merely may or even will) go along the pre-ordained way, a way which was bound to involve humiliation and suffering:

And he began to teach them that the Son of man must suffer many things, and be rejected by the elders and the chief priests and the scribes, and be killed, and after three days rise again (Mark 8.31).

From that time Jesus began to show his disciples that he must go to Jerusalem and suffer many things (Matt. 16.21).

Everything that is written of the Son of man by the prophets will be accomplished (Luke 18.31).

First he [the Son of Man] must suffer many things and be rejected by this generation (Luke 17.25).

The authenticity of these predictions has often been questioned, but their theme is so central to the purpose of Jesus himself that this insistence on the unconditional obligation of the Son of Man to suffer is not an historical problem, even though the actual wording of the predictions may, in some cases, reflect the tendency to fill in details after the event.

The form of the mission of Jesus, then, was part of its content. The 'Way of the Son of Man' which Jesus followed carried clear indications in action and in word that this was none other than God's 'Way' for Israel demonstrably being lived out in full obedience before men's eyes. The 'Way' of Jesus had indeed the same threefold character as the 'Way of Israel' in the Old Testament: it was the Way of Sonship, the Way of Knowledge, and the Way of Torah.

The Way of Sonship. The Gospels make it quite clear that Jesus was aware of being in a unique and intimate relationship to the Father. The evidence for this is the Synoptic account of the Baptism[1] and the fact that the Father was so intimate and near to Jesus that he only spoke of God as Father either in prayer or in talk with disciples.[2] The probability that there was, so to speak, a characteristic tone of voice in Jesus' speech about the Father is suggested by the fact that the actual Aramaic word *Abba* has remained in the transmission of the tradition,[3] and that St Paul found himself using the same word when speaking of Christians addressing the Father as 'sons in the Son'.[4] The historical expression and manifestation of this sonship would naturally take the form of actualizing the vocation of Israel. Certainly it is in just those three books which had most influence on the mind of Jesus—Deuteronomy, Isaiah, and Ezekiel—that we find most prominently the idea of a salvific miming of the initial saving history of Israel. The Way of Sonship for Jesus was, as Stauffer puts it, a 'doxological' way, a glorification of the Father. This Israel must fulfil the old Israel's obligation to be in the 'things of the Father' (Luke 2.49).

The Way of Knowledge. This feature of the 'Way' of Jesus is specially brought out in the Fourth Gospel, but it has a firm base in the Synoptic tradition. In Jesus the Father perfectly 'knows' Israel, and in Jesus Israel perfectly 'knows' the Father. The Father 'knows' Jesus in choosing him, endowing him with the Spirit, and giving him 'signs' as he walks along the 'Way'. Israel in Jesus 'knows' the Father in true reverence and humility, in alert recognition of the 'signs' given, and readiness to seek out the poor and outcast: 'I came not to call the righteous, but sinners' (Mark 2.17). This mutual knowledge of the Father and the Son which becomes one of the main themes of the Fourth Gospel is already found in the Q tradition which lies behind Matt. 11.27 and Luke 10.22:

> All things have been delivered unto me of my Father: and no one knoweth the Son, save the Father; neither doth any know the Father, save the Son, and he to whom the Son willeth to reveal him (Matt. 11.27).

'No prophet', says W. D. Davies, 'claimed that he *knew* Jehovah. Full knowledge was always an object of desire, not of attainment, a mark of the Messianic Age, not of present experience . . . It is this fulness of knowledge that Jesus claims for himself, . . . and this unique relationship is expressed by saying that Jesus knew God fully—claimed a knowledge of God that before not even the prophets had claimed.'[5]

The Way of Torah. We have noted that obedience to the Torah was one of the expected features of the Messianic Age, and, as W. D. Davies points

---

[1] Cf. pp. 74 ff. below.   [2] Cf. T. W. Manson, *The Teaching of Jesus*[2], 1935.
[3] Mark 14.36.   [4] Gal. 4.6; Rom. 8.15.
[5] *Paul and Rabbinic Judaism*, p. 158.

out, the possibility that Jesus was consciously fulfilling the expectation of a Messianic Torah, as surely as he fulfilled other elements in the Messianic expectation, has not been the object of sufficient interest.[1] In Old Testament thought, walking in the 'Way of the Lord' and 'knowing' him are synonymous with obeying the Torah and with true sonship, and Matthaean sayings like 'It is fitting for us to fulfil all righteousness' (3.15) and 'Think not that I have come to abolish the law and the prophets; I have not come to abolish them but to fulfil them' (5.17) are authentic expressions of a vocation which Jesus accepted as central to his whole mission.

We saw that in the Old Testament tradition the three figures of prophet, king and priest appear as ideal imitators of God. In them the functions and duties of Israel as the elect covenant people of God are concentrated. It is certain that these figures were prominent in the background of Jewish Messianic expectation to which Jesus came, and one can trace their influence in his own thought and practice. Kingly, priestly and prophetic functions were already merged in the role to which he believed that he had been summoned if we assume, as I believe we must, that the Servant-songs exercised a decisive influence on Jesus' thinking about the form which his ministry must take. We can certainly detect in the Gospel tradition about Jesus kingly, priestly and prophetic elements, and this in a way which suggests that they probably go back to actual features of the historical mission.

Jesus saw his own role as being, in one chief aspect, that of a king. The inscription on the cross and the taunt 'Hail, King of the Jews' suggest that the mission of Jesus was widely interpreted as having a royal character. There are sufficient direct references and implications in the Gospel tradition to make this most probable. The Way of Sonship itself involved kingship, as we have seen from the Old Testament background. The entry into Jerusalem was a carefully contrived royal procession, although sufficiently veiled to be a sign of royalty only for those who were prepared to see the Messiah as the king who visited his capital in humiliation. The mission of Jesus was a summons to a kingship which he must have realized was unlikely to be welcomed and accepted. His temptation was to tempt the Father by assuming, say, a kingship that would have pleased the Zealots, in order to force the issue. He was tempted to proclaim himself in a way more congenial and seemingly more effective by appearing as king on the top of Zion. He went up to Jerusalem and entered his capital for coronation, but it was the Father who would crown him—he must not

---

[1] *Torah in the Messianic Age and/or the Age to Come*, p. 4.

seek to crown himself. There was no kingdom but that which the Father would give, and no king but him whom the Father would crown. The irony of it is that Jesus was being crowned king at the very moment when it would seem that his humiliation was far removed from any possible kingship. This ironical situation is characteristically seized upon by the author of the Fourth Gospel and the crown *is* placed on the head of Jesus in his capital. The King-Messiah is in fact presented to the people by those who believe that he has not yet appeared.

The prophetic character of the mission of Jesus needs no detailed substantiation here.[1] Jesus quite clearly regarded himself as a prophet and the manner both of his words and works shows that he saw himself as standing in the line of the prophetic tradition.

It is also clear that Jesus saw his mission as having a priestly content. Two things in particular seem to suggest this. Jesus certainly saw himself as commissioned to enact the way of Israel personified in the Isaianic Servant-poems. This was in his mind when he spoke of the Son of Man who had come to give his life a ransom for many. There is very likely a reference here to the priestly character of the Servant's mission as a 'sin offering' (*'asham*). Jesus had come to carry out in his life and work what was a primary priestly task. Further he was a priestly intercessor. He made direct reference to his intercession for Peter,[2] and it would seem that one of the primary roles of the Son of Man for Jesus was that of intercession. This is indicated in such a saying as 'Everyone who shall confess me before men, him shall the Son of man also confess before the angels of God' (Luke 12.8).

The mission of Jesus was to fulfil an historical task: to walk himself in the 'Way of Israel' and thereby express his sonship in terms applicable to the situation to which he came. In action and in word Jesus willed to mime the significant features of his nation's history. The form of the ministry of Jesus was an extended act of prophetic symbolism.

Jesus was himself the 'Way', and therefore the perfect imitator of the Father. Perception of his mission as a 'sign' and decision to act upon it was a matter for which those confronted with it were accountable. Upon whether they saw 'sign' or '*skandalon*' judgment turned.

---

[1] The evidence is set out and discussed in C. H. Dodd's essay 'Jesus as Teacher and Prophet' in *Mysterium Christi*, edited by G. K. A. Bell and A. Deissmann, 1930.
[2] Luke 22.32.

6

The 'Sign' and 'Scandal' of the Son of Man

THE FOUR GOSPELS all agree in associating the beginning of the mission of Jesus with that of John the Baptist,[1] and there is sufficient evidence to show that this is not a case of early Christian interpretation being read back into the tradition, but a juxtaposition to which Jesus himself had frequently referred in a significant and characteristic way.

When asked a direct question about his 'authority' it is significant that the mind of Jesus went back at once to the movement of John the Baptist: 'I will ask you a question: answer me, and I will tell you by what authority I do these things. Was the baptism of John from heaven or from men? Answer me' (Mark 11.29 f.). Jesus had himself taken John the Baptist's appearance as a 'sign' from the Father that the penultimate stage[2] of the Kingdom had been reached, and he seems here to have assumed that his questioners were capable of perceiving this sign also. Inability to see John as a 'sign' will mean inability to see Jesus as a sign. For Jesus, John was the sign of the Elijah to come,[3] and therefore, by implication, Jesus himself was being indicated as the Messiah who comes after the Elijah. Rejection of John the Baptist and his movement was, for Jesus, rejection of the will of God.[4]

[1] It would seem probable that 'the beginning of the Gospel' was almost a technical term for John the Baptist's movement. The anti-Marcionite prologue to St Luke speaks of John the Baptist 'who is the beginning of the Gospel' (ὅς ἐστιν ἀρχὴ τοῦ εὐαγγελίου). The Acts of the Apostles also reflects a tradition which associated John the Baptist in a special way with the 'beginning': 1.21 f.: 'All the time that the Lord Jesus went in and went out among us beginning (ἀρξάμενος) from the baptism of John'; 13.24, RV: 'when John had *first* preached (προκηρύξαντος) before his coming'; 10.37: 'beginning (ἀρξάμενος) from Galilee after the baptism which John preached'. Some early Fathers support this interpretation. Basil of Caesarea, for example, writes in *Contra Eunomium* II, 15 (PG 29.601), 'Mark made the preaching of John the beginning of the Gospel (ἀρχὴν τοῦ εὐαγγελίου)'. These considerations strengthen C. H. Turner's suggestion (*A New Commentary on Holy Scripture*, ed. Gore, Goudge and Guillaume, 1928, *ad loc.*) that Mark 1.2 f. is in parenthesis and that vv. 1 and 4 read consecutively: 'The beginning of the gospel of Jesus Christ . . . was John the Baptist's preaching . . .'   [2] 'The law and the prophets were until John', Luke 16.16.
[3] Mark 9.11–13.   [4] Luke 7.30.

The close juxtaposition of the mission of John the Baptist and that of Jesus in the Gospel tradition may well reflect something which was in the forefront of the mind of Jesus himself. He responded to the movement of John the Baptist by taking it as a 'sign' from the Father that the Kingdom of God was about to appear. He acted on this sign and was baptized. This was not the only 'sign' which Jesus perceived in the mission of the Baptist. It seems likely that the imprisonment of John was taken by Jesus as a sign that his own mission must now begin, and further, that the death of John the Baptist was taken by Jesus as a sign that he must now be 'up to Jerusalem'. This is suggested in the saying of Jesus which Mark locates after the Transfiguration: 'I tell you that Elijah has come, and they did to him whatever they pleased, as it is written of him' (9.13). The death of John the Baptist is written up at surprising length and in great detail, and it would seem that Dr Farrer is right in suggesting that Mark wishes to suggest that the 'passion' and death of John is in prefiguration of that of Jesus.[1] The saying just quoted is associated with a saying about the Son of Man having to suffer in similar fashion. The death of John the Baptist points, for those who can discern these things, to the death of the Messiah. The lengthy and elaborate treatment of the death of John the Baptist may be a reflection of the significance, as a sign, which Jesus himself attached to it.

The mission of John the Baptist and Jesus' reaction to it is followed in the Gospel tradition by accounts of the Baptism and Temptation.

A critical problem of first importance here, especially for our purposes, is to determine whether these narratives of the Baptism of Jesus and his Temptation are legends which have been read back into the tradition, or whether they go back to some real extent to Jesus himself. The latter seems to me more likely. The Baptism and Temptation of Jesus are so indelibly associated with the basic character of his mission as he conceived it as to make it highly unlikely that the accounts of them are of secondary origin. This conclusion if accepted has most important consequences, because in both cases it means that we have some knowledge of the interpretation which Jesus himself placed on these happenings. The accounts of the Baptism and the Temptation which we now find in the Gospel tradition may well be founded on an account of these happenings which Jesus gave to his disciples at some point during the ministry, probably after the confession of Peter at Caesarea Philippi during that phase when he was primarily concerned with the nature and function of the mission laid upon his disciples. The significance of these two happenings we must now analyse in detail.

[1] *A Study in St Mark*, 1951, p. 92.

Jesus, we have suggested, seeing in John's mission a sign from the Father that his action as King was about to come to a head, identified himself with it and was baptized. What followed is given in these words by St Mark's Gospel:

And when he came up out of the water, immediately he saw the heavens opened and the Spirit descending upon him like a dove; and a voice came from heaven, 'Thou art my beloved Son; with thee I am well pleased' (Mark 1.10 f.).

We have here a complex of various images: the heavens opening, the dove, and the two figures suggested by the words of the voice: the king and the prophet-servant. Before discussing these more fully it is important that we should remind ourselves that Jesus was a poet, a dramatic poet, giving much of his teaching in verse form, and making many of his actions conform to the character of prophetic symbolism. The importance of this is that literary criticism, as students of literature understand this term, is of prime importance for an understanding of the form of the ministry of Jesus. Particularly is this true of the critical appreciation of poetry and drama. The study of poetic sensibility is of great importance for New Testament study, since Jesus' mode of perception and apprehension was clearly that of a poet.[1]

To take the significance of the words of the voice first. In relation to all the evidence available, it would seem from this that Jesus was finally and completely aware of unique and intimate sonship, that God was his Father in a unique sense. One says 'finally and completely' because the Lucan infancy narrative in its story of Jesus in the temple may well be evidence of a consciousness of standing in a quite unique relation of sonship: 'I must be in the things of my Father' (Luke 2.49).

This unique sonship would not have been dissociated in the mind of Jesus from the vocation of Israel, which, as we have seen, is presented in the Old Testament as a call to be Son of Yahweh by walking in the 'Way'. The sonship of Jesus is to take the form of an enactment of the Way of Israel. The sonship of Israel in the Old Testament is focused in the king, and it would seem to be the figure of the king which Jesus had before him after the baptism by John. This is suggested by the fact that the words 'Thou art my Son' echo Ps. 2, which recent Old Testament scholarship

---

[1] One reason why one welcomes the work of Dr Austin Farrer is that he makes use of the methods of literary criticism. The exegesis of the Gospels has for too long been in the hands of academics whose primary interests are linguistic or historical. Mr T. S. Eliot's *Four Quartets* give one a vision of the way a commentary on the Fourth Gospel ought to go.

associates with kingship.[1] This psalm has been described by Mowinckel as a 'royal initiation oracle', and it may well be that it suggested the image of kingship for Jesus himself. In that case it looks as if Jesus interpreted the incident after his Baptism as a token of the Father's will to anoint[2] and enthrone him as king. This was the form his earthly sonship must take. This image of kingship must have included the consciousness of a summons to be himself Israel. Ps. 2 gives a picture of a king summoned to lordship over the nations, or rather, to be prepared to *receive* this lordship from God (vv. 8 f.). The Temptation narrative was to show that Jesus, summoned by the Father to kingship, was tempted to receive lordship from the Devil.

The fact that at one and the same time Jesus *is* Israel and yet has a mission *to* Israel may suggest a difficulty to the modern mind, but this kind of oscillation of reference is characteristic of the Old Testament conception of the roles to be played by, significantly, the king, the *Ebed Yahweh* of the Book of Isaiah, and the Messiah. As ruler and guardian the king had a responsibility *to* Israel the nation, but in Hebrew thought, the king *is* Israel in a special sense. In him the sonship of Israel is focused in a unique manner. Furthermore, as we have seen,[3] by obediently discharging his commission from Yahweh to Israel the king appears as an ideal figure, the ideal *imitator Dei*.

The latter words of the voice seem to echo the opening of the first of the 'Servant-songs',[4] and other passages in Isaiah relating to the 'Servant'.[5] For Jesus himself, of course, there was no 'Deutero-Isaiah' nor was there a quartet of 'Servant-songs' obviously detachable from the rest of the Book of Isaiah. Consequently the scholar's distinction between the Servant of the main body of the book of Second Isaiah, and the Servant of the Songs would have been quite foreign to Jesus himself. In any case, here again, the oscillation between the Servant who *is* Israel and the Servant who has a mission *to* Israel is a main feature of 'Deutero-Isaiah', and the same kind of fluidity of reference in the mind of Jesus regarding the 'Israel' character of his mission may reflect the extent of the influence of this book on his thought. Jesus saw the Father calling him to enact Israel's kingship but in terms of an obedience, humility and martyrdom like that of the Isaianic Servant, and this would mean that its significance would be concealed from all but those who by their own childlike sim-

---

[1] Cf. S. Mowinckel, *He that Cometh*; H. Ringgren, *The Messiah in the Old Testament*; A. Bentzen, *King and Messiah*.
[2] Acts 10.38 suggests that the early Church took the incident as a royal anointing with Spirit.
[3] Cf. p. 61 above.   [4] Isa. 42.1.   [5] Isa. 44.2.

plicity and unsophisticated trust had a certain affinity with it. It is precisely this kind of kingship which Jesus was to enact publicly on such an occasion as the entrance into Jerusalem.

The symbolism of the dove points in the same direction. It is usual to see in the description of the descent of the dove an allusion to the Spirit of God hovering (like a bird, said the rabbis) over the deep in the Genesis account of creation. It is interesting to note, however, that in rabbinic literature the dove is a common symbol for Israel, particularly for Israel in its 'gentleness, fidelity, its persecution, its submission',[1] which are just those features of Israel's life which, as we shall see, Jesus believed it was his task to embody in his own personal version of Israel: 'the Son of Man'. I. Abrahams quotes the following as a 'characteristic Rabbinic passage': 'As the dove knows her mate and never forsakes him, so Israel, once recognising the Holy One as God, never proves faithless to him. All other birds, when they are about to be slaughtered, wince, but the dove holds out its neck to the slayer. So there is no people so willing as Israel to lay down its life for God. Just as the dove (after the flood) brought light to the world, so God said unto Israel, who are likened to the dove, Take olive oil and light thy lamp before me.'[2] In view of the fact that the various elements in the narratives of the Baptism and the Temptation are all related to the mission of Israel, it is quite likely that the dove symbolism belongs to the same complex. In the mind of Jesus his mission is perceived in a poetic fusion of the symbols of the King, the Servant, and the Dove.

The language in which the setting of the Baptism of Jesus is described may well corroborate this point by suggesting a fourth image which points to Israel. The heavens *opened* and the Spirit *coming down*[3] echo several Old Testament passages. There is first Isa. 64.1 (Heb.):

> Oh that thou wouldst rend the heavens,
> that thou wouldst come down.

The context in which this passage is found makes it clear that the expectation of a decisive intervention by God is being expressed in terms meant to recall the great dramatic intervention of Yahweh at Sinai when he came down upon the mountain for the establishment of the Covenant. The other passages where 'opening the heavens and coming down' is found are again reminiscent of the scene at Sinai:

> He bowed the heavens also, and came down;
> And thick darkness was under his feet (II Sam. 22.10=Ps. 18.9).

[1] I. Abrahams, *Studies in Pharisaism and the Gospels*, Series I, 1917, p. 48.
[2] *Ibid.*   [3] Matt. 3.16; Luke 3.21.

Bow thy heavens, O Lord, and come down:
Touch thy mountains, and they shall smoke (Ps. 144.5).

In St John's Gospel before the account of the ministry begins the disciples (and readers!) are given the pledge that they will see the heaven opened and the 'angels of God ascending and descending upon the Son of man' (1.51). If the rabbinic interpretation[1] is being followed here the meaning is that they will see the ascent and descent on Jesus as Israel. Belief in Jesus will result in a sharing in his heavenly vision of the Father; 'in' him they will see the heavens opened.

The four images which can be detected in the Gospel accounts of the Baptism, namely, Son-King, Servant, Dove, heavens opened, all suggest Israel.

If this is the case, then the Synoptic accounts of the Baptism indicate that the significance of his mission was initially perceived by Jesus through a poetic fusion of images suggesting the call and command of Israel, and this in turn throws light on the meaning of the Temptation.[2]

Here again, there is no good reason for doubting that the source of the narratives of the Temptation given in the Q tradition was Jesus himself. They explain so much of the activity and teaching of Jesus, and are so closely related to the *manner* of his mission and to what would seem to have been a continuing 'temptation' that it is most likely that we have here Jesus' own presentation of the experience given to the disciples at some stage later in the ministry, again presumably after the confession of Peter at Caesarea Philippi. If this is so, it means that we have here the interpretation which Jesus himself put on the Temptation, and it seems likely from the way it has been written up that he saw it as a temptation of Israel in the wilderness.

The main reason for thinking this is that the replies of Jesus all come from that section of the Book of Deuteronomy which is concerned with the vocation and the temptation of Israel. The replies of Jesus show that he had in mind the sequence of Deut. 6–8 which has as its theme Israel's vocation to walk in the 'Way' of Torah, knowledge and sonship, and Israel's temptation to avoid this 'Way'. Israel is to 'remember all the way' which God had led him 'these forty years in the wilderness' (8.2) by obeying all the commandment (v. 1) 'that he might make you *know*' (v. 3) and so realize true sonship: 'As a man disciplines his son, so the Lord your God disciplines you' (v. 5). The accounts of the Temptation of Jesus

---

[1] Cf. C. H. Dodd, *The Interpretation of the Fourth Gospel*, 1953, pp. 245 f.
[2] Cf. Dom J. Dupont, 'L'Arrière-fond Biblique du Récit des Tentations de Jésus', *New Testament Studies* 3, 1956/57, pp. 287–304.

in St Matthew and St Luke suggest that Jesus saw himself going through again the trial of Israel. Jesus was, first, tempted to doubt the reality of the vocation which he had accepted after the Baptism, and to seek some satisfying proof from the Father. In acute hunger, he saw the plenty of the Promised Land[1] and was tempted to anticipate, for his own satisfaction, the bounty which God would give in his own time: 'If you are the Son of God command these stones to become loaves of bread' (Matt. 4.3). Jesus clearly saw himself following in Israel's 'Way', and subject to the temptations of Israel.[2] But this New Israel rejected the temptation to put the Father to the test: 'Man shall not live by bread alone.' As so often, the meaning of this is aptly summarized by a phrase from the Fourth Gospel: 'My food is to do the will of him who sent me' (John 4.34). His was the obedience; the rest, vindication and personal satisfaction, was not his concern, but the Father's. Here was an Israel who did not demand τέρατα for himself, and it was because the Pharisees sought after 'signs from heaven' of their own choosing that they missed the sign which was actually being given them—Israel in Jesus himself. Jesus was to see them as symbols of 'disobedient Israel; an adulterous and sinful generation'.

Again the second Temptation (following the order in St Matthew)[3] suggests that in the mind of Jesus there was a necessary link between Messiahship and the 'Way' of Israel. In fact he now believed himself faced with Israel's fundamental and continuing temptation—that of Massah. Ps. 95 with its reference to 'The day of Massah in the wilderness' suggests that this became almost a technical term for basic apostasy. This temptation was fundamental because it concerned the unique vocation of Israel as the covenant people of Yahweh to seek a certainty and assurance of their own choosing, to demand a 'sign from heaven' which would make it unequivocally clear whether 'the Lord is among us or not' (Ex. 17.7). If we may refer to the Johannine account of the 'sign' at Cana of Galilee here (behind which, as we shall see, there lies the temptation motif), we could say that Jesus lived through again Israel's temptation to force God's hand to supply the life-giving water in an unambiguous τέρας, rather than to remain obediently confident that God would supply it in his own time and way, just as, in St John, Jesus is tempted to anticipate the redemptive wine-giving of his Passion which must however wait

---

[1] Cf. Deut. 8.1–10.

[2] 'C'est la tentation d'Israel que le Christ revit, en tirant profit de la leçon que l'Ecriture lui avait degagée', Dom J. Dupont, *op. cit.*, p. 289.

[3] Matthew's order is probably nearer the original. Luke may well have changed the order because he wished to make a general comment about the Temptation (cf. Luke 4.13), and it therefore suited his purpose to end on the reply, 'Thou shalt not tempt the Lord thy God.'

upon the Father's directives. To cast himself from the temple would be to commit Israel's sin at Massah but, as Dom Dupont puts it: 'Là où Israel avait péché, Christ reste fidèle.'[1] This Israel did not stop in the 'Way' to which he had committed himself and say 'When?' or 'Where?'[2] In this the Master is the exemplar for his disciples who will be tempted to seek from him τέρατα of their own choosing:[3] 'Thou shalt not tempt the Lord thy God.'

In the first Temptation Jesus was tempted to doubt that the call to be Israel had really come to him. He had so identified himself with Israel as to experience Israel's perennial desire for a certainty of his own choosing. In the second he experienced another form of the temptation to force God's hand by seeking a 'sign from heaven'. In the third he experienced Israel's temptation to idolatry, to 'walk after other gods'. The reply of Jesus, 'Thou shalt worship the Lord thy God, and him only shalt thou serve', suggests, from the context in which these words are found in Deut. 6, that Jesus saw himself as Israel brought to the Promised Land[4] and there tempted to rely entirely on his own sufficiency[5] and to avoid the service which is costly and humiliating.

In St Luke's Gospel there are suggestions that Jesus saw the whole of his ministry as a tempting of Israel. After the initial account of the Temptation St Luke comments: 'And when the devil had ended every temptation, he departed from him until an opportune time' (4.13). In the Lucan account of the Last Supper Jesus addresses his disciples as those 'who have continued with me in my temptations' (22.28), and the context in which he speaks of his kingship which they are to share with him suggests that the fundamental temptation of Jesus, and after him of the disciples (because the form of his mission was to determine theirs also) was to 'exercise lordship' (v. 25) rather than to be 'the servant' (v. 27), to seek acclaim by open declaration rather than accept the obscurity of faithful obedience.

While it is true that St Luke makes quite explicit that the ministry of Jesus was, by its very nature, bound to be a temptation, this is a feature of the ministry clearly perceptible in the other versions of the Gospel tradition, and it is very likely that this is an aspect of the ministry which goes back to the interpretation which Jesus himself put upon it. Certainly the

---

[1] *Op. cit.*, p. 290.   [2] Cf. Luke 17.20 f.   [3] Luke 17.22 f.
[4] Cf. Deut. 6.10 f. 'Sonship' of Yahweh and supremacy over the nations are complementary ideas in the Old Testament, and it may be that here again we have a reminder of the sensitivity of Jesus to the form which his kingship must assume. Cf. A. R. Johnson in *The Labyrinth*, ed. S. H. Hooke, 1935, p. 108.
[5] Perhaps by going the way of the Zealots. Cf. O. Cullmann, *The State in the New Testament*, 1957, and Mark 12.15.

references to temptation occur at just those points where one can easily
see the influence of Jesus' commitment to walk in the way of Israel in the
form of a servant. To the question about tribute to Caesar[1] Jesus reacted
as to a temptation, a temptation, probably, to declare himself unambiguously as a King-Messiah of the Zealot type.[2] But this would have been to
appear as false and faithless Israel. Again, the tenor of Jesus' words after
the confession at Caesarea Philippi, 'Get behind me, Satan!' (Mark 8.33),
suggests that he experienced in the rebuke of Peter a temptation to turn
from the way of the Son of Man to which he had just alluded (v. 31).
Peter's suggestion is the constant *skandalon*[3] that he must avoid. Gethsemane seems also to have been an experience of temptation for Jesus.
His words to the disciples, 'Watch and pray that you may not enter into
temptation' (Mark 14.38), may well reflect how he himself experienced this
stress. If this is so, at Gethsemane Jesus was tempted again to seek other
more direct, less obscure and shameful means of accomplishing his task than
the path to which the Father had called him. This 'Way' he had elsewhere
referred to as a cup,[4] and his willing and complete identification of himself
with Israel as God's obedient servant he now experienced as specially
costing. The other certain reference to a circumstance which constituted
a temptation for Jesus was the question about divorce.[5] This may have
been no more than a temptation to come down on a party side, either that
of Hillel or Shammai. On the other hand it may have been a temptation
to doubt the reality of the Father's vocation to walk in the 'Way' of
Torah, as himself a new and greater Moses not subservient to the old
Mosaic Torah. Finally we come to the Lord's Prayer with the injunction:
'Lead us not into temptation.' In this, as in all things, the life of the disciple is an *imitatio Christi*. The disciple will be tempted to put his Lord to
the test, to demand confirmation or certainties of his own choosing. But
it was his Lord who said: 'Not what I will, but what thou wilt' (Mark
14.36).

It seems possible to conclude from the narratives of the Temptations
and the other references which have just been discussed that Jesus saw
his mission in history to be not the verbal direct proclamation of himself,
but the obedient moulding of his life to a form which the Father would
indicate, through 'signs', as the fulfilment of his purpose as divine King.

---

[1] Mark 12.15.
[2] 'From the beginning of his public ministry until its decisive close Jesus consistently
regarded the Zealot—that is, political—interpretation of the Messiah as a satanic
temptation, and consequently combatted it.' O. Cullmann, *The State in the New Testament*, p. 30.
[3] Matt. 16.23.   [4] Mark 10.38 f.   [5] Mark 10.2: cf. Matt. 19.3.

F

Jesus was primarily aware of the Father, of his nearness and uniquely intimate relation to himself, and of the Father's mission committed to him. To turn in on himself in an introspective way, to exercise lordship in Gentile fashion,[1] would be to succumb to the age-old temptation of Israel to be a 'saved' rather than a 'saving' remnant.

The threefold Temptation of the Q account suggests that Jesus himself interpreted his experience after the Baptism as a re-enactment of the election of Israel at the Exodus and the testing of Israel in the wilderness. There is other evidence in the Gospel that the classic 'Way' of Israel from Egypt to Jerusalem[2] exercised a powerful influence on the character of the mission of Jesus. There are certain clearly deliberate acts of Jesus during his ministry which suggest that he believed that his mission as Son must take the visible form of enacting, in 'prophetic symbolism',[3] the 'Way' of Israel from the Exodus, through the wanderings in the wilderness, to the entry into the Promised Land and the ascent of Zion. There can be no doubt of the influence on Jesus of the Book of Isaiah, particularly of that section of our present book known generally as Deutero-Isaiah. There, as we have seen,[4] the redemption of Israel is pictured as a New Exodus across the desert into the Promised Land and up to Zion. A similar picture is given, in miniature, in Isa. 35, a scripture to which Jesus attached special importance since he referred to it on an important occasion at the beginning of his Galilean ministry.[5] The movement of thought in this chapter is from the wilderness and desert, along the new 'Way', to Zion.[6] In this context it is instructive to examine the three events in the ministry of Jesus which he clearly planned with care: the entry into Jerusalem, the cleansing of the temple and the Last Supper.

We can certainly speak of the entry into Jerusalem as a prepared piece of miming. Mark 11.1–6 (the sending for the colt) indicates that Jesus had made careful and detailed preparations beforehand. This planning of the entry suggests that Jerusalem occupied a decisive and critical place in Jesus' thought on the course of his mission.

Jerusalem the holy city and Zion the throne of David[7] have a prominent place in Hebrew and Jewish Messianic expectations, both of which looked

---

[1] Luke 22.25.   [2] Cf. pp. 31 ff. above.

[3] That the mission of Jesus was, in one respect, a mime of the 'Way' of Israel is suggested, but not developed in, for example, J. A. T. Robinson, *Jesus and his Coming*, 1957, p. 59: 'The whole of his ministry, and particularly its climax, was seen by him, *one could almost say staged by him*, as a deliberate coming of the representative of God to his people'; and O. Cullmann, *The Early Church*, 1956, p. 153: 'He must *play the part of the Servant of God for the sake of humanity*' (my italics).

[4] Cf. p. 45 above.   [5] Luke 7.18–22.   [6] Isa. 35.1–2, 8, 10.

[7] Cf. A. G. Hebert, *The Throne of David*, 1941, pp. 49 ff., pp. 80 ff.

for the coming of the Lord to his Zion. It is interesting to note, further, that Jerusalem was the locale of the ministries of the three key figures of the Old Testament whom we have seen to be presented as ideal *imitatores Dei*:[1] the king, the prophet and the priest. 'The *kings* of the line of David rule and die there [cf. II Chron. 9.31; 16.14; 21.1, etc.], the *priests* carry out their duties in the Temple there, and the *prophets* do not cease to declare that the fortunes of Jerusalem and of the people of God are bound up together.'[2] The sayings and actions of Jesus relating to Jerusalem and the temple may indicate the influence of this background of Messianic imagery. He entered Jerusalem as king and prophet, and exercised in the temple the powers of king and priest.

Certainly there is evidence, particularly from St Luke's Gospel, that Jesus felt himself under a compulsion to go 'up to Jerusalem': 'He set his face to go to Jerusalem' (9.51); 'His face was set towards Jerusalem' (9.53); '[Moses and Elijah] spoke of his exodus which he was to accomplish at Jerusalem' (9.31). The use of the phrase 'up to Jerusalem' in the Gospels suggests that the journey to the holy city was a frequently reiterated theme of Jesus in discourse with disciples.[3] A passage like Mark 10.32 f., for example, indicates that the 'ascent to Jerusalem' had become a familiar, indeed almost a technical term, in relation to the mission of Jesus: 'And they were on the way (ἐν τῇ ὁδῷ), going up to Jerusalem'; 'Behold, we are going up to Jerusalem' (Matt. 20.17; Luke 18.31). These passages together with the Q apostrophe to Jerusalem strengthen the suggestion of Professor J. J. von Allmen when he writes: 'The question may be put whether Jesus, when going up to Jerusalem with the Twelve, who are the representatives to the people of God, did not bring to fulfilment— in secret, like all the promises which He fulfilled at the time of His first coming—the great eschatological gathering together to the holy city.'[4]

Although for Jesus the Messiah was more than Son of David,[5] he was at least that, and it would seem that he looked to Jerusalem as the place where he would be enthroned as Messiah at a time and in a way the Father would choose. The execution of John the Baptist, who was taken by Jesus as the Elijah to come, may well have been received by him as a 'sign' from the Father that the 'ascent to Jerusalem' must now be made. In the Fourth

---

[1] Cf. p. 61 above.
[2] Article on 'Names (Geographical)' in *Vocabulary of the Bible* (edited by J. J. von Allmen), ET 1958, pp. 284 ff.
[3] Luke 19.28.
[4] *Op. cit.*, p. 284.
[5] Mark 12.35–37.

Gospel not only is this 'up to Jerusalem' theme given special emphasis, but there is an interesting passage which also suggests that Jesus' move to Jerusalem was in response to some token given him by the Father.[1] And if the comment in Luke 19.11[2] is accepted it would seem that Jerusalem and kingship were frequent topics in Jesus' converse with disciples. The entry then was the carefully prepared 'sign' of the nature of the kingship which, in obedience to the Father, Jesus came to inaugurate in Jerusalem. Acting on the prompting of the Father[3] he was coming to his throne. This was the King-Messiah's visitation of his capital.[4] In St John, as W. R. Farmer has pointed out, the use of palm branches suggests a crowd receiving Jesus as the very reverse type of King from that which Jesus believed himself called to be.[5] This may be a typical piece of Johannine irony, but it may also be that there were those who took Jesus to be the Zealot king which, in spite of temptation, he refused to be.

Jerusalem is indissolubly linked with the temple in Jewish thought, particularly in Messianic and eschatological speculation.[6] Mount Zion was the mountain of God and the mountain of the temple of God. An oracle with a very powerful influence in the history of the image of a return to Zion in the Messianic times was Isa. 2.2 f.:[7]

It shall come to pass in the latter days that the mountain of the house
    of the Lord
shall be established as the highest of the mountains
and shall be raised above the hills;
and all nations shall flow to it,
and many peoples shall come, and say:
'Come, let us go up to the mountain of the Lord,
to the house of the God of Jacob;
that he may teach us his ways
and that we may walk in his paths.'
For out of Zion shall go forth the Law (*torah*),
And the word of the Lord from Jerusalem.

[1] John 7.8–10.
[2] 'He proceeded to tell a parable, because he was near to Jerusalem, and because they supposed that the kingdom of God was to appear immediately.'
[3] Cf. John 6.15. This action of Jesus may have been determined by his conviction that the 'hour' for coronation had not yet come.
[4] Luke 19.44.
[5] 'The presence of palm branches would seem to indicate that there may well have been within the rejoicing crowd those who looked to Jesus as one who, following in the footsteps of the Maccabees, would lead the nation to victory in its struggle to throw off the "yoke of the heathen" and reassert the sovereignty of God over Israel', W. R. Farmer, 'The Palm Branches in John 12.13', *JTS*, n.s. 3, 1952, pp. 65 f.
[6] Cf. A. G. Hebert, *The Throne of David*, pp. 49–52; pp. 80–92.
[7] Cf. Micah 4.1 f. If Micah was a disciple of Isaiah of Jerusalem he may have taken this oracle over from his master.

Zion was especially the seat of royalty, the throne of David. It seems very likely that in pre-exilic times the temple was the scene of an enthronement of Yahweh at the New Year Festival, and that the king took part in the liturgical mimes.[1] Certainly Jerusalem and Zion became symbols for royalty in the subsequent literature. Jerusalem was the 'city of the great King' (Ps. 48.2),[2] and in the Messianic Age was to be the centre of the world with life-giving streams flowing from her.[3]

The evidence of the Gospels indicates that the temple in Jerusalem occupied a central place in the mind of Jesus. It is not without significance that the temptation narrative includes a scene of Jesus placed on the top of the temple in Jerusalem. He saw himself coming to Jerusalem and appearing dramatically on the temple, there to reveal himself.[4] But that temptation was put aside, and when he did come to Jerusalem and the temple it was to give a sign of himself as the destroyer and rebuilder of the temple.[5] Again, he asserted in his action of 'cleansing' the temple that he came as King indeed. The accusation brought against Jesus[6] that he threatened to destroy the temple indicates that the subject of the temple may have occupied a more prominent place in his teaching and actions than the Gospel tradition suggests.[7] A new and greater David comes to the temple to pray and finds it turned into an emporium. He enacts the coming destruction of the temple as it now is, and places himself as the foundation of the New Temple.

If the Last Supper was a Passover meal then it would have for Jesus all the associations which we have noted previously. Its unique character would be that before he went to his death in this final Passover he intended to go through for the last time the history he had sought to embody in the sign of his mission. It not only looked to the past, to Israel's covenant at Sinai, but it was a prefiguring, an anticipation of the kingly banquet to come. The King and the Kingdom would then be indissolubly one, and this was affirmed proleptically in the Last Supper.

A study of key events like the Baptism, the Temptation, the entry into Jerusalem, the cleansing of the temple and the Last Supper has suggested that Jesus very probably took it to be a necessary part of his mission that he should indicate, at the relevant points, that he was deliberately representing the history of Israel as King-Messiah. His life was not just an

[1] Cf. S. H. Hooke (ed.), *Myth and Ritual*, 1933, and *The Labyrinth*, 1935.
[2] Cf. the words of Jesus in Matt. 5.35.   [3] Zech. 14.8 f.
[4] Cf. a midrash, which may go back to time of Jesus: 'At the time when King Messiah reveals himself he will come and stand on the roof of the temple' (Pesikta Rabba, 162a).
[5] John 2.13–22.
[6] Mark 14.58. Cf. Acts 6.14.
[7] Cf. Matt. 12.6 (RV): 'One greater than the temple is here.'

individual pageant of the history of Israel. There was always sufficient indication of the Israel form it was assuming but, as well, equally clear tokens for those willing to receive them that something greater than Israel was here. To quote J. G. H. Hoffmann: 'He took upon himself the task of manifesting himself as Messiah-King, not only during the last hours of his earthly ministry but in the whole length of it, actualizing in each of his actions this royal and Messianic ideology which he made not only an integrating part of his message but the essence of his mission.'[1] Jesus, in the manner of the Old Testament prophets (for example, Ezekiel),[2] saw his whole life in words and actions as, in one aspect, an extended *mimesis* of Israel's vocation, a 'sign' of the times. We must now examine other features of the Gospel material about Jesus which corroborate this.

The calling of the Twelve. There can be no gainsaying the cardinal importance which Jesus attached to the Twelve and the large place given to the training of them. As we shall see when we discuss his teaching on discipleship, Jesus summoned the Twelve to follow in his 'Way'. He and they together constituted one sign: the sign of Messiah and his Israel. The words of Jesus in the 'high-priestly' prayer of John 17, 'I have manifested thy name unto the men whom thou gavest me out of the world: thine they were, and thou gavest them to me' (v. 6), suggest the words of Isaiah of Jerusalem: 'Behold I and the children whom the Lord hath given me are for signs and for wonders in Israel from the Lord of hosts, which dwelleth in Mount Zion' (8.18). Certainly for Jesus the kingdom came in their mission as in his.

The Wanderings. Jesus is an embodiment of wandering nomadic Israel. Apparently this was a feature of his mission which he believed to be a necessity laid upon him by the Father: 'Let us go on to the next towns that I may preach there also; for that is why I came out' (Mark 1.38; cf. Luke 4.43). The Son of Man (and the Twelve) are called to a wandering mission: 'Foxes have holes, and birds of the air have nests; but the Son of Man has nowhere to lay his head' (Luke 9.58). Everybody has a home except, as usual, wandering Israel. The verb πορεύομαι is used in the Septuagint particularly of Israel proceeding in the Way of Yahweh, and the frequent use of the verb in the Gospels may be evidence of the same idea in the mind of Jesus.

Sabbath signs. There can be no doubt that Jesus deliberately chose the Sabbath as the occasion of many of his 'mighty works'. The fact that so

---

[1] 'Jésus messie juif', *Aux sources de la tradition chrétienne* (Mélanges Goguel), 1950, p. 112.
[2] Cf. p. 59 above.

many incidents occurred on the Sabbath is not likely to have been due simply to chance. It is very probable that Sir Edwyn Hoskyns[1] was right in his suggestion that the timing of incidents on the Sabbath was deliberate, as a sign of the presence of the Messianic age, for those who were willing to be confronted with this great reality because they had not 'hardened their hearts'.

Desert feedings. Dr Austin Farrer's arguments against the hitherto very prevalent critical assumption that the two accounts of the feeding of a multitude in St Mark must be doublets are convincing, and would be reinforced by the emphasis of this book that Jesus gave a large place in his ministry to acts of 'prophetic symbolism'. That these events were 'signs' is indicated by the fact that in both cases they are followed by comment about their identification:

> They were sore amazed in themselves;
> for they understood not concerning the loaves,
> but their heart was hardened (6.51 f., RV).

> Why reason ye because ye have no bread?
> Do ye not yet perceive, neither understand?
> Have ye your heart hardened?
> Having eyes, see ye not?
> And having ears, hear ye not?
> And do ye not remember?
> When I brake the five loaves among the five thousand,
> how many baskets full of broken pieces took ye up?
> They say unto him, Twelve.
> And when the seven among the four thousand,
> how many basketfuls of broken pieces took ye up?
> And they say unto him, Seven.
> And he said unto them,
> Do ye not yet understand? (8.17–21, RV).

Jesus obviously attached significance to these numbers, and intended the feedings as 'signs' of Messiah gathering in for the Royal Banquet both Israel and the Gentiles. And the references to the desert in both cases make it probable that for Jesus himself these feedings were re-enactments of the feeding of Israel with manna, the new thing being that his 'Israel' included Gentiles.

The poor and the outcast. The Gospel tradition makes it plain that the mission of Jesus was characterized by a predilection for the poor and socially outcast.[2] This is a feature of his ministry which receives special

---

[1] Cf. the essay 'Jesus the Messiah' in *Mysterium Christi* (edited by Bell and Deissmann).   [2] Cf. Mark 2.15; Luke 15.1 f.

mention, and the fact that he was a friend of 'publicans and sinners' was for many a *skandalon*. It is very probable here again that this deliberate seeking out of the poor and outcast was meant by Jesus to have the character of a *semeion*. We have noted that in the Old Testament[1] God's 'knowledge' of Israel was revealed in the way he dealt with Israel as a rejected slave, and Israel was commissioned to imitate God's manner in relations with the slave, stranger and widow. For those with eyes to see, and ears to hear, then, the actions of Jesus in consorting with the outcast could be a 'sign' of the presence of him who by this clear *mimesis* of the ways of the Father of Israel was fulfilling the vocation of Israel to be *imitator Dei*, and actualizing Israel in his own person.

We have been arguing that there is evidence in the Gospels that Jesus was conscious of a mission to give his life the form of an 'Israel', and that, in the manner of 'prophetic symbolism', he deliberately mimed certain key events in the 'Way' of Israel as it had been epitomized in Hebrew and Jewish liturgy and tradition. This gave his mission a 'cryptic', mysterious, ambiguous character. It is St Mark's Gospel which has preserved most rigorously this feature of the mission of Jesus. Jesus is for St Mark the real but hidden Messiah, an enigma to be identified. One can detect in the transmission of the Gospel material the tendency to make the enigmatical more unambiguous and plain, to make the 'secret' of who Jesus is more and more an open one. It might have been expected that St Mark would leave the reader in no doubt as to the identity and significance of the central figure of his Gospel. There is no question that he regarded such identification as of ultimate importance. The fact that he does not underline at any point what he regards as the vital reaction to Jesus, not even Peter's confession at Caesarea Philippi (cf. Matthew's 'Blessed are you, Simon Bar-Jona . . .'), suggests that he felt himself under constraint to allow the activity and words of Jesus to speak for themselves. It is as though he believed that he could only write the Gospel about Jesus in one way—the way of Jesus himself! The nature and form of St Mark's Gospel may well bear witness to the importance which Jesus himself attached to the form and method of his mission. It was such a deep and constant preoccupation of his (because it was part of his obedience) that it left a lasting impression on the first disciples and the Gospel tradition which derives from them. The manner of Jesus in his ministry has controlled to a large extent the form and manner in which that ministry has been related in the Gospels.

The cryptic character of the mission of Jesus is focused in his designa-

---

[1] Cf. p. 60 above.

tion of it as the 'Way of the Son of Man'. It is very likely that Jesus chose this title just because of its enigmatical character. Not that 'Son of Man' was anything like an ingeniously difficult riddle. By its Old Testament background it pointed to the theme of God's purpose for Israel: the formation of a people, the 'saints of the Most High' (Dan. 7). But it posed the question only. Upon those who were confronted with it lay the inescapable burden of making an answer. A passage in St John's Gospel has preserved evidence that Jesus' use of Son of Man was oblique and ambiguous: 'How can you say that the Son of man must be lifted up? Who is this Son of man?' (12.34).

The Synoptic Gospels suggest that 'Son of Man' was used in a detached, almost impersonal way by Jesus. He sketched out in teaching, and, we can now say, he enacted in his life, the Way of the Son of Man. But what this 'Way' was, and who the Son of Man was, that he could not say.[1] He came to accomplish a task. The response to it was something which he must leave in the Father's hands.

This 'Way' which Jesus set himself to fulfil in the mission of the 'Son of Man' was the 'Way of Israel' as we have traced it in the Old Testament, particularly as he saw it portrayed in terms of a human life in the Isaianic Servant-songs. The main pattern of the 'Way' of the 'Son of Man' as lived by Jesus has a significant resemblance to the 'Way' of the *Ebed Yahweh*:

The 'Way' of the 'Son of Man'

1. The Son of Man is *called* to a mission which is not his own but laid upon him by the Father, and he accepts it in obedience: Mark 14.21; 10.45; Luke 19.10.
2. The 'Way of the Son of Man' is a '*sign*' of the times, and recognition of it as such involves repentance: Luke 11.30; Mark 2.9 f., 28.
3. It is a way of *humiliation* and *obscurity*: Luke 7.34; 9.58.
4. It is a way of *suffering*: Mark 8.31; 9.12, 31.
5. The 'Son of Man' is *advocate* or *intercessor*: Luke 12.8.
6. His 'Way' will be vindicated in *glory*: Mark 8.38; 9.9, 31; 13.26; 14.62; Matt. 19.28.

The 'Way' of the Servant

1. He is *called* in the eternal purpose of God: Isa. 49.1; 42.1.
2. He is a '*sign*' to the nations: Isa. 42.6; 49.6.

---

[1] The actual question put by Jesus at Caesarea Philippi may well have been 'Who do you say the Son of Man is?' (cf. Matt. 16.13) and the reply of Peter: 'You are!'

3. The Servant's way is one of *humiliation* and *obscurity*: Isa. 42.2; 53.7.

4. *Suffering*: Isa. 50.5 ff.; 53.7.

5. *Intercession*: Isa. 53.12.

6. *Vindication*: Isa. 52.13; 53.10 ff.

There are some features of the Way of the Servant which we do not find explicitly referred to in the 'Son of Man' sayings of Jesus. The Servant's endowment by the Spirit is an obvious example. But for Jesus to speak of his endowment by the Spirit directly would have been a self-reference which contradicted the way to which he had committed himself. As Professor C. K. Barrett[1] has emphasized, the paucity of references to the Spirit in the Synoptic tradition has to be related to the nature of the Messianic secret. His endowment by the Spirit is not a matter about which he must speak but a reality upon which he must act. Similarly, because the 'Way' of the Servant in the 'Son of Man' is a thing to be recognized, we should not expect to find direct descriptive or explicatory teaching about it. This would have been to declare himself in a wrong way. As Jeremias has put it: 'Does the uniqueness of Jesus consist of the fact that he set forth a new Messianic theory in which he combined, for the first time, Isa. 53 and Dan. 7—and not rather in the fact that he lived out and fulfilled the very content of both these passages?'[2]

It is interesting to note that there is the same kind of oscillation of reference to one who *is* Israel and one who has a mission *to* Israel in both the figures of the Isaianic Servant and Jesus' Son of Man. It is very doubtful whether any sense of contradiction would have been experienced by Jesus himself. What Dr E. L. Allen[3] has written of Deutero-Isaiah was probably also true of Jesus. Dr Allen speaks of Deutero-Isaiah's 'concealment of himself behind his mission' and continues: 'Second-Isaiah possesses to an extraordinary degree the power to transcend himself and to enter by sympathetic insight into the experience of others; this is what enables him to describe the relation between Yahweh and Israel in such intimate fashion, so that we forget that the latter is not an individual but a community. As the counterpart of this he is able to view his own experience from outside and to describe what actually happened to himself as though it concerned another.'[4]

---

[1] *The Holy Spirit and the Gospel Tradition*, 1947, p. 158.

[2] J. Jeremias, 'Zum Problem der Deutung von Jes. 53 im palästinischen Spätjudentum', *Aux sources de la tradition chrétienne* (Mélanges Goguel), p. 113.

[3] *Prophet and Nation*, 1947.

[4] *Op. cit.*, p. 118.

Again the two figures of the 'Son of Man' and the Servant are associated with the imagery of kingship.[1] If we are right in stressing the important place of kingship in the mind of Jesus, it may well be that Jesus accepted the picture given of the Servant in Isaiah as a divine indication of the way in which his royal mission as 'Son of Man' must be accomplished. This was how he as King of Israel ought to come to the throne which the Father would give him.

To sum up the argument of this chapter so far. The evidence of the Gospel tradition would suggest that the form of his mission was of prime concern to Jesus. It had to exhibit a definite shape because it was the 'sign' of the times for those with eyes to see and ears to hear. This meant that Jesus sought to mime, in the manner of the Old Testament prophet whose work he believed he had to fulfil, the pattern of Israel's destiny as it had become stylized in Jewish tradition. His mission to Israel involved for him being himself Israel the martyr.

If this is so, if his mission was, in one chief way, a *mimesis*, it explains what we have noted as the cryptic character of so much of his ministry, and it would explain the so-called 'Messianic secret' associated with the name of Wrede. The works and words of Jesus were constituted by the Father a 'sign' to the house of Israel, and it was he alone through the Spirit who would reveal them as such.

The 'Way of the Son of Man' was the way of the 'sign', first of all in deed. Those who were confronted with the actions of Jesus had to take heed as to what they saw in them. They were accountable for the significance which they attached to them and this meant the extent to which they were prepared to act on them. Any discussion of the miracles of Jesus ought to begin with the significance which he himself attached to them, and the Gospels give us sufficient material for forming a judgment on this.

We may start with the reply of Jesus to the query of John the Baptist, 'Are you he who is to come, or shall we look for another?'[2] This is a good place to begin because it illustrates how the manner of Jesus in replying to direct questions about himself was dictated by the 'Way' of the Son of Man in which he must walk. The temptation of Jesus, which continued throughout his ministry, was to anticipate, by some explicit verbal declaration, the manifestation of himself as Messiah-King of Israel which the Father would bring about. The 'mighty works' of Jesus were identification marks which those who knew the Scriptures might understand:

---

[1] Cf. H. Ringgren, *The Messiah in the Old Testament*; S. Mowinckel, *He that Cometh*; I. Engnell, *Studies in Divine Kingship in the Ancient Near East*, Uppsala, 1943.
[2] Matt. 11.3 ff.; cf. Luke 7.19 ff.

Go your way and tell John the things
which ye do hear and see:
'The blind receive their sight, and the lame walk,
the lepers are cleansed, and the deaf hear,
and the dead are raised up',
and 'the poor have good tidings preached to them'.
And blessed is he whosoever shall find
none occasion of stumbling in me.

The Baptist's question was answered by a summons to make his own deductions from the evidential signs which accompanied the mission of Jesus. The reply of Jesus is in verse form,[1] and is clearly a poetic blending of various pictures of the Age to Come in Isaiah.[2] The dominant image however is that used in Isa. 35.5 ff. and, significantly, this is the Exodus from the wilderness up to Zion along the new 'Way'. The reply of Jesus was a summons to John the Baptist, and others, to identify the things which they heard and saw, as milestones, so to speak, along the 'Way' which was being traversed before their eyes. They were responsible for their willingness to discern in what took place during the ministry of Jesus an enactment of Israel, at last, walking patiently, consistently, obediently, gladly along the 'Way' to which he had been summoned from the time when he was first brought into existence.

The meaning of the actions of Jesus was disputable. The Kingdom of God did not come in the actions of Jesus with the kind of certainty which would enable one to say 'See, here it is!' or 'There' (Luke 17.20). The actions of Jesus were not 'signs from heaven' in the sense of indisputable, unambiguous, manifestly unquestionable 'miracles' in the modern sense.[3] At one and the same time it was possible to see Jesus as a 'sign' *ab inferis* ('He has Beelzebul') as well as a 'sign' *a superis* ('Thou art the Messiah'): 'You say that I cast out demons by Beelzebul. And if I cast out demons by Beelzebul, by whom do your sons cast them out? Therefore they shall be your judges' (Luke 11.19; cf. Matt. 12.27). 'Signs and wonders' may betoken the presence of the false as well as the true Messiah.[4] To yield to the pressure of the moment and give 'signs from heaven' in a self-regarding way would have been to yield to the Temptation:

And the Pharisees came forth,
and began to question with him,

[1] Cf. C. F. Burney, *The Poetry of our Lord*, 1925, p. 117.
[2] E.g. 26.19; 29.18 f.; 35.5 f.; 61.1.
[3] The words of Jesus in Mark 8.14–21 about the meaning of the feedings (cf. 6.52) are of a similar character to his saying about parables in Mark 4.11 f.
[4] Mark 13.22; cf. Matt. 7.22.

> seeking of him a sign from heaven,
> tempting him (Mark 8.11).

The words of Jesus in the Q version of this incident, 'an evil and adulterous generation seeks for a sign',[1] suggest that he had in mind again Israel's temptation at Massah, which was to seek from God an indubitable indication that the Lord was among them. Jesus, obediently going through the journey of Israel, must not succumb to the Massah type of temptation, but must point to the signs which the Father is giving to those who have the repentant eyes to see. The response to the 'miracles' which Jesus looked for was not astonishment (although he could not prevent people staying content with that) but repentance:

> Then he began to upbraid the cities where most of his mighty works were done, because they did not repent. 'Woe to you, Chorazin! woe to you, Bethsaida! for if the mighty works done in you had been done in Tyre and Sidon they would have repented long ago in sackcloth and ashes (Matt. 11.20 f.).

If there was no readiness or inclination to read the signs of the times in this 'way' no amount of sheer 'wonder' would make any difference:

> But Abraham said, 'They have Moses and the prophets; let them hear them!' And he said, 'No, father Abraham; but if some one goes to them from the dead, they will repent!' He said to him,' If they do not hear Moses and the prophets, neither will they be convinced if some one should rise from the dead' (Luke 16.29–31).

Yet while the miracles were 'signs' they were not hopelessly esoteric. There was a real analogy between ability to make deductions about the weather from the 'signs' given and ability to discern the 'signs' accompanying the mission of Jesus:

> He also said to the multitudes, 'When you see a cloud rising in the west, you say at once, "A shower is coming"; and so it happens. And when you see the south wind blowing, you say, "There will be scorching heat"; and it happens. You hypocrites! You know how to interpret the appearance of earth and sky; but why do you not know how to interpret the present time?' (Luke 12.54–56).

The mighty works which Jesus found accompanying his mission as he sought to fulfil it constituted a temptation to turn in on himself, and place the emphasis there rather than on the Father to whose glory it all pointed. The principle which he enunciated in this matter for his disciples who

---

[1] Matt. 16.4. Cf. Mark 9.19. Luke (11.29) may have dropped 'adulterous' as being an unfamiliar idiom to Gentile ears; cf. T. W. Manson, *The Sayings of Jesus*, 1949 (Part II of *The Mission and Message of Jesus*, 1937), p. 89.

were to follow in his way undoubtedly points to a conviction which he held about his own miracles:

> Nevertheless do not rejoice in this, that the spirits are subject to you; but rejoice that your names are written in heaven (Luke 10.20).

The miracles were taken by Jesus himself as 'tokens' of the Father's continuing fidelity and presence. This would certainly seem to be the implication of the *agalliasis* passage which in St Luke's Gospel is placed immediately following the saying just quoted, and in St Matthew comes immediately after the upbraiding of the unrepentant cities: 'I thank thee, Father, Lord of heaven and earth, that thou hast hidden these things from the wise and understanding and hast revealed them to babes; yea, Father, for such was thy gracious will' (Luke 10.21). These happenings were indications that God's purpose for Israel was being fulfilled in Jesus, and blessed were the eyes which could see that this was so:

> Blessed are your eyes, for they see,
> and your ears, for they hear.
> Truly, I say to you,
> many prophets and righteous men
> longed to see what you see,
> and did not see it,
> and to hear what you hear,
> and did not hear it (Matt. 13.16 f.).

Discernment of the work of the Holy Spirit is the great matter at stake. For this a man is ultimately accountable. Upon it turns judgment to come. The blasphemy against the Holy Spirit is persistently to identify Jesus as a 'sign' *ab inferis*: ' " Whoever blasphemes against the Holy Spirit never has forgiveness, but is guilty of an eternal sin"—for they had said, "He has an unclean spirit" ' (Mark 3.29).

It was not only the actions of Jesus which constituted 'signs' summoning the beholder to identification, repentance, and 'following'. The 'Way of the Son of Man' in the course of the ministry of Jesus was to be discerned in what was heard as well as seen. The disciples were to take heed how they heard (Mark 4.24). They were to be alert and sensitive to hear the words of Jesus as a *shema Yisrael*, or as rubrics to the enactment of Israel's vocation which was taking place concurrently in his ministry. This character of the mission of Jesus determined the nature of his speaking. The characteristic form of the 'teaching' of Jesus was the 'parable'. This included not only the narrative simile but the brief epigrammatic aphorism.[1] The parables of Jesus were, like the Old Testament

---

[1] The first 'parable' in St Mark's Gospel is 'How can Satan cast out Satan?' (3.23).

mashal, riddles—but this not in the sense of esoteric puzzles for the clever but enigmas which made moral demands on the repentant. Like the miracles they had a necessarily elusive ambiguous character. There was, so to speak, a *teras* and a *semeion* element in those parables (the majority) which Jeremias calls 'Christological self-witness'.[1] 'Every parable', says T. W. Manson, 'is significant in two ways. It has its own meaning as a story and a further meaning—and this is the important thing—by application to persons or events or both together. It is possible for a hearer to follow and appreciate the former meaning without having the slightest inkling of the latter.'[2] This would certainly seem to be the implication of the words of Jesus about the purpose of speaking in parables in Mark 4.11 f.,[3] and of the frequent refrain, 'He who has ears to hear let him hear.' Not one of the parabolic sayings or narratives in St Mark's Gospel, for instance, is simply elucidatory. They all have their background in Old Testament imagery relating to God's purpose for Israel: sowing and harvesting, vineyard, fig-tree, watchman. As Jeremias puts it: 'All the parables of Jesus compel his hearers to come to a decision about his person and mission.'[4]

The cryptic, reserved element in the mission of Jesus sprang from his profound conviction that the Father had summoned him to give himself to be fashioned into a *semeion* for the times. He had been sent not to reveal himself or preach himself, but to go along a 'Way', remaining confident that the Father would use this for his own redeeming purposes. The works and words pointed to fulfilment of the Father's purpose for Israel. To proclaim himself would, as we have seen, violate the Father's commission. In this connection it is instructive to study the replies which Jesus made to direct questions about himself. They suggest that he regarded such questions as temptations to make the unambiguous verbal self-identification, and thus violate the nature of his works and teaching as a 'sign'. The question of his identity could not be treated as a mere point of information, but had to be faced by the questioner himself as a summons to faith and obedience. Confronted by such questions Jesus believed himself to be on trial as the obedient Son. Summoned to a life of obedience by means of a *mimesis* of Israel the Servant he must therefore open not his mouth, but let the Father declare him.

To take some examples. The question sent by John the Baptist, 'Art thou he that cometh?' (Matt. 11.3; Luke 7.19) has already been discussed

---

[1] J. Jeremias, *The Parables of Jesus*, ET 1954, p. 165.
[2] T. W. Manson, *The Teaching of Jesus*, pp. 64 f.
[3] For a discussion of this passage cf. T. W. Manson, *The Teaching of Jesus*, pp. 75 ff.; J. Jeremias, *The Parables of Jesus*, ch. 1.   [4] *Ibid.*, p. 159.

in another connection.[1] Here we need simply to note again that the reply to the Baptist's query took the characteristic form of a summons to the questioner to make his own reply to his own question. The things which are happening through Jesus are actualizations of the 'signs' which were to accompany the arrival of the Messianic age. One had to decide for or against these events as 'signs'. As 'signs' they could constitute only a *skandalon*, and the blessed ones are those who have the courage, the penitence, and the patience to discern here the 'sign of the Son of Man'.[2] The reply of Jesus, therefore, cannot be simply the supplying of elucidatory information. It is a Messianic summons to repentance.

Mark 11.27 f. Here the chief priests and scribes and elders confronted Jesus with what amounted to a direct question about himself: 'By what authority are you doing these things? or who gave you this authority to do them?' Once more the procedure was as before. Jesus insisted that his questioners alone might properly answer their own question: 'I will ask of you one question . . . was the baptism of John from heaven, or from men? Answer me.' In other words, if we may paraphrase what appears to be the argument behind the words of Jesus here: 'Did you see in John's movement the very activity of God, and were you ready to face his demands? If you were not, if you saw there nothing more than another reform movement and not primarily the activity of God through his prophet, then you are necessarily precluded from seeing the significance of my movement, for it too is the activity of God—come to completion. If you cannot recognize the activity of God when it is about to come to a head, you cannot, as the posing of your question itself implies, recognize it when it has come to a head, for a process completed is a new thing. . . . Neither will I tell you, then, by what authority I do these things.' Unwillingness to identify John's movement meant *a fortiori* unwillingness to identify his.

Mark 14.62. This is the crucial passage. In the presence of the Sanhedrin Jesus was asked by the High Priest to identify himself verbally and unambiguously with the Messiah: 'Are you the Christ, the son of the Blessed?' The reply of Jesus in the more commonly accepted text is: 'I am (ἐγώ εἰμι), and you will see the Son of man sitting at the right hand of power, and coming with the clouds of heaven.' If this is accepted as the authentic reading, it means that on this occasion, and only there, Jesus made an unequivocal direct verbal claim to be the Messiah. Consequently, if our conclusions about the nature of the Messianic task, as Jesus conceived it, are sound, this kind of reply would have run counter

---

[1] Cf. pp. 91 ff. above. [2] Matt. 11.6; Luke 7.23.

to a manner of speech and action which Jesus believed had been laid upon him by the Father. One could argue, however, that this situation before the Sanhedrin was unique and provided the reason for the exception to the rule. Here Jesus was confronted with the nation of Israel in solemn assembly, and this was the very moment for him to reveal himself. It is more likely however that the second half of the reply concerning the coming of the Son of Man referred to Jesus' consistent belief that it was the Father who would reveal him openly, and that the moment for this was not far off. There is more to be said for thinking that Jesus would have held this as precisely a moment for *not* making a verbal asseveration. He must preserve, as part of his mission, the martyr-like silence of the Isaianic Servant.

The text given by an important group of manuscripts, mainly 'Caesarean' (Θ, fam. 13, 543, 472, 565, 700, 1071, Georgian, Armenian, Origen), has the reply: 'You have said [that] I am . . .' ($\sigma\grave{\upsilon}$ $\epsilon\mathring{\iota}\pi\alpha\varsigma$ $\grave{\epsilon}\gamma\acute{\omega}$ $\epsilon\mathring{\iota}\mu\iota$). This has the obliqueness which we have seen to be characteristic of the words of Jesus used in answer to other similar direct questions about himself, and is most likely both to be the original reading in St Mark and to give the historical reply of Jesus. There is a further important consideration which supports this interpretation. Both St Matthew and St Luke in the parallel passages have the equivocal kind of reply which we believe to have been characteristic of Jesus. St Matthew, who is clearly using the Marcan tradition at this point, has: 'You have said so' ($\sigma\grave{\upsilon}$ $\epsilon\mathring{\iota}\pi\alpha\varsigma$, 26.64), and St Luke, who is also probably using Marcan material here, has a similar evasive reply: 'If I tell you, you will not believe, and if I ask you, you will not answer.'[1] It is not easy to see why, if the reading 'I am' is original in St Mark, subsequent tradition should move in the direction of making this direct reply more ambiguous and indirect. The tendency is for later tradition to make the ambiguous and equivocal more explicit and obvious, and one can trace this process in the history of the Gospel tradition from St Mark to St John. It is particularly difficult to see why St Matthew should have preferred $\sigma\grave{\upsilon}$ $\epsilon\mathring{\iota}\pi\alpha\varsigma$ $\grave{\epsilon}\gamma\acute{\omega}$ $\epsilon\mathring{\iota}\mu\iota$ to the direct explicit $\grave{\epsilon}\gamma\acute{\omega}$ $\epsilon\mathring{\iota}\mu\iota$, since it is characteristic of his method to clarify the ambiguities of the Marcan tradition,[2] and when on other occasions he has made less explicit words of Jesus about himself quite unmistakably direct.[3]

[1] Luke 22.67 f.; Luke 22.70 seems to suggest further that Luke's version of Mark had $\sigma\grave{\upsilon}$ $\epsilon\mathring{\iota}\pi\alpha\varsigma$.
[2] Cf. G. D. Kilpatrick, *The Origins of the Gospel according to St Matthew*, 1946, and Austin Farrer, *St Matthew and St Mark*, 1954, ch. 1.
[3] Matt. 14.33; cf. Mark 6.52; Matt. 16.28; cf. Mark 9.1.

G

If this interpretation of Mark 14.62 is accepted, it might then be asked:
Why did the High Priest tear his clothes after hearing this kind of reply?
But the blasphemy of Jesus would be located by the Jewish authorities
not simply in his verbal Yes or No to the question of Messiahship (whether
expressed directly or indirectly) but in his quite direct and unambiguous
claim to being vested with a kingship which belonged to God alone. As
Professor J. Y. Campbell has expressed it: 'It is not clear, and I think it is
improbable, that it was Jesus' implicit claim to be Himself the Son of
Man that called forth the high priest's declaration that He was guilty of
blasphemy, but rather His explicit assertion that He would be seen seated
"on the right hand of the Power".'[1]

Mark 15.2 (*Matt. 27.11–14*; *Luke 23.2 f.*). All three Synoptic evangelists, and the Fourth Gospel, agree that to the direct question of Pilate no
direct unequivocal answer was given by Jesus. In the Synoptists the reply
is: 'You have said so' (σὺ λέγεις). In St John Jesus is said first to have
replied in a way reminiscent of the ambiguity of the Synoptic tradition,[2]
and then to have been silent.[3] It is significant that in the Fourth Gospel,
where the author does not hesitate, when occasion demands, to report
Jesus as having verbally and explicitly identified, described and explained
his own person, the veiled cryptic manner of Jesus during his Passion
should have been preserved. This would suggest that the historical tradition on this issue was so strong as to prevent any modification, in spite of
the opportunity it would have given a later generation like that of the
author of the Fourth Gospel to provide an apologia for the attitude of
Jesus. If this is so, it would corroborate the argument above that the
replies of Jesus to questions about his own person were equivocal throughout his ministry, because anything else would, for him, have amounted to
a self-display and self-vindication and a yielding to a temptation which
he had continually to put on one side.

Luke 23.9. In the Lucan trial before Herod the manner of Jesus is to
make no reply to the questioning of Herod.

The manner of Jesus in indicating the meaning of his own person and
mission was always of such a kind that men were left to pass judgment on
themselves by the attitude they adopted to him. His method in dealing
with questions about himself was the same as the indirect but challenging
way of pointing men to see in John the Baptist the Elijah to come, or
telling the parable of an only son sent into the vineyard. The 'Way' of
Jesus was a 'sign'—and therefore a *skandalon*!

---

[1] 'The Origin and Meaning of the Term Son of Man', *JTS* 48, 1947, p. 145.
[2] John 18.34, 36.   [3] John 19.9.

The true significance of the mission of Jesus was, in principle, disputable. If that had not been so it would have meant that Jesus had deviated from the vocation of obedience to the Father in order to explain himself or defend himself. This would have amounted to usurping the Father's work of 'revealing' and 'convicting'. His mission therefore was bound to have the character of a *skandalon*. The dominant association of this word *skandalon* in the Gospels is that of the Hebrew word *mikshol*, meaning 'a stumbling-block', 'a hindrance', and it is mostly used in such a way as to emphasize moral responsibility. The *skandalon* does not accidentally trip one up. It is a situation which confronts us in such a way that whether we act or (as is more frequent!) refuse to act, we are accountable. The 'sign' when discerned and gladly recognized becomes a blessing; the 'sign' wilfully ignored or falsified is a *skandalon*:

> Blessed are your eyes for they see . . . blessed is he who takes no offence at me (Matt. 13.16; 11.6; cf. Luke 10.23; 7.23).

Neutrality is not possible, in spite of appearances!

29189

7

The 'Sign' of the Disciple

IT WOULD SEEM CLEAR that there is abundant testimony in the Gospel tradition that Jesus took the basic outline of the history of Israel in the Old Testament as a 'sign' from the Father of the pattern which his own mission must assume. His being Israel himself would constitute the mission to Israel. The Father would, in his own time and way, reveal his mission as the 'sign' of the presence of the Israel of God walking obediently in the way of true sonship. The 'Way of the Son of Man' was to imitate his Father, what Stauffer has called the *doxological way*, whereby the Father would be glorified.

But Jesus intended that his way should be that of his disciples also. Their mission as bearers of the Gospel was to be expressed in the deliberate walking in his 'Way'. If his life was the imitation of the Father, their life as disciples was to imitate him. Thereby in fact they would realize sonship: loving their enemies, as he did, and praying for their persecutors, they would behave as the sons of their Father in heaven.[1] They were to be perfect as their Father in heaven was perfect, and there was a quite concrete way in which this was to be done: walking in the 'Way' as it had been manifested in the life of their Lord. The Way of the Son of Man was to be the way of discipleship also.

There are indications in the Gospel tradition that Jesus regarded the disciples as intimate participants in his own mission and destiny. It is almost as if, like Isaiah of Jerusalem, he saw himself and those whom the Father had given him as sent for 'signs and wonders' to Israel.[2] Indeed, as we shall see, this is precisely the association which the author of the Fourth Gospel suggests.[3]

The word $\mu\alpha\theta\eta\tau\acute{\eta}s$ itself may reflect something of the intention of

---

[1] Matt. 5.44 f.; cf. Luke 6.35.

[2] Isa. 8.18. Jesus also followed Isaiah's practice of giving symbolic names to those intimately involved in his mission. Cf. G. Östborn, *Tōrā in the Old Testament*, p. 158 n. 2: 'Bentzen maintains . . . that Isaiah's circle constituted a model for Jesus' circle of disciples: that Jesus saw his work in the same light as Isaiah had looked upon his mission.'

[3] John 17.6, 9.

Jesus. If the argument of T. W. Manson is sound, Jesus did not use for his disciples the customary word *talmidha'* which was regularly used of pupils of the rabbis. Manson suggests that Jesus preferred the more unusual word *shewilya'* and for this reason:

> It is tempting to see in the choice of the word a definite opposition to the whole scribal system. The *talmid* of the Rabbinical schools is primarily a student. His chief business was to master the contents of the written Law and the Oral Tradition. The finished products of the Rabbinical schools were learned biblical scholars and sound and competent lawyers. The life of a *talmid* as *talmid* was made up of study of the sacred writings, attendance on lectures, and discussion of difficult passages or cases. Discipleship as Jesus conceived it was not a theoretical discipline of this sort, but a practical task to which men were called to give themselves and all their energies. Their work was not study but practice. Fishermen were to become fishers of men, peasants were to be labourers in God's vineyard or God's harvest field. And Jesus was their master not so much as a teacher of right doctrine, but rather as the master-craftsman whom they were to follow and imitate. Discipleship was not matriculation in a Rabbinical College but apprenticeship to the work of the Kingdom.[1]

The 'imitation of Christ' is not a late Christian ideal but has real roots in the New Testament, although some of the forms which it has taken represent deviations from this norm. The *imitatio Christi* has its roots in the Lord's insistence that the life of the disciple, like his own life, had to have a clearly recognized form, because, like his again, the Spirit would reveal it as a sign, a sign of Christ, to those who had eyes to see such a thing. If the life of the Lord is an imitation of the Father, the life of the disciple is an imitation of Christ.

The disciple was first summoned to 'follow' Jesus and the call 'Follow me' became, as J. W. Bowman says, a *terminus technicus* with Jesus.[2] When it is used by others than Jesus it is in such a way as to suggest that it was a well-known characteristic of him: 'And as they were going along the way, a man said to him, "I will follow you wherever you go." . . . Another said, "I will follow you, Lord. . . ." ' (Luke 9.57, 61; cf. Matt. 8.19, 21). Again, Peter's summary of discipleship of the Lord in Mark 10.28 suggests that this way of speaking about it had become stereotyped because of the Master's own usage: 'Peter began to say to him, "Lo, we have left everything and followed you." The evidence about Jesus' own use of the term is found in the Synoptic Gospels as follows:

[1] T. W. Manson, *The Teaching of Jesus*, pp. 239 f.
[2] J. W. Bowman, *The Intention of Jesus*, 1945, p. 147.

And Jesus said to them, 'Follow me and I will make you become fishers of men.' And immediately they left their nets and followed him (Mark 1.17 f.).

And as he passed on, he saw Levi the son of Alphaeus sitting at the tax office, and he said to him 'Follow me.' And he rose and followed him (Mark 2.14).

And he called to him the multitude with his disciples, and said to them, 'If any man would come after me, let him deny himself and take up his cross and follow me' (Mark 8.34).

You lack one thing; go, sell what you have, and give to the poor, and you will have treasure in heaven; and come, follow me (Mark 10.21).

Truly, I say to you, in the new world, when the Son of man shall sit on his glorious throne, you who have followed me will also sit on twelve thrones, judging the twelve tribes of Israel (Matt. 19.28).

It would seem that the idea of 'following' was exclusively associated with discipleship in the teaching and practice of Jesus. The term occurs either in actual calls to discipleship or in descriptions of it. Now this 'following' of Jesus was of greater significance than the actual physical accompanying of him, although of course it involved that. It meant that there was a specific 'Way' of discipleship, and behind this language of Jesus there was certainly the Old Testament imagery of the 'Way' with all that we have seen this involved for him. There are occasions, in fact, when it is possible that the language used by an evangelist reflects the importance of Jesus as the 'Way' and discipleship as a *mimesis* of his way. Mark 10.52 is a good example. Blind Bartimaeus had faith and was made whole. This means that he was able to see again and the consequence was that he 'followed Jesus in the way'.

It is very probable that behind the two terms for 'following' in the Gospels (ἀκολουθέω, δεῦτε ὀπίσω μου) there was one word in the Aramaic[1] and that this reflected the Old Testament usage of *halak 'ahere*. Now, as we have seen, the associations of this phrase are primarily of Israel being commissioned to walk in the 'Way' of the Lord, and thereby obey the Torah. Jesus was summoning his disciples to walk in the same 'Way' to which he had committed himself, only they were to do it by allowing the form of his life and mission to be reproduced in theirs. If Jesus is the 'bridegroom' they are the 'sons of the bride-chamber'. The 'Way' he went needed copying by them because it was of final paradigmatic significance. Just as they could see in the 'Way' he went the presence

---

[1] J. W. Bowman (*op. cit.*, p. 217 n. 26) points out that in Syriac both phrases are translated by the one term *to botori*.

of the Messianic Israel, so men could see in the 'Way' his disciples went the presence of him in whom Messianic Israel was embodied. Jesus' summons to 'follow' him was more than an invitation to accompany him on a teaching tour. It was a 'Messianic summons':[1] a summons to give oneself to share the fate of him who was going as it had been written of him, and to remain confident, as he did, that there would be the end in glory, the coming of the Son of man in triumph in a way and at a time which the Father would determine. Jesus regarded it as inevitable that his twelve disciples would share, to some real extent, his own fate: 'If they have called the master of the house Beelzebub, how much more them of his household!' (Matt. 10.25); but they would share too in the triumphant vindication: 'Ye who have followed me, in the regeneration when the Son of Man shall sit on the throne of his glory, ye also shall sit upon twelve thrones, judging the twelve tribes of Israel.'[2]

The character of the mission of Jesus as a 'sign of the times' was extended in the mission of the Twelve. 'The Kingdom is the future breaking into the present, and manifesting itself in the things which the disciples are to do in addition to their preaching. This combination of preaching and beneficent activity is their task as it is the task of their Master.'[3] We must now examine in more detail the call and mission of the Twelve.

The call of the Twelve is described in Mark 3.13–19 and the parallel passages in Matthew (10.1–4) and Luke (6.12–16). Mark is insistent that the calling into being of the body of the Twelve is a deliberate act of Jesus (v. 13), and that they are to be an 'extension' of his mission. They are summoned to undertake the two activities which have characterized his own mission: to preach and to have authority to cast out devils (vv. 14 f.).

In the Q tradition the affirmation of the nearness of the Kingdom of God characteristic of Jesus is ascribed to the disciples also: 'Heal the sick in it and say to them, "The kingdom of God has come near to you" ' (Luke 10.9). They were to announce in any place which did not receive them: 'Even the dust of your town that clings to our feet, we wipe off against you; nevertheless know this, that the kingdom of God has come near' (Luke 10.11).

As mentioned previously, the Twelve were called into being to constitute a sign of the 'Israel' character of Jesus' mission. They were to be 'with him' and the boundary of his mission included theirs. The old

---

[1] Cf. Kittel's article on ἀκολουθέω in *TWNT* I, p. 214.
[2] Matt. 19.28 (RV); cf. Luke 22.28–30.
[3] T W. Manson, *The Teaching of Jesus*, p. 180.

Israel could be thought of, in one way, as the twelve tribes, and the twelve disciples of Jesus were a *semeion* of the presence of the new Israel. In another way, one might think of the three pillar patriarchs, Abraham, Isaac and Jacob, who stood in such a relation of intimacy and obedience to Yahweh that 'the God of Abraham, Isaac and Jacob' came to be used as a technical term for the God of Israel.[1] In the Israel which came with the mission of Jesus there were three pillar patriarchs also: Peter, James and John, surnamed, as were the patriarchs Abraham and Jacob, and given an intimate share, at the Transfiguration, in the awareness of Jesus as recapitulating in himself the history of Israel given in the Law (Moses) and the Prophets (Elijah).

In the 'mission charge' to the Twelve given in Mark 6.6–13 their essential activities are listed as summoning to repentance, casting out devils, and anointing and healing the sick. Then come the instructions about the equipment which was required for their mission. There seems to have been some confusion in the transmission of the material about this. In Mark there are two, and only two, things insisted upon as being of obligation for the 'way' (ὁδός): a staff (ῥάβδος), and sandals (σανδάλια). Bread, wallet, money, overgarment are forbidden. There can be no doubt from this that Jesus attached great importance to the appearance of the Twelve on their mission. Most commentators are content to suggest that they are to appear as itinerants, 'travelling light', but there is sure to have been more to it than that. If the argument is sound that Jesus' conception of the 'Way of Israel' was influenced by the liturgical celebration of the Exodus in the Passover ritual, so that the whole of his mission was, so to speak, an extended Passover mime, and if his 'Way' was to be 'followed' by the Twelve, then this might well explain the problem before us. The participants in the Passover feast, says Pedersen, repeated the Exodus by eating the meal in the greatest haste, with staff in hand, with sandals on their feet, and with girded loins.[2] It is interesting to compare here the text of this Passover injunction as it is given in the Septuagint:

αἱ ὀσφύες ὑμῶν περιεζωσμέναι
τὰ ὑποδήματα ἐν τοῖς ποσὶν ὑμῶν
αἱ βακτηρίαι ἐν ταῖς χερσὶν ὑμῶν (Ex. 12.11).

ὑποδήματα (the word used, incidentally, in Matthew and Luke) is synonymous in meaning with σανδάλια, and so is βακτηρία with ῥάβδος. The mission of the Twelve would suggest therefore some kind of Passover re-enactment. They were actually on the journey which was repeatedly

---

[1] Ex. 3.6; cf. Mark 12.26.   [2] Cf. Pedersen, *Israel* III–IV, p. 401.

'rehearsed' in the Passover celebration. This would seem to be the meaning if we follow Mark's account. If, however, we follow the Q tradition and accept the prohibition of staff and sandals, this might suggest that, as with Jesus himself, the mission of the Twelve was to be dominated by the urgency of being up to the temple in Jerusalem. In the Mishnah there is the regulation that 'a man may not enter the Temple Mount with his staff or his sandal or his wallet'.[1] It is possible then, as T. W. Manson suggests, that 'the mission of the disciples is meant to be regarded as a specially sacred undertaking, and that they are to set out upon it as if they were setting out to worship in the Temple'.[2] Either way, therefore, there seems every reason to suppose that the manner in which the Twelve were to conduct their mission was held by Jesus to have a similar 'signful' nature to his own.

This is further borne out by Mark 6.10–11 and its parallel versions in Matt. 10.11–15, Luke 9.4–5, and in the charge to the seventy in Luke 10.5–12. An examination of this material suggests that the following further instructions were given. Like him they were to proclaim the advent of the Kingdom of God (Luke 10.9, 11) 'whether they would hear or whether they would forbear'. Nevertheless men would be as accountable for the way in which they received the mission of the disciples of Jesus as they would for the mission of Jesus himself. Would men discern in their coming a decisive 'sign' and repent? If they did not, dust must solemnly be shaken from the feet εἰς μαρτύριον αὐτοῖς. This is the same phrase which is used earlier in Mark in the story of the healing of the leper. Jesus bade the leper go to the priest and make the prescribed Levitical thank-offering εἰς μαρτύριον αὐτοῖς. In both cases μαρτύριον is apparently being used in a sense practically equivalent to σημεῖον. The leper's thankoffering would constitute a *semeion* to the Jewish authorities that a mighty work had been accomplished in their midst. The disciple's action in shaking off the dust from the feet would be a *semeion* to warn of the near presence of the Kingdom of God (Luke 10.9). The words and actions of the disciples on the proclamation tours were to have the same *semeion* character as those of Jesus himself. The cities which refused to receive his disciples were judged in the same terms as those which refused to receive him. In them, as in him, the Kingdom came, and judgment turned on recognition of this fact and acting upon it by repentance. 'It shall be more tolerable on that day for Sodom than for that town' (Luke 10.12), said Jesus of the city which refused to receive his disciples, and 'It shall be

---

[1] Berakoth 9.5, quoted in Manson, *The Sayings of Jesus*, p. 181.
[2] *Ibid.*

more tolerable on the day of judgment for the land of Sodom than for you' (Matt. 11.24) of Capernaum's rejection of him.

In the mind of Jesus himself, to be confronted by a disciple of his was tantamount to being confronted by him, and judgment turned upon what men saw and heard either in the disciple or in their Lord: 'He who receives you receives me, and he who receives me receives him who sent me' (Matt. 10.40). 'He who hears you hears me; and he who rejects you rejects me; and he who rejects me rejects him who sent me' (Luke 10.16). As T. W. Manson has expressed it: 'The messengers are, in a sense, the Kingdom of God itself. The solidarity is impressive. The disciple represents in the fullest sense Jesus, and Jesus represents in the fullest sense the Kingdom of God. What they offer is God's offer and what they claim is God's claim.'[1] Jesus would seem to have shared the belief expressed in the much-discussed saying of the Mishnah: 'He who is sent is as he who sent him.'[2]

The place where the influence of the idea of discipleship as the imitation of Christ can be most fully and clearly perceived is, as one might expect, Luke-Acts.[3] Indeed, it is very likely that this was the motif which determined the structure and theology of the work, not primarily because of a personal predilection of St Luke's, although the theme was specially congenial to him, but because this concept of the Christian life had indisputable dominical authority in the tradition which he inherited. The figure of Jesus in St Luke's Gospel is presented, much more than in the other evangelists, as the ideal man, the pattern humanity, and the Christian life and activity in Acts, as exemplified in the Christian apostles, is shown to be necessarily an imitation of Christ. The influence of the *imitatio Christi* motif in the Gospel is unmistakable. The Christian ideal of taking up the cross *daily*, to which St Luke specially draws attention (9.23), finds its visible embodiment in Simon of Cyrene who is presented by the evangelist as carrying his cross behind Jesus (ὄπισθεν τοῦ ᾿Ιησοῦ) (Luke 23.26). The Lucan passion narrative presents Jesus as the model martyr, and it is significant that St Luke places the saying about the disciple having to imitate the Lord as *diakonos* on the occasion of the Last Supper (24.26–30). The disciples too will be involved in a reproduction of his *mimesis*, but for them (as for him) there is to be a throne.

It has often been pointed out that Luke-Acts was composed to bring

---

[1] *The Sayings of Jesus*, p. 78.   [2] Berakoth 5.5.

[3] Professor G. W. H. Lampe's essay, 'The Holy Spirit in the Writings of St Luke', in *Studies in the Gospels* (ed. D. E. Nineham), 1955, is very instructive in this connection. Cf. also H. J. Cadbury, *The Making of Luke-Acts*, 1927, and R. Leivestad, *Christ the Conqueror*, 1954.

out the parallelism between the mission of the Lord and that of his disciples, but, in connection with the present argument, it will be convenient to examine again first the general resemblances between the mission of Jesus and that of his apostles, and then the particular models of the imitation of Christ in Stephen, Peter and Paul.

In his prologue to the Gospel St Luke had indicated what was to be the subject of his work: Jesus as 'the sign to be spoken against' (2.34). This phrase is picked up again towards the end of Acts where we are reminded that what was true of Christ must also be true of those who walk in his 'Way': they too will be spoken against (28.22). The beginning of the mission of Jesus was marked by a special anointing[1] by the Holy Spirit.[2] So it is with the mission of the apostles whether to Jews or to Gentiles. The Jewish mission of the Church is anointed with the Spirit in Jerusalem at Pentecost,[3] and the Gentile mission in Caesarea.[4] If Jesus was a man 'approved by signs and wonders'[5] the same is true of the apostles of Jesus,[6] and their ministry is described in exactly the same way as that of Jesus.[7] The words and works of the apostles were intended to be taken as *semeia* of Christ. The promise of the Lord to the disciples about the help which will be given them in the future has this characteristic form: 'I will give you a mouth and wisdom (σοφίαν) which none of your adversaries wiil be able to withstand (ἀντιστῆναι) or contradict (ἀντειπεῖν)' (Luke 21.15). In Acts we see this promise fulfilled and are meant to take the things which the apostles do and say as 'signs' of the Lord's presence. There are places in Acts where the Lord's promise of help seems to be deliberately alluded to: for instance, the comment that when confronted with the lame man healed the opponents of Peter and John could not contradict it (οὐδὲν εἶχον ἀντειπεῖν, 4.14), or, as we shall see later, the description of the reaction to the speech of Stephen.[8] In Luke 12.12 Jesus says to his disciples: 'The Holy Spirit will teach you in that very hour what you ought to say.' In Acts this is seen in fulfilment.[9] It is in the Lucan writings, in fact, that the intimate organic relation between the *manner* of the Master's proclamation and that of his apostle is specially stressed. In Luke 4.43 the purpose for which Jesus was 'sent' is to preach the Gospel of the Kingdom of God (εὐαγγελίσασθαί με δεῖ τὴν βασιλείαν τοῦ Θεοῦ). In Acts εὐαγγελίζειν is used of the proclamation of the apostles (e.g. 8.4). In the Gospel Luke places in an initial and prominent place the *kerygma* of Jesus in the synagogue at Nazareth. He it is who

---

[1] Acts 10.38. [2] Luke 4.18. [3] Acts 2.1–11.
[4] Acts 10.44–46. [5] Acts 2.22. [6] Acts 2.43.
[7] Cf. Luke 4.40 f. and Acts 5.12–15.
[8] Cf. p. 110 below. [9] E.g. Acts 4.8.

mentions specifically that Jesus went into the synagogue on the Sabbath 'as his custom was' (κατὰ τὸ εἰωθός).[1] The form of the *kerygma* in the Nazareth synagogue was first a citation from Isa. 61.1 f. describing the mission of one whose work would usher in the Age to Come, and then the announcement that this was now happening—for those with 'ears to hear': 'Today this scripture has been fulfilled in your ears' (4.21). Again, the discourse of the risen Jesus on the road to Emmaus takes the form of an 'opening of the scriptures':

> 'O foolish men, and slow of heart to believe all that the prophets have spoken! Was it not necessary that the Christ should suffer these things and enter into his glory?' And beginning with Moses (ἀρξάμενος ἀπὸ Μωυσέως) and all the prophets, he interpreted to them in all the scriptures the things concerning himself (Luke 24.25–27).

This manner of reasoning from scriptures has certainly been taken by St Luke as the necessary model for the apostolic preaching in Acts. The mission of Philip the Evangelist is obviously modelled in its form and content on that of the Master. He evangelized the Samaritans. It may well be significant, as Dr Austin Farrer notes, that in the Gospel it is St Luke, 'and he alone of the Synoptists, who records a long journey of Christ in or about the Samaritan country (9.51–18.30) as though anticipating the mission in Samaria begun by St Philip the Evangelist and continued by St Peter and St John (Acts 8.5–25)'.[2] Philip went to Samaria to proclaim (ἐκήρυσσεν), and the multitudes acted upon the words spoken by him and the signs done by him (which were the signs of the Master: driving out unclean spirits, healing of paralysed and lame).[3] Philip's method of proclaiming the Gospel to the Ethiopian eunuch echoes the speech of the Lord on the Emmaus Road, and in the synagogue at Nazareth. The scriptural passage for interpretation was Isa. 53.7 f., and the Ethiopian posed the problem of identification: 'About whom, pray, does the prophet say this, about himself or about someone else?' (Acts 8.34). Then, in words which are reminiscent of Christ on the road to Emmaus, Philip pointed to Jesus as the one alluded to: 'Then Philip opened his mouth, and beginning with this scripture (ἀρξάμενος ἀπο τῆς γραφῆς ταύτης) he told him the gospel of Jesus (εὐηγγελίσατο αὐτῷ τὸν Ἰησοῦν).' The kerygmatic method of the apostles in the Acts is clearly meant to be taken as a

---

[1] Luke 4.16. Cf. the references in the Acts to the Apostles proclaiming the Gospel in the synagogues on the Sabbath, 13.5; 17.2: 'Paul went into the synagogue as his custom was (κατὰ δὲ τὸ εἰωθός), and for three weeks he argued with them from the scriptures, explaining and proving that it was necessary for the Christ to suffer, and to rise from the dead.'

[2] Austin Farrer, *St Matthew and St Mark*, p. 53.   [3] Acts 8.6 f.

repetition of that of Jesus himself. It is possible to argue[1] that Luke starts from the kerygmatic practice of his day and that this has determined the form in which he presents the proclamation of Jesus in such passages as 4.16–30 or 24.13–35. It is equally possible, and, in view of the considerations discussed earlier about the form which Jesus himself believed that his mission should assume, more likely, that the manner of apostolic proclamation was regarded by the early Church as one of the ways in which the Christian life as *imitatio Christi* was realized.

The same motif underlies the way in which the works of the apostles are presented in the Acts. There is a deliberate parallelism between the account of the healing of the paralytic in Luke 5.17–26 and the healing of the lame man by Peter in Acts 3.1–10. To the paralytic Jesus said ἔγειρε καὶ περιπάτει (v. 23); Peter took the lame man by the right hand and raised him up (ἤγειρεν) and he walked (περιεπάτει, v. 7). It is only the Lucan account of the healing of the paralytic which ends with the comment that an ἔκστασις took hold of all and they praised God (ἐδόξαζον τὸν Θεόν, v. 26). Similarly the people present at the healing of the lame man at the Beautiful Gate were filled with ἔκστασις when they saw him walking and praising God (αἰνοῦντα τὸν Θεόν, v. 10). The raising of the paralytic led to Jesus' first clash with the authorities, and so it was with his apostle also. The healing of the lame man produced the first clash between Peter and the authorities (4.1 ff.).

Perhaps the most striking early example in the Acts of the influence of the *imitatio Christi* on the formation of the tradition about his followers is the account of the death of Stephen in Acts. In fact the whole mission, speech and death of Stephen is presented in such a way as to recall the Master. Stephen first appears on the scene, like his Lord, full of grace and power, doing great wonders and signs (τέρατα καὶ σημεῖα μεγάλα) among the people (6.8). As with Jesus, so now with Stephen, his opponents were not able to withstand the wisdom and the Spirit with which he spoke.[2] Evidence against Jesus was taken from false informers, and the same was true of his follower Stephen (vv. 11, 13). The people are stirred up against him; the elders and scribes have him seized and brought before the Sanhedrin (v. 12). The charges brought against Stephen were the same as those brought against Christ (vv. 13 f.). The speech of Stephen with its historical review of Israel's history is reminiscent of the same kind of historical judgment found in the Lord's speech in the synagogue

---

[1] Cf. C. F. Evans, 'The Kerygma', *JTS*, n.s. 7, 1956, pp. 25–41.

[2] Acts 6.10: καὶ οὐκ ἴσχυον ἀντιστῆναι τῇ σοφίᾳ καὶ τῷ πνεύματι ᾧ ἐλάλει; cf. Luke 21.15: ἐγὼ γὰρ δώσω ὑμῖν στόμα καὶ σοφίαν.

at Nazareth (Luke 4.25–27), or in the woes on the scribes and Pharisees (Luke 11.47–51). It seems certain that we are meant to have the Nazareth scene in mind, from the similar circumstantial notes in both narratives. Before Jesus begins his 'sermon' in the synagogue at Nazareth we are told that the eyes of all in the synagogue were fastened on him (καὶ πάντων οἱ ὀφθαλμοὶ ἐν τῇ συναγωγῇ ἦσαν ἀτενίζοντες αὐτῷ, v. 20). The setting for Stephen's speech is similarly described: καὶ ἀτενίσαντες εἰς αὐτὸν πάντες οἱ καθεζόμενοι (Acts 6.15).[1] After the synagogue sermon Jesus was cast out of the city (ἐξέβαλον ἔξω τῆς πόλεως, Luke 4.29). Stephen also is thrust outside the city for stoning: ἐκβαλόντες ἔξω τῆς πόλεως ἐλιθοβόλουν (Acts 7.58).

The death of Stephen is narrated in such a way as to constitute a veritable *passio Stephani* having a basic similarity to the *Passio Christi* of St Luke's Gospel. Just as Jesus on trial before the Sanhedrin was sustained by the vision of the triumph of the Son of man in glory (Luke 22.69), so Stephen, full of the Holy Spirit as promised, saw the heavens opened and Jesus standing as Son of man in glory at the right hand of God (Acts 7.55 f.). As Jesus prayed for the forgiveness of those who were putting him to death (Luke 23.34), Stephen did the same (Acts 7.60). The final committal of Jesus is found only in St Luke: Πάτερ, εἰς χεῖράς σου παρατίθεμαι τὸ πνεῦμά μου (23.46); and this is echoed by the words of Stephen: Κύριε Ἰησοῦ, δέξαι τὸ πνεῦμά μου (Acts 7.59). Jesus was buried by Joseph of Arimathaea, whom St Luke is careful to describe as a good and righteous man (ἀνὴρ ἀγαθὸς καὶ δίκαιος, Luke 23.50). In Acts this seems to be echoed in the note that devout men (ἄνδρες εὐλαβεῖς) buried Stephen (Acts 8.2). In the Gospel tradition it is Luke alone who mentions the lamentations for Jesus (23.27); these are paralleled by lamentations for Stephen (Acts 8.2).

We know that very soon in the early Church, as for example in the letters of St Ignatius of Antioch, the martyr was regarded as *the* imitator of Christ. The treatment of the death of Stephen suggests that this sentiment goes back to the apostolic age, and is in fact based upon the necessity for the 'Way' of the disciple to correspond to the 'Way' of the suffering Son of Man, and this we have seen is likely to have been a belief of Jesus himself. 'The whole intention of St Luke', writes Dr Austin Farrer, 'is to show that in his martyrdom St Stephen becomes a second Christ.'[2]

The mission of the apostles Peter and Paul is presented, as we would

---

[1] Cf. Luke 22.56, which suggests that more is at stake than a stylistic feature, and strengthens the idea that Luke presents the questioning of Peter as a trial, a kind of sub-plot to the main drama.
[2] *A Study in St Mark*, p. 267.

now expect, in a way which reminds us that behind their words and works there is the activity of the Lord himself conforming their lives to the pattern of his own.

Peter's mission began, like his Lord's, after a special endowment of the Holy Spirit. This came at Pentecost in Jerusalem.[1] Then came the healing of the lame man which, as we have seen, is reminiscent of the Lord's raising of the paralytic. The speeches of Peter follow the formula we have found to be characteristic of the Lord's addresses in St Luke's Gospel. Peter's healing of Aeneas again has reminiscences of Jesus' curing of the paralytic.[2] Peter's raising of Dorcas from the dead has unmistakable echoes of the account of the raising of Jairus' daughter.[3] It is interesting, as Professor Lampe notes,[4] that in St Luke's Gospel the raising of Jairus' daughter is followed by the sending out of the Twelve, and in Acts the raising of Dorcas is followed by the proclamation of the Gospel to the Gentiles. The way in which the imprisonment and release of Peter is written up in Acts 12.1–17 is reminiscent of the Crucifixion and Resurrection appearances of Jesus. In fact Acts 12 begins what can be termed a prefigurative *passio Petri*. Peter, like his Master, was seized on the days of unleavened bread (Acts 12.3; cf. Luke 22.1). He was imprisoned with two soldiers and taken outside the city (vv. 6, 10). Through the action of God he was raised ($\dot{a}\nu\dot{a}\sigma\tau a$ $\dot{\epsilon}\nu$ $\tau\dot{a}\chi\epsilon\iota$, v. 7) and appeared in Jerusalem (v. 12), and like his Master his reappearance was not believed.[5] Like the risen Jesus Peter calmed his brethren (v. 17; cf. Luke 24.36, 38), and bade them tell these things to James and the others.

St Paul was also sent on his mission by the Holy Spirit (Acts 13.4). With Barnabas he proclaimed the Gospel in the synagogues. Paul's first healing, that of the lame man at Lystra, is told in a way unmistakably reminiscent of Peter's healing of the lame man at Solomon's Porch and this, in turn, echoes the Lord's raising of the paralytic at Capernaum. This man, like the man at Solomon's Porch, was 'lame from his mother's womb' ($\dot{\epsilon}\kappa$ $\kappa o\iota\lambda\dot{\iota}as$ $\mu\eta\tau\rho\dot{o}s$ $a\dot{v}\tauo\hat{v}$, Acts 14.8; cf. 3.2). Fixing his eyes on him ($\dot{a}\tau\epsilon\nu\dot{\iota}\sigma as$, 14.9; cf. 3.4) Paul healed him. The reaction of the crowd was very like that of those who were present at Peter's healing in Jerusalem. They thought that they were confronted with gods (14.11), just as the crowd gazed at Peter and John ($\tau\dot{\iota}$ $\dot{a}\tau\epsilon\nu\dot{\iota}\zeta\epsilon\tau\epsilon$) as if they were wonder-working deities (3.12), and we remember that the reaction to Jesus at Capernaum was 'Who can forgive sins but God only?' (Luke

---

[1] Acts 2.1–21. [2] Acts 9.32–35.
[3] Acts 9.36–43; cf. Luke 8.49–55. [4] In *Studies in the Gospels*, pp. 194 f.
[5] Acts 12.15: 'It is his angel'; cf. Luke 24.37: 'They . . . supposed that they saw a spirit.'

5.21). This provided Paul with an opportunity of proclaiming the Gospel *ad Gentiles* (Acts 14.15 f.) just as the incident in Solomon's Porch had provided Peter with an opportunity of proclaiming the *kerygma ad Judaeos*. Both incidents resulted in a clash with the authorities (14.19 f.; cf. 4.1 f.). The general account of healings and exorcisms at Ephesus resembles the similar account of healings and exorcisms at Jerusalem.[1] Paul's raising of Eutychus (20.7 ff.) recalls Peter's raising of Dorcas.

We now come to the later part of Paul's mission as narrated in Acts, and this is presented in such a way as to suggest a *passio Pauli*. The account begins with a 'prediction of the passion' made by the prophet Agabus: 'So shall the Jews at Jerusalem bind the man that owns this girdle, and deliver him into the hands of the Gentiles' (21.11). Paul was seized in the temple and charged with teaching everywhere 'against the people' (κατὰ τοῦ λαοῦ, v. 28) just as Jesus, in Luke's Gospel, had been charged with 'perverting the people' (ἀποστρέφοντα τὸν λαόν, 23.14). The crowd shouted out after Paul 'Away with him' (αἶρε αὐτόν, 21.36; cf. 22.22), which was the cry of the crowd given in Luke 23.18. There were those who wished to release Paul and they echoed the words of Pilate in Luke's Gospel: 'We find nothing wrong in this man' (Acts 23.9; cf. Luke 23.14). The words of Pilate about Jesus, that nothing to justify the death penalty had been found (οὐδὲν ἄξιον θανάτου, Luke 23.15), were echoed by the words of Claudias Lysias in his letter to Felix (μηδὲν δὲ ἄξιον θανάτου, 23.29; cf. 26.31). Paul followed Jesus in appearing before both Jewish and Roman courts. St Luke's Gospel closes with the risen Christ opening the minds of the apostles to the things 'written about me in the law of Moses, and the prophets, and the psalms' (24.44). Similarly Acts closes with the picture of St Paul 'testifying to the Kingdom of God, and persuading them concerning Jesus, both from the law of Moses, and from the prophets, from morning till evening' (28.23).

It would seem to be the clear intention of St Luke to stress that the 'Way' of the follower of the Lord Jesus had necessarily to take on the likeness of the 'Way' of the Lord himself.[2] In this he is articulating a belief which was powerfully at work in the early Church and which had its roots in the mind and purpose of Jesus as disclosed to his disciples during his mission. One could sum up this part of the argument by referring to the function of the apostles as 'witnesses' (μάρτυρες). As we have seen, the

---

[1] Acts 19.11 f.; cf. 5.14–16.

[2] This seems to me more likely than the suggestion of H. J. Cadbury that the phenomenon is purely fortuitous: 'He [St Luke] may have been affected by a tendency to assimilation or to the stereotyping of incidents of which he himself was quite unconscious.' *The Making of Luke-Acts*, p. 232.

mission of the disciples had in the eyes of Jesus the character of a μαρτύριον.[1] The background to this usage would seem to be the distinctive meaning of 'witnessing' which is to be found in the Book of Isaiah. There *'edh* is used to describe the mission of Israel:

'You are my witnesses (*'edhim*),' says the Lord
'and my servant whom I have chosen' (Isa. 43.10).

Fear not, nor be afraid;
have I not told you from of old and declared it?
And you are my witnesses! (Isa. 44.8).

Israel's faith and obedience are a sign pointing to Yahweh himself, 'the faithful witness'. 'Witness' (*'edh*) and 'sign' (*'oth*) are used synonymously in Isa. 19.20. In the Age to Come an altar and a pillar will be 'a sign (*'edh*) and a witness (*'oth*) to the Lord of hosts in the land of Egypt'. The royal Messiah will be given to Israel as a 'witness': 'Behold I made him a witness to the peoples' (Isa. 55.4). Israel will be the true witness when he has eyes to see and ears to hear. To recognize the 'signs' which God gives is to become oneself a 'sign'. The function of the disciples as 'witnesses' reflects this Old Testament background and again suggests that the 'Israel' character of the mission of Jesus went back to the consciousness of Jesus himself. The disciples as 'witnesses' is an emphasis of the Lucan and Johannine writings, and this is yet another way of illustrating that the disciples ('witnesses') are, as such, engaged in the *mimesis* of him who was the perfect 'witness' (μάρτυς).[2] The words and works of the disciple 'testify' to him who through the spirit is the ἀρχηγός and τελειωτής of their lives. This is the conception of the nature of the mission of the disciples which is expressed in both the 'longer' and 'shorter' endings of St Mark:

(1) And they went forth and preached everywhere while the Lord worked with them and confirmed the message by the signs which attended it (16.20).
(2) Jesus sent out by means of them, from east to west, the sacred and imperishable proclamation of eternal salvation.[3]

We have previously discussed certain external features of the mission of the disciples which were to mark it as an obedient following in the 'Way' of Israel which had been pioneered for them by Jesus himself.[4] We must turn now to consider the attitudes and behaviour which are required of the disciple as an imitator of his Lord.

---

[1] Mark 6.11; 13.9.
[3] The text given after 16.8 by L, Ψ, and others.
[2] Rev. 1.5; 3.14; John 18.37.
[4] Cf. pp. 100 ff. above.

H

Like the mission of Jesus, the mission of the disciple was a summons to walk in the way of *sonship*. In his teaching Jesus presented the sonship of God to which the disciples were called as involving essentially the *imitatio Dei*. There was to be on their part, for example, the indiscriminate uncalculating love for enemies because this would be a practicable replica of the love which the Father has:

> Love your enemies and pray for those who persecute you, so that you may be sons of your Father who is in heaven.[1]

Where the exemplar of this was to be found Jesus did not, of course, explicitly state. This would have been a 'witnessing to himself' which was alien to his mission. A passage like I Peter 2.21–23 is however evidence that the early Church inherited from the first disciples a belief that the Lord himself was the embodiment of his own teaching, and that the *imitatio Dei* took for them the form of the *imitatio Christi*.

The summons of the disciples to the life of the *imitatio Dei* is given in a saying of Jesus which has come down in two versions:

> You, therefore, must be perfect (τέλειοι) as your heavenly Father is perfect (Matt. 5.48).

> Be merciful (οἰκτίρμονες), even as your Father is merciful (Luke 6.36).

τέλειος is characteristic of St Matthew's Gospel[2] and looks back to the Old Testament idea of 'perfection'. There[3] to be 'perfect' on the part of man is associated with the ideas of 'walking with God', 'fearing God', 'walking in the way of the Lord', 'eschewing evil', and is thus part of the complex imagery used to express the idea of the *imitatio Dei*. This saying of Jesus occupies the place in the life of his community which the Levitical saying, 'You shall be holy; for I the Lord your God am holy' (Lev. 19.2), held in the Old Israel. In St Luke's Gospel the word used is οἰκτίρμονες, 'merciful'. From Old Testament usage it would seem that 'merciful' (*hasidh*) and 'perfect' (*tamim*) have practically the same meaning: 'With the merciful (*hasidh*) thou wilt show thyself merciful, with the perfect (*tamim*) thou wilt show thyself perfect' (II Sam. 22.26). Christian discipleship as the road to 'perfection' through following in the 'Way' of Christ doubtless had its origin in such sayings of Jesus as this. Relevant also are sayings like that in Matt. 10.25, 'It is enough for the disciple that he be

---

[1] Matt. 5.44 f.; cf. Luke 6.27. Cf. B. S. Easton, *Christ in the Gospels*, 1930, p. 136.
[2] Cf. Matt. 19.21 where 'to be perfect' (τέλειος) means 'following' Jesus.
[3] Gen. 6.9; 17.1; Job 1.1; Deut. 18.13; Ps. 119.1.

like his master', and Luke 6.40, 'The disciple is not above his master: but everyone when he is perfected shall be as his master.'

The 'Way' of the disciple is one of *renunciation*: 'If any man would come after me let him deny himself and take up his cross and follow me' (Mark 8.34). 'So therefore, whoever of you does not renounce all that he has cannot be my disciple' (Luke 14.33). This austerity and simplicity in the manner of life of the disciple will point to the destitution of the Son of man who had nowhere to lay his head. If this renunciation means, as it often will, the surrender of family life and affection,[1] they will be following one who had himself done this before them. This renunciation will involve an entire self-giving which may have to be expressed in death itself, but this is how a disciple will follow the 'Son of Man' who came to give up himself in redemption for many.[2]

The 'Way' of the disciple is one of *obedience*: 'Whoever does the will of God is my brother, and sister and mother' (Mark 3.35). 'Why do you call me "Lord, Lord", and not do what I tell you' (Luke 6.46). St Matthew, and St Luke to a lesser extent, present the teaching of Jesus as a new Torah which is fulfilled in his own life, and therefore the disciples' obedience to the Torah will take the form of the imitation of his life.

The way of the disciple is pre-eminently a life of *humility*, which will most likely be expressed in humiliation and suffering. In Mark 10.42 ff. there is a direct exhortation to the *mimesis* of the διακονία of the Son of Man:

> You know that those who are supposed to rule over the Gentiles lord it over them (κυριεύουσιν) and their great men exercise authority over them. But it shall not be so among you; but whoever would be great among you must be your servant (διάκονος), and whoever would be first among you must be slave (δοῦλος) of all. For the Son of man also came not to be served (διακονηθῆναι) but to serve, and to give his life as a ransom for many.[3]

Jesus here, in characteristic indirect fashion, pointed to the 'Son of man' as the true model of greatness. The true κύριος is the διάκονος, and the greatness of the disciple will take the same form: διακονία. With this passage we may compare Mark 9.35:

> And he sat down and called the twelve; and he said to them, 'If anyone would be first, he must be last of all and servant of all' (πάντων διάκονος),

and the saying in Luke 22.27:

---

[1] Matt. 10.37; cf. Luke 14.26; Mark 10.29 f.   [2] Mark 10.45; cf. 8.35.
[3] 'La leçon que donne Jésus est confirmée par son exemple', M.-J. Lagrange, *Évangile selon S. Marc* (Etudes Bibliques), Paris, 1911, *ad loc.*

Which is the greater, one who sits at table, or one who serves (ὁ διακονῶν)? Is not the one who sits at table? But I am among you as one who serves (ὁ διακονῶν).

The *mimesis Christou* in humility is practically certain to involve suffering. Discipleship must involve therefore a 'following' of the *Passio Christi*: 'The cup that I drink you shall drink, and with the baptism with which I am baptized, you will be baptized' (Mark 10.39); and, as with himself, he cannot seek to anticipate for them, as James and John request, the vindication in glory which it is the Father's alone to give as and when he will. The way in humility will, in fact, certainly involve the shame and humiliation of non-resistance: 'I say to you, Do not resist (ἀντιστῆναι) one who is evil. But if anyone strikes you (ῥαπίζει) on the right cheek (σιαγόνα), turn (στρέψον) to him the other also; and if anyone would sue you (κριθῆναι) and take your coat, let him have your cloak as well' (Matt. 5.39 f.). As Professor W. Manson pointed out,[1] the words given in Greek above are found in the Septuagint version of the third of the Servant-songs (Isa. 50.6, 8). 'We ought to infer', says A. G. Hebert commenting on this fact,[2] 'that the hearers are not being given merely precepts of the spiritual life, clothed in picturesque oriental language, but are being told that they must reproduce in their lives the pattern of the servant of the Lord.'

There is an evident similarity between the 'Way' of the 'disciple' as it is presented in the Synoptic tradition and the 'Way' which Jesus himself went.[3] In fact, if we put side by side the 'Ways' of the Isaianic Servant,[4] the Son of Man,[4] Jesus himself, and the disciple of Jesus we find the same basic pattern:

The 'Way' of the Isaianic Servant

He is *called* in the eternal purpose of God and endowed by the spirit to be a '*sign*' to the nations, and this will involve *humiliation, obscurity* and *suffering*. He is *tempted* to turn aside. The Servant will be *intercessor* for others and will be *vindicated in glory*.

The 'Way' of the 'Son of Man'

He is *called* to a mission which will be a '*sign*' of the times, and this will involve *humiliation, obscurity* and *suffering*. He is *tempted* to disobey. The Son of Man will be *intercessor*, and will be *vindicated in glory*.

---

[1] *Jesus the Messiah*, 1943, p. 31.   [2] *The Authority of the Old Testament*, 1947, p. 126.
[3] An interesting paper by J. J. Vincent, 'The Parables of Jesus as Self-Revelation', in *Studia Evangelica*, ed. K. Aland and others, Berlin, 1959, pp. 79 ff., demonstrates the importance of the parables of Jesus as presentations of the pattern of discipleship.
[4] Cf. p. 89 above.

The 'Way' of Jesus

He is *called*[1] and *Spirit-endowed* for his mission which is one of *humiliation, obscurity and suffering*. He is *tempted* to turn aside from the task. He *intercedes*[2] and is *vindicated in glory* in resurrection.

The 'Way' of the Disciple

He is *called* to follow in the 'Way' of the Lord, and endowment by the *Spirit* is promised to him. He is *tempted* to disown his task which brings him *humiliation, obscurity* and *suffering*. He *intercedes*[3] and will be *vindicated in glory*.[4]

The force at work in the formation of the tradition which has produced these parallel patterns was the central place which the early Church gave to the Christian life as the *imitatio Christi*. But this was a motif which did not begin in the early Church. It has exercised this controlling force because it was something indelibly associated with the life and mission of the Lord himself. This means, as we shall see later,[5] that the activities of the Church which interested the 'form-critics', such as worship, proclamation and teaching, were themselves controlled by the form of the historical mission of Jesus.

The themes which we have been discussing are taken up and underlined in a fresh and significant way by the author of the Fourth Gospel. The theme of this Gospel could well be termed: 'Jesus the perfect *imitator Patris*.' The 'Way' of Jesus is the 'Way' of Israel as obedient Son, the 'Way' of Torah, and the 'Way' of knowledge, and the disciple bears witness to his Lord by following in his 'Way' as the *imitator Christi*. It is to the treatment of these themes in the Fourth Gospel that we must now turn.

---

[1] 'To this end came I forth', Mark 1.38.
[2] Luke 22.32.
[3] Luke 6.28; cf. Matt. 5.44.
[4] Matt. 19.28; cf. Luke 22.30.
[5] Cf. pp. 176 ff. below.

8

Jesus the Imitator of the Father
in St John

THE AUTHOR of the Fourth Gospel treats afresh the Synoptic presentation of the 'Way' of Jesus as a *semeion*. He is interested in the actual historical course of the ministry of Jesus, which forms the framework of his Gospel, but he is also determined to press upon the reader the question of Thomas, 'We do not know where you are going; how can we know the way?' (14.5). Discerning the true dimensions of the 'Way' of Jesus focuses the problem of belief in the Fourth Gospel. The 'Way' of Jesus is a great deal more than the actual historical *curriculum vitae*, although it includes that. It is important, but not sufficient, to say: 'Is not this Jesus, the son of Joseph, whose father and mother we know?' (John 6.42). One has constantly to be on guard against asserting knowledge which may in fact be culpable ignorance: 'We know where this man comes from; but when the Christ appears, no one will know where he comes from' (John 7.27).

The origin and goal of the 'Way' of Jesus is continuously presented as the issue upon which a man must make his decision.[1] The crucial point is whether a man can see in the historical 'Way' of Jesus a 'sign' of the 'Way' from and to God which he is, whether he can discern in the 'Son of Joseph, whose father and mother we know' the 'bread which came down from heaven' (John 6.41 f.), and the Jesus who 'had come from God, and was going to God' (13.3). The 'Way' of Jesus was, in reality, a descent and an ascent: 'You will see heaven opened, and the angels of God ascending and descending upon the Son of man' (1.51); and this dimension of the mission of Jesus is subtly suggested by the actual movements of Jesus in the Gospel *up* to Jerusalem and *down* to Galilee. Behind the journey from Galilee to Jerusalem this author sees the 'Way' of the Son back to the Father (14.12). Just as what is implicit throughout the whole Gospel about the relation of 'seeing' and 'believing'[2] becomes explicit in

---

[1] Cf. John 7.35; 8.22; 9.29; 13.36.
[2] Cf. pp. 121 ff. below.

the reply of Jesus to Thomas which forms the climax of the Gospel,[1] so the reply of Jesus to the question of Thomas in 14.5 f. makes explicit the character of the mission of Jesus as the 'sign' of the 'Way' to the Father: 'Thomas saith unto him, "Lord, we do not know where you are going; how can we know the way?" Jesus said to him, "I am the way, and the truth, and the life; no one comes to the Father, but by me." '

This theme of Jesus as the 'Way' is effectively and dramatically emphasized in the Fourth Gospel by the structural device which Stauffer has called the *Stundenschlag*—the striking of the hour-bell. 'It is the fourth evangelist', he writes, 'who has most consistently worked out that unique freedom from men and freedom towards God in which Jesus listened to the secret promptings about the way he should go.'[2] The Father's way has been accepted by the Son, and there is, so to speak, a time-table in operation for its traversal: time and time again we are told that the 'hour' of Jesus had not yet come, and the Gospel works up to the climax when the hour for the Son of man to be glorified has arrived (17.1). This major theme of the striking of the destiny bell along the Israel journey which the Son of man takes is dramatically linked with the actual notes telling the time in the Fourth Gospel.[3]

There are instructive treatments of this 'hour-bell' theme in two passages of St John. First: 2.4: 'And Jesus said to her, "O woman, what have you to do with me? My hour has not yet come." ' As Son of Man Jesus has committed himself to walk in the way put before him by the Father. To turn away from it, to disobey or alter the time-calls, would be an act of filial disobedience to the Father, even if it were at the behest of his mother. This is the temptation which he must unhesitatingly put aside.[4] The hour for the giving of the wine (in his death) has not yet come, and in any case will not be of his choosing. There must be no premature hastening or foreshortening of the 'Way' of the Son of Man which the Father has determined. The 'sign' of the giving of the wine points, for believers, to the place where the eternal Wine will be given—the Cross.

The second illustration is found in chapter 7. Jesus is here urged by his disciples to make a clear unambiguous declaration of himself; no longer must he act ἐν κρυπτῷ but ἐν παρρησίᾳ (v. 4). But to make his own manifestation to the world in his own way would have meant yielding to

---

[1] If, as is probable, the work originally ended at 20.31.
[2] E. Stauffer, *New Testament Theology*, p. 27.   [3] Cf. 1.39; 4.6; 19.14.
[4] Cf. Loisy, *Le Quatrième Evangile*, 1st ed., Paris, 1903, p. 273: 'Ce qu'elle dit ressemble à la proposition de Satan dans l'histoire de la tentation: "Si tu es le Fils de Dieu, ordonne que ces pierres deviennent des pains," sauf que ses paroles excluent le doute et que son intention est bienveillante.'

the fundamental temptation which beset him. On a first reading it might seem that the temptation theme had disappeared altogether from the Fourth Gospel. In fact, the Fourth Evangelist has his own way of bringing out, just as clearly as in the Synoptic Gospels, that it was the Father who would validate the mission of Jesus. Jesus had to put aside all temptation to anticipate the Father's καιρός (v. 6) for this. So in this passage, Jesus says to the disciples: 'Go to the feast yourselves; I am not going up to the feast, for my time (καιρός) has not yet fully come' (v. 8). Almost immediately, however, we read: 'But after his brethren had gone up to the feast, then he also went up, not publicly but in private' (οὐ φανερῶς ἀλλ' ὡς ἐν κρυπτῷ, v. 10).[1] As Stauffer says,[2] the obvious inference is that the Father has given him a 'sign'. The Father had appointed a καιρός for the open proclamation of the kingship of Jesus, and Jesus must not accept any move that would anticipate this, like the incident which followed the feeding of the multitude (6.15). The connection of this incident with the tradition about the temptation of Jesus is made very probable by the comment: ἀνεχώρησε πάλιν εἰς τὸ ὄρος αὐτὸς μόνος.[3] Again, as in the Synoptists, the 'Way' given him by the Father is described by Jesus as a cup which he must drain. Any action, like that of Peter, which suggested other methods, was a temptation to be put aside (18.11).

The Fourth Evangelist has dramatized most effectively the Synoptic theme of the 'Way' of the Son of Man by his treatment of what we have called the time-table which Jesus accepted as belonging to the mission the Father had assigned to him. He has also underlined the fact that the mission of Jesus had a uniquely significant form, and that on men's perception of this turned their eternal destiny. This has been done by the treatment of the 'works' and 'words' of Jesus both of which point to the presence of a truly obedient Israel, the *imitator Patris*, Jesus the unique Son.

On a first reading it would appear that the 'signs' in St John's Gospel are not signs as understood by the Synoptic tradition but open unambiguous *terata*. But a careful reading of the Fourth Gospel makes it clear that the author was in fact wishing to make the same point in a startling way.

---

[1] Cf. Loisy, *op. cit.*, p. 490, who speaks of the exhortation to Jesus, 'Show yourself to the world' (John 7.4), as 'une nouvelle forme de la second tentation du Christ dans Matthieu'.

[2] *New Testament Theology*, p. 27.

[3] Cf. Matt. 4.8 f., and cf. again Loisy, *op. cit.*, p. 431: 'Déjà dans le premier Évangile il y a une sorte de parenté mystique entre tous ces sommets, montagne de la tentation, montagne du discours, montagne de la transfiguration, montagne de la résurrection. Ce qu'on lit ici du projet de la foule est tout ce que le quatrième Évangile pouvait retenir de la tentation diabolique pour un royaume terrestre.'

There is a cryptic element about the Johannine 'signs', and even when the *teras* character of a mighty work is most pronounced, as in the raising of Lazarus, it does not therefore immediately lead to faith, or perception of it as a 'sign'. Seeing is not necessarily believing.[1] Seeing matters,[2] but is not sufficient by itself. It must lead on to faith, and this by no means follows automatically. On examination the 'signs' of the Fourth Gospel are only recognizable as such to those who both see and believe.

The episode at Cana of Galilee was not an open *teras*. Only the servants who had drawn the water were in possession of facts which would suggest that the occurrence was a *teras*. To the 'ruler' of the feast and the rest there was nothing extraordinary happening, except the holding back of good wine. But nevertheless the glory of Christ was to be perceived in this, and the disciples who 'believed on him' saw it (2.11). In the episode of the nobleman's son at Capernaum there is again a similar reticence. Only the nobleman knew sufficient to be deflected into concentrating only on the *teras*, without believing, as Jesus himself emphasized: 'Except ye see signs and wonders ye will in no wise believe.' But the nobleman did believe, and the inference is that it is because he was an *obedient* disciple.

Again, in spite of the fact that a crowd of sick folk were lying at the Pool of Bethesda the healing of the lame man has a similar cryptic character. When they were informed that the healing had been performed by Jesus the Jews interpreted it as a sign from below rather than from above. They perceived not the sign of the Messianic Lord of the Sabbath but a sacrilegious blasphemer (5.18).

The account of the feeding of the five thousand suggests at first that this was an event seen and believed by the multitude and therefore interpreted rightly as a Messianic 'sign'. But the comment of Jesus in the discourses which follow suggests that the Evangelist wishes us to see here again a further instance of seeing and not believing: 'You seek me, not because you saw signs, but because you ate your fill of the loaves' (6.26). This would seem to be made certain by the use here of a Johannine device to emphasize that to be present when Jesus gave a 'sign' was not inevitably to accept it as such:[3] 'So they said to him, "Then what sign do you do, that we may see, and believe you?" ' (6.30 RV).

The same thing is true of the account of the man born blind in chapter 9. The Pharisees either refused to see any sign at all, or they were guilty of

---

[1] Cf. an interesting article by O. Cullmann, 'Εἶδεν καὶ ἐπίστευσεν. La vie de Jesus, objet de la "vue" et de la "foi" d'après le quatrième Evangile', in *Aux sources de la tradition chrétienne* (Mélanges Goguel).

[2] John 1.14; 11.15; 12.30; 20.8, 27.

[3] Cf. John 2.18.

blasphemy against the Holy Spirit by ascribing the power of Jesus to its contrary source. The fact that they cast him out with the words, 'You were born in utter sin, and would you teach us?' (v. 34), brought them under the judgment of Jesus whose words at the beginning of this narrative are: 'It was not that this man sinned, or his parents: but that the works of God might be made manifest in him' (v. 3). The judgment which came in the actions of Jesus forced the issue: either that 'those who do not see may see' or that 'those who see may become blind' (v. 39).

Finally the raising of Lazarus. This is the most dramatic illustration in the Fourth Gospel that seeing is not automatically believing. It repeats, in an uncompromising manner, the principle enunciated in the parable of Dives and Lazarus: 'If they do not hear Moses and the prophets, neither will they be convinced if some one should rise from the dead' (Luke 16.31). All that the chief priests and the Pharisees could see in the 'sign' of the raising of Lazarus was a *teras* which would bewitch people and lead to the end of their own power through Roman retaliation. They would not discern there the 'sign' of 'the Resurrection and the Life'.

The 'works' of Jesus, then, were done in the Father's name, and it was he who brought them about. To those with the sight which issued in faith they were works *given* to Jesus by the Father (John 5.36). Turning now to the words of Jesus we find a similar emphasis. If in the case of the miracles 'seeing' was very far from necessarily 'believing', so with the words of Jesus 'hearing' was not necessarily 'believing'. There was hearing *and* hearing. True audition of the words of Jesus meant discerning in them the Father speaking through the Son: 'The word (λόγος) which you hear is not mine but the Father's who sent me' (14.24). If the works of Jesus were inevitably a *skandalon* to some,[1] St John makes it clear that the same was true of the speech of Jesus: 'Many of his disciples, when they heard it, said, "This is a hard saying; who can listen to it?" But Jesus, knowing in himself that his disciples murmured at it, said to them, "Do you take offence?" ' (6.60 f.). To hear the word (λόγος) of Jesus meant to believe in him as sent by the Father (5.24). It was this perception which enabled a person to see in the λαλία of Jesus the λόγος of God. The Jews did not 'know' his speech (λαλία) because they were not able to hear his word (λόγος). Hearing the words of Jesus meant acting upon them, and was thus equivalent to obedience, to being 'of God': 'He who is of God hears the words of God; the reason why you do not hear them is that you are not of God',[2] said Jesus to the Jews.

Jesus is himself in the Fourth Gospel the model of the true 'seeing' and

---

[1] Cf. pp. 96 ff. above.   [2] John 8.47; cf. 12.47.

'hearing': 'He who sent me is true, and I declare to the world what I have heard from him' (8.26); 'You seek to kill me, a man who has told you the truth which I heard from God.'[1] This would be true also of the Paraclete: 'He shall not speak on his own authority, but whatever he hears he will speak' (16.13).

The Fourth Gospel thus underlines in its own way an important belief of the Synoptic Evangelists: the words of Jesus constituted a Messianic summons to be on the alert to recognize in him and his mission the 'word' of the Father. This word Jesus possessed because he was himself the obedient executor of the Father's commission. He was himself the perfect example of that readiness to take the paternal 'signs' as they are given and act upon them which he demanded of his followers. If, as we have seen, the *semeia* of St John's Gospel were not the unambiguous *terata* which at first they seem to be, so too there is an emphasis on the cryptic character of the Johannine παροιμίαι which at first sight seem easily decipherable allegories. After the παροιμία about the shepherd and the hireling in chapter 10 there is the comment: 'This παροιμία Jesus used with them, but they did not understand what he was saying to them.'[2]

The Pharisees, who have just 'seen' the 'sign' of the healing of the man born blind without believing, now 'hear' a parable, and again it is without believing. There is a similar contrast in St John between the words of Jesus ἐν παροιμίαις and ἐν παρρησίᾳ (16.25, 29) to that which we have noticed between the 'works' ἐν κρυπτῷ and ἐν παρρησίᾳ. As C. K. Barrett puts it: 'The Synoptic similitudes and the Johannine "allegories" have often been contrasted; in fact, neither are the Synoptic speeches pure parable nor the Johannine pure allegory. The Christo-centric tendency of the Synoptic parables is accentuated by John, who composes symbolic discourses which bring out the fact that the death and exaltation of Jesus are the life of men.'[3]

The 'Way' of Jesus as the 'Way' of *Sonship, Torah,* and *Knowledge* is specially prominent in the Fourth Gospel. It is in fact the Gospel of the Father-Son relationship. The perfect relationship of the Father and the Son which exists in the eternal Godhead was mimed on the historical scene in the life of Jesus,[4] and, as we shall see later, was in turn to be imitated in the relationship between Jesus and the disciple. That is the threefold structure of the *imitatio Dei* in the Fourth Gospel. The three

---

[1] John 8.40; cf. 14.10, 24.   [2] John 10.6; cf. 16.25, 29.
[3] *The Gospel according to St John*, p. 307.
[4] 'The human career of Jesus is, as it were, a projection of this eternal relation (which is the divine ἀγάπη) upon the field of time', C. H. Dodd, *The Interpretation of the Fourth Gospel*, p. 262.

levels of the *imitatio* are not (perhaps deliberately) kept distinct, because that which is true of the Son in Godhead is true *at the same time* of the Son incarnate in Jesus.

The whole activity of the Son is an imitation of what he sees the Father doing: 'The Son can do nothing of his own accord, but only what he sees the Father doing; for whatever he does, that the Son does likewise' (5.19). Whatever the Father does, the Son as perfect *imitator Patris* does likewise. The Father has 'life in himself' and so it is with the Son (5.26). The Father raises the dead and gives life, and so does the Son (5.21). Between the Father and the Son there is the perfect mutual relationship of love: 'The Father loves the Son, and has given all things into his hand.'[1] 'The Father loves the Son, and shows him all that he himself is doing' (5.20). The 'work' of the Father is not cut off from the 'work' of the Son: 'My Father is working still, and I am working' (5.17). There is a unique and intimate unity of the Father and the Son: 'He who sent me is with me; he has not left me alone.'[2]

A very important passage on the Father-Son relationship in the Fourth Gospel is the exchange between Jesus and the Jews in 8.38–47:

'I speak of what I have seen with my Father, and you do what you have heard from your father.' They answered him, 'Abraham is our father.' Jesus said to them, 'If you were Abraham's children, you would do what Abraham did, but now you seek to kill me, a man who has told you the truth which I heard from God; this is not what Abraham did. You do what your father did.' They said to him, 'We were not born of fornication; we have one Father, even God.' Jesus said to them, 'If God were your Father, you would love me, for I proceeded and came forth from God; I came not of my own accord, but he sent me. Why do you not understand what I say? It is because you cannot bear to hear my word. You are of your father the devil, and your will is to do your father's desires. He was a murderer from the beginning, and has nothing to do with the truth, because there is no truth in him. When he lies, he speaks according to his own nature, for he is a liar and the father of lies. But, because I tell you the truth, you do not believe me. Which of you convicts me of sin? If I tell the truth, why do you not believe me? He who is of God hears the words of God; the reason why you do not hear them is that you are not of God.'

The contrast here is between two genuine cases of 'sonship'. True sonship means imitation of the father. Jesus is truly Son of his Father in his obedience. The Jews are also genuinely sons through their obedience —to the Devil!

---

[1] John 3.35; cf. 13.3.   [2] John 8.29; cf. 16.32; 17.5, 21.

The Father-Son relationship is one of perfect *Knowledge*. The Father perfectly 'knows' the Son and the Son perfectly 'knows' the Father in complete reciprocity: 'The Father knows me, and I know the Father' (10.15). Israel's vocation to 'know the Lord' is now fulfilled. Here in Jesus God 'knows' his Israel and Israel 'knows' the Lord.[1] On the Father's side this means, as in the Old Testament, providential endowment for the chosen task. On the side of the Son this means perfect obedience to the Father's will. Jesus as Son walks in the way of *obedience to the Torah*. Östborn suggests,[2] with a good deal of probability, that the Fourth Gospel takes up, for special emphasis, the theme of Jesus as the New Law which is a prominent feature of St Matthew's Gospel. He sees John 14.6 as an expression of this idea of Jesus as personified 'Torah' and refers to the frequent association in Hebrew tradition of the 'Way' (*derek*), 'truth' (*'emeth*) and 'life' (*hayyim*) with 'law' (*torah*).[3] Östborn refers further to the observation of Odeberg[4] that in the Gospel of St John Jesus applies expressions to himself which are otherwise used in Jewish tradition of the 'Torah', e.g. 'water', 'bread', 'light'. Certainly there is no mistaking the emphasis in this Gospel on Jesus as the perfectly obedient one:

My food is to do the will of him who sent me, and to accomplish his work (4.34).

I seek not my own will, but the will of him that sent me (5.30).

I have come down from heaven, not to do mine own will, but the will of him who sent me (6.38).

I honour my Father (8.49).

I know that his commandment is eternal life. What I say, therefore, I say as the Father has bidden me (12.50).

I know him [the Father] and I keep his word (8.55).

I have not spoken on my own authority; the Father who sent me has himself given me commandment what to say and what to speak (12.49).

I have kept my Father's commandments and abide in his love (15.10).

I glorified thee on earth, having accomplished the work which thou gavest me to do (17.4).

In his unique sonship, which is expressed in perfect obedience and knowledge, Jesus is the one true *imitator Patris*, and his historical mission

---

[1] In Jesus Israel is perfectly known: he has an instinctive recognition of a true Israelite, John 1.47 f.; 2.24 f.; 5.42.

[2] G. Östborn, *Tōrā in the Old Testament*, p. 161.

[3] Cf. Mal. 2.5-9.   [4] In *The Fourth Gospel*, Uppsala, 1929.

is the fulfilment of Israel's vocation to walk in the 'Way' of the Lord. But, as we have seen, in the Synoptic tradition this pattern of the Lord's life was not self-evident except to the eyes and ears of those who were prepared to act upon the summons to repentance and faith. The Fourth Evangelist has his own startling way of underlining the ambiguous *semeion* character of the mission of Jesus. In spite of what would seem to be most direct and explicit declarations in word and action about the significance of his own person and mission, there is more reference to unbelief than belief in the Fourth Gospel. St John's Gospel bears witness in its own way to the original enigmatic nature of the ministry of Jesus.

We have noted previously the constant recurrence of the figures of the king, the prophet and the priest in the Old Testament conception of the *imitatio Dei*, and how they can be seen exercising an influence on the role which Jesus believed his sonship must assume. In the Fourth Gospel the Evangelist has, here again, given his own particular emphasis to this feature of the tradition. The prominence of the kingship of Jesus in St John has often been pointed out and there is no need here to repeat the examination of the material in detail. Suffice it to mention that it is only in this Gospel that we find a reference to an attempt to crown Jesus King (6.15); he is recognized as King of Israel by Nathanael (1.49); and the Johannine treatment of the entry into Jerusalem with its reference to the palm branches (12.13) underlines its royal character. The soldiers in the garden do homage to Jesus as King, and the kingship of Jesus is clearly the theme of the Johannine Passion narrative.[1] It is very probable also that in the image of the vine and the branches there may be some reference to the tree of life with its royal associations.[2] Jesus is pointed out as the Prophet by the woman of Samaria (4.19), by the people after the feeding of the five thousand (6.14), and at the feast of Tabernacles (7.40); and he acts as a prophet not only by imparting *torah* but by prediction.[3] In the figure of the Lamb (1.29, etc.) we are probably meant to discern Christ as both the priest who offers and the victim who is offered in sacrifice. In the 'high-priestly' prayer Jesus appears as the high priest who makes intercession in a way very similar to the picture in the Epistle to the Hebrews. The 'seamless robe' would also appear to be a reference to Christ as high priest.

We have seen that in the mind of Jesus himself discipleship necessarily assumed a clearly recognized pattern, the life of the disciple being a 'sign'

---

[1] Cf. especially John 18.33–38, 39; 19.1–15, 21 f.
[2] Cf. G. Widengren, *King and Saviour*: 4, 'The *King and the Tree of Life in Ancient Near Eastern Religion*, Uppsala, 1951.
[3] John 1.48; 2.25; 4.29.

of his own presence and activity through the Spirit. To this theme the Fourth Evangelist has given special emphasis. The disciple of Jesus is by definition, so to speak, the *imitator Filii* following in the way of Jesus the *imitator Patris*. What is implicit in the Synoptic tradition is given special explicit treatment in St John.

First of all, there is the scene in chapter 13 which forms the preface to the explicatory last discourses. Here Jesus is presented as the Exemplar for his disciples, especially of διακονία, and he explicitly exhorts them to *mimesis* of himself:

> When he had washed their feet, and taken his garments, and resumed his place, he said to them, 'Do you know what I have done to you? You call me Teacher and Lord; and you are right, for so I am. If I then, your Lord and Teacher, have washed your feet, you also ought to wash one another's feet. I have given you an example, that you also should do as I have done to you. Truly, truly, I say to you, a servant is not greater than his master; nor is he who is sent greater than he who sent him. If you know these things, blessed are you if you do them. . . . Truly, truly, I say to you, he who receives anyone whom I send receives me; and he who receives me receives him who sent me.'[1]

Here we have a dramatic illustration of the distinctive feature of the concept of the *imitatio Christi* in the New Testament. *It is an* imitatio *which is possible only because of a prior act of redemption.* The foot-washing of the disciples is a *semeion* that self-giving in love is the characteristic action of the Godhead (cf. vv. 1 and 3) and an enactment of the life of the disciple which imitates the action of God. 'The act of washing is what the Crucifixion is, at once a divine deed by which men are released from sin and an example which men must imitate.'[2]

Of what does the *imitatio Christi* in the Fourth Gospel consist? First of all, the disciple is one who 'follows' Jesus. The theme of 'following in the Way' is as prominent in St John as in the Synoptic Gospels,[3] and, as we might expect, the Evangelist seems to have welcomed the ambiguity of the word (ἀκολουθεῖν) which indicates at one and the same time the actual physical historical accompanying and the spiritual and ethical *mimesis*:

> The next day again John was standing with two of his disciples; and he looked at Jesus as he walked, and said, 'Behold, the Lamb of God!'

---

[1] John 13.12–17, 20; cf. 15.15 f.
[2] C. K. Barrett, *The Gospel according to St John*, p. 364.
[3] For the summons ἀκολούθει μοι in St John cf. 1.43; 12.26; 13.36; 21.19, 22; cf. also 10.4, 27.

The two disciples heard him say this, and they followed Jesus (ἠκολούθησαν). Jesus turned, and saw them following, and said to them, 'What do you seek?' And they said to him, 'Rabbi, where are you staying?' (μένεις). He said to them, 'Come and see.' They came and saw where he was staying (μένει), and they stayed with him that day (1.35–39).

Discernment of the signs of the times issues in the 'following' of Jesus. This has as its objective the knowledge of his abode, and to company with Jesus brings fruition of the quest—vision. In the Fourth Gospel there is an intimate link between 'following' Jesus (ἀκολουθεῖν) and 'abiding' with him (μενεῖν).[1]

If, as Odeberg suggests, Jesus as the Light is meant to suggest Jesus as the New Torah,[2] then these passages about 'following' and 'walking' show that the *mimesis Christou* means obedience to his commandments:

I am the light of the world; he who follows me will not walk in darkness, but will have the light of life (8.12).[3]

Are there not twelve hours in the day? If anyone walks in the day, he does not stumble, because he sees the light of this world. But if anyone walks in the night, he stumbles because the light is not in him (11.9 f.).

The light is with you for a little longer. Walk while you have the light, lest the darkness overtake you; he who walks in the darkness does not know where he goes (12.35).[4]

Obedience to Jesus is the disciple's way to 'knowledge' (7.17).

The disciple in his relation to Jesus will imitate the relation of love and knowledge which exists between the Son and the Father in Godhead. Running through the Gospel there is a clear parallelism between the Father-Son relationship and the Jesus-disciple relationship. This can be seen most conveniently if the material is set out in two columns:

FATHER-SON	JESUS-DISCIPLE
1. *Dependence*	
The Son can do nothing of his own accord but only what he sees the Father doing; for whatever he does, that the Son does likewise (5.19).	Apart from me you can do nothing (15.5).

[1] Cf. Hoskyns, *The Fourth Gospel*, p. 179.
[2] Cf. p. 125 above.
[3] Cf. I John 1.7.
[4] Cf. I John 2.11.

As I live because of the Father . . .

. . . He who eats me will live because of me (6.57).

All that I have heard from my Father . . .

. . .I have made known to you (15.15).

The Father who sent me has given me a commandment, what I should say, and what I should speak (12.49).

I have given them the words which thou gavest me (17.8).

The words that I say to you I do not speak on my own authority, but the Father who dwells in me does his works (14.10).

2. *Mission*

As thou didst send me into the world, . . .

. . . so I have sent them into the world (17.18).

As the Father has sent me, . . .

. . . even so I send you (20.21).

. . . He who receives me receives him who sent me (13.20).

He who receives any one whom I send receives me (13.20).

3. *Love* (*in obedience*)

As the Father has loved me, . . .

. . . so have I loved you (15.9).

A new commandment I give to you, that you love one another, even as I have loved you, that you also love one another. By this all men will know that you are my disciples, if you have love for one another (13.34 f.; cf. 15.12).

The Father loves the Son and shows him all that he himself is doing; and greater works than these will he show him, that you may marvel (5.20).

He who believes in me will also do the works that I do; and greater works than these will he do, because I go to the Father (14.12).

I have kept my Father's commandments and abide in his love (15.10).

If you keep my commandments, you will abide in my love (15.10).

I

FATHER-SON   JESUS-DISCIPLE

4. *Union*

Do you not believe that I am in the Father and the Father in me?
... Believe me that I am in the Father and the Father in me (14.10 f.).

I am in my Father, ... and you in me, and I in you (14.20).

The Father who abides (μενεῖ) in me (14.10).   Abide (μείνατε) in me, and I in you (15.4).

I and the Father are one (10.30).

Thou in me ...   ... I in them (17.23, 26).

                                        You will abide (μενεῖτε) in the Son, and in the Father (I John 2.24; cf. vv. 27 f.).

The relationship between Jesus and the disciple, brought into being and maintained by the Spirit,[1] is a *mimesis* of the perfect relationship of unity and love which exists between the Father and the Son in Godhead.

It is St John, of all the Evangelists, who seems to have been most intent to present Jesus and his disciples as the actualization of the 'Sign of Isaiah'.[2] The language used, for example, in John 6.37 and 39 is reminiscent of Isa. 8: 'All that the Father gives me will come to me; and him who comes to me I will not cast out'; and especially is this true of the discourse in chapter 17:

... to give eternal life to all whom thou hast given him (v. 2).

I have manifested thy name to the men whom thou gavest me out of the world; thine they were, and thou gavest them to me, and they have kept thy word (v. 6).

I am not praying for the world but for those whom thou hast given me (v. 9; cf. 18.9).

The life of the Christian disciple as *imitator Christi* is not any kind of yoga of self-endeavour. It is not a process which is initiated and sustained

---

[1] Cf. I John 3.24 and 4.13.   [2] Cf. p. 58 above.

by the Christian believer, as if the *imitatio Christi* were some kind of literal mimicry. It is a process initiated and sustained by the Spirit as Paraclete, and in it he conforms the pattern of the life of believers to that of the Lord so that men may become aware that they are his disciples. The Spirit as Paraclete will guide the disciples along the way which is Christ himself (16.13), and bring into their remembrance all the things that he said (14.26).

Where and how will this be done? The answer is 'In liturgy and in life'. The life of the disciple as *imitator Christi* in ἀγάπη we have touched on above. 'Christian ethics' is a term to describe the form of living determined for the Christian by his vocation to the *mimesis* of Christ. And there is one activity where the basic features of this life are mimed in such a way that the relationship between the Exemplar and his followers is experienced in a uniquely intimate way. This activity is worship. Cullmann has recently discussed in a very illuminating way the influence of worship upon the structure and contents of the Fourth Gospel.[1] One of the chief concerns of the Gospel, he writes, is 'to set forth the connection between the contemporary Christian worship and the historical life of Jesus'.[2] The author starts from the experience of Christian worshippers in his own day. They are aware of the presence of the life-giving Son given them through the Spirit, particularly so in the assembly for the Lord's Supper. The author then seeks to show his readers how they may feel their way back to the historical events which lie behind this liturgical action and also, if the Apocalypse comes from the same background,[3] how they are anticipating the Messianic banquet to come. The Lord who speaks to the reader in the Last Supper discourses is at one and the same time the Lord of the upper room in Jerusalem and the Lord of present Christian experience who speaks in this way with special unique intimacy at every eucharistic assembly.

The union of the believer and his Lord is thus, as presented in the Fourth Gospel, one of special intimacy, so much so that it may not improperly be taken as a *mimesis* of the union which exists between the Father and the Son. If, as we have seen, one of the essential features of that type of experience which is called 'mystical' is a profound sense of union or oneness with the object of the experience, then there need be little hesitation about speaking of mysticism in the Fourth Gospel, especially since it is in worship that this author seems to have been primarily aware of that experience of oneness between the 'sign' and the

---

[1] O. Cullmann, *Early Christian Worship*, ET (SBT 10), 1953.   [2] *Op. cit.*, p. 37.
[3] As suggested again recently by E. Stauffer in his *New Testament Theology*.

reality signified which is always suggested by the early Christian use of μυστικός.[1] We might say that the 'essential' union of the Father and Son with the Spirit in Godhead is imitated, and thereby participated in, through the 'mystical' union which exists between the believer and Jesus by the action of the Spirit as Paraclete.

When we come to consider the teaching of St Paul it will be found that there the *imitatio Christi* can take the quite concrete form of the imitation of the apostle of Christ. There is no explicit teaching of this kind in the Fourth Gospel, but certain figures in the narrative would seem to be presented as ideal disciples, exemplars of the *imitatio Christi*.[2]

Nicodemus, for instance, is a true disciple coming from the darkness of Judaism to the light of Christ, not like Judas who leaves this light for the darkness of night. Nicodemus is alert to recognize in Jesus the 'signs' that God is with him (John 3.2).

The story of the man born blind in chapter 9 is told in such a way as to remind the reader that the life of a Christian believer has features which are inevitably reminiscent of his Lord. The man's discipleship begins with a washing followed by illumination suggesting the baptism of Jesus himself (v. 7). There is the same kind of disputing as to his identity as happened in the case of Jesus himself: ' "Is not this the man who used to sit and beg?" Some said, "It is he"; others said, "No, but he is like him" ' (vv. 8 f.); and the man's direct answer ἐγώ εἰμι produces, like the same words on the lips of his Lord, a confused and hostile reaction. Like his Lord he is brought before the Jewish authorities for investigation, and under trial he bears faithful witness and, in the end, he too is cast out.

The figure of Lazarus in the Fourth Gospel may also be intended as an example of a disciple raised from death to life through the action of Jesus. Whether or not Lazarus is the beloved disciple, as some have suggested, there would seem to be no doubt that the latter is meant to be taken as a model *imitator Christi*. Just as the Son is in the bosom (εἰς τὸν κόλπον) of the Father (1.18), so the beloved disciple lies in the bosom (ἐν τῷ κόλπῳ) of Jesus (13.23). He is the first to believe in the resurrection, and holds, in this sense, as C. K. Barrett says, a primacy of faith.[3] He is quick to see and believe, and this makes him a model believer. Perhaps Peter is the *imitator Christi par excellence* since he will suffer and die to glorify

---

[1] Cf. p. 21 above.

[2] This move towards visible exemplars of the imitation of Christ is perhaps already perceptible within the Synoptic tradition. The anointing at Bethany (Mark 14.3–9) presents the woman as a concrete illustration of Christian humility and devotion to the Lord.

[3] *The Gospel according to St John*, p. 466.

God in a manner very close to that of his Lord (21.18). As in the Lucan writings, so here, the martyr in this sense is the norm of the *imitatio Christi*. He is to succeed to the shepherding of the sheep (21.15–17). 'Like Christ, the Shepherd, he is not only to find pasture for the sheep, but he is also to be prepared to lay down his life for them.'[1]

The Johannine teaching on discipleship as the *imitatio Christi* is summed up clearly and cogently in the First Epistle of St John. In this epistle the *imitatio Christi* is the test for the authentic Christian character of any spirituality—one might say also of any mysticism. The 'new commandment' is realized in Jesus, and in the disciple in so far as he is an *imitator Christi*: 'As he is, so are we in this world' (4.17). The test for the true 'knowledge' of Christ is walking in the 'Way' of Christ: 'By this we may be sure that we are in him: he who says he abides (μένειν) in him ought to walk in the same way in which he walked' (2.6). Commenting on I John 2.10 ff., C. H. Dodd writes: 'To obey the command of Christ, to follow his example, and in particular to obey and follow him in the way of love, this is to be sure we know him, to be sure we are in him, and to be in the light.'[2] That the *imitatio Christi* is the form which the *imitatio Dei* necessarily assumes for the Christian is the subject of the passage I John 3.2 f. Through the *imitatio Dei* men become sons of God, and likeness to Christ, which is the form the *imitatio Dei* takes, begins now in pureness of life: 'Beloved, we are God's children now; it does not yet appear what we shall be, but we know that when he appears, we shall be like him, for we shall see him as he is. And everyone who thus hopes in him purifies himself as he is pure.' The love of Christ, exemplified in his death, is to be imitated in the same kind of self-giving: 'By this we know love, that he laid down his life for us; and we ought to lay down our lives for the brethren' (3.16; cf. II John 6). 'It is clear,' writes C. H. Dodd, 'that from the outset the "law of Christ" (Gal. 6.2) by which Christians are bound to direct their conduct, was defined in the Church's teaching, not only by the traditional precepts of Jesus, but also by his example.'[3]

[1] Alf Corell, *Consummatum Est*, ET 1958, p. 40.
[2] C. H. Dodd, *The Johannine Epistles* (Moffatt New Testament Commentary), 1946, p. 35.
[3] *Op. cit.*, p. 85.

9

The Imitation of Christ in St Paul

1. *The more excellent Way*

THE 'WAY' as a term for the Christian religion occurs most frequently in the Acts of the Apostles in association with St Paul, and this fact, together with the use made of the term and its cognate imagery in the Pauline literature, both early and late, suggests that he thought of the Christian life as pre-eminently 'walking' in the 'Way of Christ':

You should walk worthily of God (I Thess. 2.12).

You received from us how you ought to walk and please God, and you are so walking (I Thess. 4.1).

. . . that you may walk honestly toward them (I Thess. 4.12).

Withdraw yourselves from every brother who walks disorderly (II Thess. 3.6).

We hear of some who walk among you disorderly (II Thess. 3.11).

. . . as God has called each, so let him walk (I Cor. 7.17).

. . . not walking in craftiness (II Cor. 4.2).

We walk by faith, not by sight (II Cor. 5.7).

Though we walk in the flesh, we do not war according to the flesh (II Cor. 10.3).

Did we not walk by the same spirit? (II Cor. 12.18).

All who walk by this rule (Gal. 6.16).

We were buried therefore with him through baptism into death; that like as Christ was raised from the dead . . . so we also might walk (Rom. 6.4).

We who walk not after the flesh, but after the spirit (Rom. 8.4).

Let us walk honestly, as in the day (Rom. 13.13).

. . . you are no longer walking in love (Rom. 14.15).

For we are his workmanship, created in Christ Jesus for good works, which God prepared beforehand, that we should walk in them (Eph. 2.10).

... to walk worthily of the calling to which you have been called (Eph. 4.1).

Be imitators of God, as beloved children, and walk in love, as Christ loved us ... (Eph. 5.2).

Brethren, join in imitating me and mark those who so walk as you have an example in us (Phil. 3.17).

... to walk worthily of the Lord (Col. 1.10).

As therefore you received Christ Jesus the Lord so walk in him (Col. 2.6).

Walk in wisdom toward those outside (Col. 4.5).[1]

The metaphor of the 'Way' occurs in I Cor. 12.31 in the preface to the hymn on ἀγάπη in the following chapter: '... a still more excellent way I show you.' The significance of this passage will be discussed later in this chapter, but in view of the character of I Cor. 13 as a description of the life of Christ as lived in his disciples, it seems very probable that the new and more excellent way is Christ himself. That is to say, for both St John and St Paul the 'Way' is first and foremost Jesus himself. The apostle's 'ways' in Christ (I Cor. 4.17) are part of the 'Way' of the Lord Christ himself. For St Paul the coming of Christ meant that the ideal of the *imitatio Dei* had now, for the Christian, inevitably to take the form of the *imitatio Christi*. This Christian 'Way' is associated in St Paul's mind with Sonship, Torah, and Knowledge, which we have seen to be the three features of the 'Way' of the Old Israel, and of Jesus himself.

The 'Way' of Sonship. Jesus was, for St Paul, the unique 'model' Son, the image of the invisible God, the first-born of all creation,[2] the 'form' of God.[3] There is nothing comparable in St Paul to the treatment of the Father-Son relationship in St John's Gospel. This is perhaps because St John, like the Epistle to the Hebrews, was more concerned with meditation on Jesus as the *object* of the Christian life, whereas St Paul was an 'active' mystic, primarily aware of Jesus as the *means*, through the Spirit, of the life of the Christian. Jesus is not only unique Son in a purely objective static sense. Through the Spirit he conforms Christians to his own image, and they become 'sons' through the Son:

But we all with unveiled face, reflecting as a mirror the glory of the Lord, are transformed into the same image from glory to glory, even as from the Lord the Spirit (II Cor. 3.18).

For those whom he foreknew he also predestined to be conformed to the image of his Son (Rom. 8.29).

[1] Cf. also Eph. 5.15; Phil. 3.16.   [2] Col. 1.15; cf. II Cor. 4.4.   [3] Phil. 2.6.

St Paul would seem to have taken the view that in this life Christians are fashioned according to the body of Christ's humiliation. In other words there is to be about them the marks of the Son of man who came in humiliation, degradation and suffering. In the life to come the same process of 'conforming' is at work so that then we shall be 'conformed' to the body of Christ's glory (Phil. 3.21). Likeness to Christ remains the operative principle.[1] 'Just as we have borne the image of the man of dust, we shall also bear the image of the man of heaven' (I Cor. 15.49); you 'have put on the new nature which is being renewed in knowledge after the image of its creator' (Col. 3.10).

The 'Way' of the Christian has therefore the form of sonship, and it is moulded into this shape by the action of the Spirit. The Christian's cry 'Father' is a *mimesis* of the Son's unique 'Abba' (Rom. 8.15). Through the Christians' mystical *koinonia* with Christ his sonship becomes in a sense theirs (I Cor. 1.9). That Christians are 'sons' means that they participate 'mystically' in the life and action of him who is uniquely and pre-eminently Son:

> God sent forth his Son, born of woman, born under the law, to redeem those who were under the law, so that we might receive adoption as sons. And because you are sons, God has sent the Spirit of his Son into our hearts, crying 'Abba! Father!' So through God you are no longer a slave but a son, and if a son then an heir (Gal. 4.5 f.).

In union with the Son, by means of the Spirit, Christians are caught up into his prayer to the Father, so that they can now say, with a full sense of reality, 'Our Father', or rather, the Son's eternal 'Abba' prayer is prayed in and through their filial prayers. The Christian's sonship is only a possibility because of the Son's redemptive work. As L. S. Thornton has commented: 'The possibility of this Christian life of Sonship turns on the redemptive action in Incarnation and Atonement, wherein by becoming slave he liberated us from slavery to Sonship, a Sonship which is made effectual through the action of the Spirit.'[2]

The 'Way' of Torah. W. D. Davies in his *Paul and Rabbinic Judaism* has argued that Paul saw in Jesus a personalization of the Torah. Jesus in his own obedience and in the commands he gave was the New Torah, the νόμος ἔμψυχος. 'Christ is for him [Paul] both the New Torah and also the example of a perfect obedience to that New Torah.'[3] Obedience to the Torah was now for the Christians a matter of the personal disciple-

---

[1] Cf. I John 3.2.
[2] L. S. Thornton, *The Common Life in the Body of Christ*, 1942, pp. 120 ff.
[3] *Op. cit.*, p. 266.

ship of Christ who was the τέλος of the Law in the sense of being himself
the embodiment of it. No doubt St Paul felt the term νόμος was unsatis-
factory in relation to the Law of Christ because Jesus was the fulfilment of
the Law not in a barely literal way, but had refashioned the Torah into
the 'Way' of ἀγάπη.

The 'Way' of Knowledge. The Christian life is also a 'Way' of knowledge
for St Paul. The metaphor of 'walking in the way' is associated with
knowledge in such a passage as Col. 1.9 f.:

> . . . that you may be filled with the knowledge of his will in all spiritual
> wisdom and understanding, to walk worthily of the Lord . . .

Christians are able to 'know' God only because they have first been
'known' by God:

> Now that you have come to know God, or rather to be known by God
> (Gal. 4.9).

> Now I know in part; then shall I know even as also I have been known
> (I Cor. 13.12).

They are now 'filled with all knowledge' (Rom. 15.14), and through the
grace of God, given in Christ, they are 'enriched in . . . all knowledge'
(I Cor. 1.5). The Christian life is a way of knowing the love of Christ
(Eph. 3.19), of attaining to the knowledge of the Son of God. The best
illustration of this element in Paul's thought about the Christian life is to
be found in Phil. 3.8–10:

> I count everything as loss because of the surpassing worth of knowing
> Christ Jesus my Lord. For his sake I have suffered the loss of all things,
> and count them as refuse, in order that I may gain Christ and be found
> in him, not having a righteousness of my own, based on law, but that
> which is through faith in Christ, the righteousness from God that
> depends on faith; that I may know him and the power of his resurrec-
> tion, and may share his sufferings, becoming like him in his death.

Being 'known' of God is a matter of the deeper obedience of the law which
is love (I Cor. 8.3).

For St Paul, as for St John, Jesus is himself the true εἰκών of 'knowledge', and the Christian life of γνῶσις is a *mimesis* of his 'knowledge':
'having put on the new man, which is being renewed in knowledge after
the image of the creator' (Col. 3.10).

Clearly for St Paul Sonship, Torah and Knowledge were now insepar-
ably related to Christ, in whom they found unique embodiment and trans-
formation. It is only because through the action of the Spirit Christians

are in Christ that they are enabled to walk in the 'Way' of their Lord. For St Paul, says W. D. Davies, 'every Christian is pledged to an attempted ethical conformity to Christ; the imitation of Christ is part and parcel of Paul's ethic.'[1]

2. *Exhortations to* mimesis

St Paul exhorts his fellow-Christians either to the imitation of Christ or to the imitation of God through Christ: for him of course the two ideas express the one reality. Behind the Christian life and its virtues, invisibly and secretly, there is the life and perfection of the Lord Christ, and blessed is the man who allows no 'stumbling-block' to hinder his perception of this great truth.

> We who are strong ought to bear with the failings of the weak, and not to please ourselves: let each of us please his neighbour for his good, to edify him. For Christ did not please himself; but, as it is written, 'The reproaches of those who reproached thee fell on me.' . . . Welcome one another, therefore, as Christ has welcomed you, for the glory of God (Rom. 15.1–3, 7).

Here the self-abnegation of the Christian is an obligation laid upon him which he ought gladly to accept, because thereby the utter self-giving of the Lord is imitated, and through this *mimesis* men are confronted with the Lord himself. The quotation from Ps. 69.9 in Rom. 15.3 is, as C. K. Barrett says, particularly significant at this point. 'It means that the example of Christ is more than an example; it belongs to the pattern of revelation.'[2] The imitation of Christ is the means whereby the Christian participates in and makes his own the saving events of the 'Way' of Israel which had been uniquely summed up and transformed in Christ.

> Have this mind among yourselves which was also in Christ Jesus, who, though he was in the form of God, did not count equality with God a thing to be grasped, but emptied himself, taking the form of a servant, being born in the likeness of men (Phil. 2.5–7).

This passage will be considered again later when we are discussing the essential marks of the Christian as imitator of Christ. But Christians are here clearly exhorted to take as their model of humility the self-giving of the eternal Son in Incarnation.

> Be kind to one another, tender-hearted, forgiving one another, as God in Christ forgave you. Therefore be imitators of God as beloved

---

[1] *Paul and Rabbinic Judaism*, p. 147.
[2] *A Commentary on the Epistle to the Romans*, 1957, p. 269.

children. And walk in love, as Christ loved us and gave himself up for us (Eph. 4.32–5.2).

Here Christ is the exemplar of love and self-giving; he is the means whereby the imitation of God is possible at all (God in Christ has forgiven, therefore . . .), and this imitation means 'walking' in the way of Christ.

Then come the significant and illuminating passages where the exhortation is to imitate Christ *through the apostle*:

I became your father in Christ Jesus through the gospel. I urge you, then, be imitators of me (I Cor. 4.15 f.).

The fundamental law of the father-son relationship applies here. If the relation between apostolic minister and Christian believer is like that of father and son, then the Christian's obligation is to be an imitator of the apostle. This involves walking in the 'way' indicated by the following verse. Timothy is 'accordingly' being sent to put them in remembrance of the apostle's ways in Christ (I Cor. 4.17).

You became imitators of us and of the Lord (I Thess. 1.6).

Be imitators of me, as I am of Christ (I Cor. 11.1).

Brethren, I beseech you, become as I am, for I also have become as you are (Gal. 4.12).

On a first reading, such passages as these might suggest that St Paul had certainly become a victim of that very καύχησις which was his characteristic temptation.[1] But there are always checks, indicated by St Paul himself, against making the *mimesis* of the apostle into a 'personality cult'.[2] In the case of each of the passages just cited the context shows that the imitation of Christ through imitation of an apostle of Christ is far from being in St Paul's mind an uncritical admiration or devotion. The check against abuse is that the particular object for imitation is either some suffering or some humiliation. 'You became imitators of us and of the Lord,' says St Paul in the I Thessalonians passage, 'for you received the word in much affliction.' The exhortation to imitate the apostle in I Cor. 11.1 is explained in the previous verse. What is to be imitated is St Paul's self-abnegation whereby, in not seeking his own advantage, he

---

[1] Cf. C. H. Dodd, 'The Mind of Paul: I' in *New Testament Studies*, 1953, pp. 67–82.
[2] 'Il ne s'agit pas d'une imitation admirative de la personnalité dans ses qualités générales, mais d'une imitation-obéissance sur tel ou tel point précis', P. Bonnard on Phil. 3.17, *L'Epître de S. Paul aux Philippiens* (Commentaire du Nouveau Testament 10), 1950, p. 70.

is pointing to the Lord Christ who did not please himself. Similarly the meaning of Gal. 4.12 is probably that the apostle's willing surrender of so many things which as a Jew he personally held dear can safely be taken as a model for a similar self-denial on the part of his readers. The injunction to imitate Paul in Phil. 4.9, 'What you have learned and received and heard and seen in me, do', has been carefully safeguarded by the preceding words: 'Whatever is honourable, whatever is just, whatever is pure, whatever is lovely, whatever is gracious, if there is any excellence, if there is anything worthy of praise, think about these things.'

For St Paul the life, teaching and activity of the apostolic minister, and through him the life of the ordinary believer, is used by the Spirit as the means, the sacramental means one ought perhaps to say, whereby a man's vocation to the *imitatio Christi* may be fulfilled. The Christian is urged to take any fellow-Christian as a living contemporary model for the *imitatio Christi* in so far as he finds there, to whatever degree, humility, self-giving, service.

Finally, a passage like I Thess. 2.14, 'You, brethren, become imitators of the churches of God in Christ Jesus which are in Judaea', suggests that in St Paul's mind the corporate life of a Christian community had a recognizable shape which other Christians could take as a means of their imitation of Christ. This form is that of humiliation and suffering whereby the Lord's servanthood is both proclaimed and mimed anew: 'for you suffered the same things from your own countrymen as they did from the Jews, who killed both the Lord Jesus and the prophets'.[1]

These passages are sufficient to demonstrate the importance of the idea of the *imitatio Christi* in St Paul's Christian thinking. We need to turn now to examine more in detail precisely what the Christian's imitation of Christ involves, and to determine the place which the historical life and work of Jesus occupied in the Pauline conception of the *imitatio Christi*.

3. *The Christian life and the Gospel of Christ*

Direct references to the life, actions and teaching of Jesus are not as frequent in the writings of St Paul as one might expect from a Christian missionary. Evidence that St Paul knew the basic features of the Lord's life, ministry, and death is clearly there in the epistles,[2] but it receives so little emphasis that an older generation of scholars was able to argue that St Paul was no longer interested in the historical ministry of Jesus.[3]

---

[1] Cf. also II Thess. 3.7, 9, and Phil. 3.17, where St Paul's fellow-Christians are termed συμμιμηταί and μίμησις is associated with 'walking' (περιπατέω).
[2] Cf. C. H. Dodd, *History and the Gospel*, 1938, pp. 63 ff.
[3] Cf. A. Schweitzer, *Paul and his Interpreters*, ET 1912.

The assumption was that, in spite of all his claims, St Paul knew himself to be a second-generation Christian, and could never quite overcome his resentment against those apostles, especially the so-called 'pillars' (Gal. 2.9) who had seen the Lord and companied with him. Consequently he tended to depreciate knowledge of the historical Jesus as compared with knowledge of the risen Lord Christ. The chief text relied upon was St Paul's statement in II Cor. 5.16:

> Wherefore we henceforth know no man after the flesh (κατὰ σάρκα); even though we have known Christ after the flesh, yet now we know him so no more.

It is very unlikely that this passage implies that St Paul in any way denied the relevance for Christian thought and spirituality of the historical Jesus. An examination of the use made by St Paul of the expression κατὰ σάρκα[1] suggests that he means by it primarily man relying exclusively on his own judgment and insight without reference to the enlightening work of the Holy Spirit.[2] Knowing κατὰ σάρκα and κατὰ πνεῦμα in St Paul is very like the contrast in St John between seeing (or hearing) and believing.[3] To know Christ κατὰ σάρκα would mean attempting to interpret him apart from the Resurrection and the work of the Spirit, and this would inevitably involve missing Christ as τὸ μυστήριον. It would mean confining the significance of Jesus to his status as a figure of the past. But in the Christian's present awareness of his Lord the Christ who was, who is now, and who is to come is experienced simultaneously. There were not for St Paul three absolutely separate dimensions of time, that of the historical Jesus in the past, that of the Christian Church in the present, and that of the Coming of the Lord, but basically the one life of the eternal Christ in his Church. The 'mystery' of Christ, of the Church, and of the individual Christian was only discernible to the eyes of faith. To such eyes, the life of Jesus was not only part of the historical past but also a present existence, the 'mystery' of 'Christ in you' (Col. 1.27), in the pattern of living of those who had given themselves to be used for this purpose. Through their lives the marks of the incarnate Lord would be evident for those with eyes to see. For them the life of the Christian pointed to the Lord Christ himself, and was in fact part of his Gospel.

An illustration of the Pauline treatment of the theme that the Christian life is an integral part of the Gospel can be taken from II Cor. 4.8–11:

---

[1] Cf. J. A. T. Robinson, *The Body* (SBT 5), 1952, pp. 17–26.
[2] Rom. 8.4–5, 12.
[3] Cf. p. 121 above.

> We are afflicted in every way, but not crushed;
> perplexed, but not driven to despair;
> persecuted, but not forsaken;
> struck down, but not destroyed;
> always carrying in the body the death of Jesus,
> so that the life of Jesus may also be manifested
> in our bodies.

This antithetical parallelism in which St Paul expresses the paradox of the Christian life recalls, as we shall see later, the paradoxical life of humiliation and glory of the Lord himself. Like his Lord the Christian is afflicted in every way[1] but, like him too, not crushed; like his Lord the Christian is perplexed, but like him also, not driven to despair; like his Lord the Christian is struck down, but not destroyed, because he is raised with Christ. The alternating rhythm of the Christian life is a *semeion* of the Lord's life for those willing to receive it and respond to it. For St Paul the willing self-donation to the afflictions, perplexities and persecutions which come the way of the Christian was the guarantee that his Lord would thereby proclaim his Gospel. It is in this way that 'we are ambassadors for Christ, God making his appeal through us. We beseech you on behalf of Christ, be reconciled to God' (II Cor. 5.20). The lives of Christians are missives from Christ sent out to all who can read this kind of address, and delivered by the apostles (II Cor. 3.3).

A close analysis of these descriptions of the life of the Christian in St Paul's epistles suggests that the apostle was making use of a tradition about the manner of life of the Lord which had already achieved normative influence in the church. As W. D. Davies puts it: 'Not only did the words of Jesus form a Torah for Paul, but so also did the person of Jesus.'[2] A good illustration of the apostolic life described in such a way as to indicate that behind it is the life of the Lord Christ himself can be seen in II Cor. 6.4–10:

> As servants (διάκονοι) of God we commend ourselves in every way: through great endurance (ὑπομονή), in afflictions (θλίψεις), hardships (ἀνάγκαι), calamities (στενοχωρίαι), beatings (πληγαί), imprisonments (φυλακαί), tumults, labours (κόποι), watchings (ἀγρυπνίαι), hunger, by purity, knowledge, forbearance (μακροθυμία), kindness (χρηστότης), the Holy Spirit, in genuine love (ἀγάπη), truthful speech (λόγος ἀληθείας), and the power of God; with the weapons of righteousness for the right hand and for the left; in honour and dishonour, in ill repute and good repute.

---

[1] Cf. Col. 1.24.
[2] *Paul and Rabbinic Judaism*, p. 148.

We are treated as impostors (πλάνοι), and yet are true,
   as unknown and yet well known,
   as dying and behold we live;
   as punished and yet not killed;
   as sorrowful yet always rejoicing;
   as poor (πτωχοί) yet making many rich;
   as having nothing, and yet possessing everything.

It is interesting to note that this description of the life of the Christian apostle is really a catena of actions and attitudes which are elsewhere, either in St Paul's epistles or in the Gospel tradition, applied to Christ himself:

διάκονοι. The Christian apostles are first διάκονοι θεοῦ, says St Paul. This is the term which Paul chooses for the Christian missionary. In I Cor. 3.5 the Christian apostles are again referred to as διάκονοι. In II Cor. 3.6 the apostles are διάκονοι καινῆς διαθήκης. In Eph. 3.6 f. Paul describes himself as a διάκονος of the Gospel,[1] and in Col. 1.25 as a διάκονος of the church.

St Paul seems to have preferred the term διάκονος for the Christian missionary rather than δοῦλος. The frequency of the description of Christians as διάκονοι must be related to the fact that Paul speaks particularly of Jesus as the διάκονος. He never speaks directly of Jesus as δοῦλος.[2] In Rom. 15.8 Christ is spoken of as a διάκονος of the circumcision, and the implication of Gal. 2.17 is that Christ is a διάκονος of righteousness.[3] As διάκονοι the role of the Christians as *imitatores Christi* appears most clearly.

If the Christian, and particularly the apostolic minister, is a διάκονος, the Christian life for St Paul is pre-eminently διακονία.[4] The various vocations in the Christian *ecclesia* are all διακονίαι.[5] The Christian Gospel is ἡ διακονία τοῦ πνεύματος and ἡ διακονία τῆς καταλλαγῆς (II Cor. 3.8; 5.18). It seems very likely that St Paul wished to stress the Christian life as above all else διακονία because that was the necessary form whereby it became a manifestation of the continuing life and activity of him who was pre-eminently and uniquely *the* διάκονος. This motif certainly underlies such a passage as II Cor. 11.23 f., where in order to authenticate himself as a genuine Christian διάκονος St Paul emphasized just those experiences wherein could be perceived a participation in the humiliations and sufferings of Christ.[6]

---

[1] Cf. Eph. 6.21 and Col. 1.23.
[2] In Phil. 2.7 the incarnate Christ is spoken of as μορθὴ δούλου.
[3] Cf. II Cor. 3.9.   [4] II Cor. 4.1; Rom. 11.13; 12.7; 15.31.
[5] I Cor. 12.5; cf. 16.15.   [6] Cf. Matt. 25.43 ff.

In all this we are justified in seeing the influence of the interpretation which Jesus himself gave to his mission. As we have seen, there is evidence enough in the Synoptic tradition that Jesus thought of himself as διάκονος and that, furthermore, discipleship of him was necessarily to take the form of an imitative διακονία of himself. And so, for St Paul, the overall shape of the Christian life must be that of διακονία.

ὑπομονή. Proceeding further with the analysis of II Cor. 6.4–10 we see lying behind the whole passage, as is the case with I Cor. 13, the life of the Master himself. The Christian apostles, as Christ's διάκονοι, commend themselves, says St Paul, ἐν ὑπομονῇ πολλῇ. ὑπομονή is named as one of the accompaniments of genuine apostleship in II Cor. 12.12. Furthermore, in other passages St Paul associates this quality specially with Christ himself. In II Thess. 3.5 he writes: 'And the Lord direct your hearts into the love of God and εἰς τὴν ὑπομονὴν τοῦ Χριστοῦ.' The love of God lies through 'imitation' of the patience of Christ. The frequent exhortations to patience and endurance, in fact, indicate that for Paul ὑπομονή is laid upon all Christians, not only because it is a good thing in itself, but because it is a necessary part of the Christian life if the latter is to be an evident *imitatio Christi*. The Lord Jesus himself was the perfect exemplar of it; their ὑπομονή is a *semeion* of his:

To those who by patience (ὑπομονή) in well-doing seek for glory and honour and immortality he will give eternal life (Rom. 2.7).[1]

We rejoice in our sufferings, knowing that suffering produces patience (ὑπομονή) (Rom. 5.7).

We wait with patience (δι' ὑπομονῆς) (Rom. 8.25).

Be patient (ὑπομένοντες) in tribulation (Rom. 12.12).

... by ὑπομονή and by the encouragement of the scriptures (Rom. 15.4).

... the God of patience (ὑπομονῆς) (Rom. 15.5).

If we are comforted, it is for your comfort, which you experience when you patiently endure (ἐν ὑπομονῇ) the same sufferings that we suffer (II Cor. 1.6).

May you be strengthened with all power, according to his glorious might, for all endurance (εἰς πᾶσαν ὑπομονὴν) and patience with joy (Col. 1.11).

... remembering ... your work of faith and labour of love and stead-fastness (ὑπομονή) (I Thess. 1.3).

[1] For St Paul Jesus was himself the embodiment of such a logion as Matt. 10.22: ὁ δὲ ὑπομείνας εἰς τέλος, οὗτος σωθήσεται.

θλᾶψις. In Col. 1.24 there is a remarkable passage which illustrates the close link between the *imitatio Christi* motif and 'mysticism': 'I rejoice in my sufferings (παθήματα) for your sake, and in my flesh I complete what is lacking in Christ's sufferings (θλίψεις) for the sake of his body, the Church.' The objections against taking this passage as an example of St Paul's 'mysticism' are often insufficiently substantiated.[1] St Paul here is not saying something which contradicts the fact of the finished redemptive work of Christ, nor is he advocating a doctrine of works. The passage we have discussed above, II Cor. 4.7–10, gives us an idea of what St Paul has in mind when he talks about sharing the sufferings of Christ. The sufferings of Christ flow over, so to speak, into the lives of his followers.[2] The sufferings of the individual Christian cannot but be a contribution to the continuing suffering of Christ in his historical Body, the Church. But it is Christ who fills up what is lacking by taking whatever Paul is willing to offer in this respect.[3] The sufferings of Paul were more than an illustration; they were a 'sign' of the sufferings of Christ; and the ability to apprehend simultaneously 'sign' and things signified we have seen to be characteristic of the mystic. There is also the possibility that St Paul regarded suffering as an essential part of the martyr-way of the Christian, and that the suffering of the Christian was for him a true *mysterion* behind which could be perceived, by those with eyes to see, Christ the redeeming martyr.

In I Thess. 1.6 the bearing of θλᾶψις is linked explicitly with the *imitatio Christi* motif. *Mimesis* of the apostle's endurance of trial is the means whereby the Lord himself is imitated:

And you became imitators of us and of the Lord, for you received the word in much affliction (ἐν θλίψει πολλῇ).

Other passages where Θλίψεις are associated with the Christian life are:

We rejoice in our afflictions (ἐν ταῖς θλίψεσιν) (Rom. 5.3).

Be patient in tribulation (τῇθλίψει ὑπομένοντες) (Rom. 12.12).

With all our affliction (τῇ θλίψει ἡμῶν) (II Cor. 7.4).

In all our distress and affliction (θλίψει) we have been comforted about you through your faith (I Thess. 3.7).[4]

ἀνάγκη. Difficulties (ἀνάγκαι) which constrain or constrict the Christian are to be used as material whereby his life as *imitator Christi* takes shape. Again there are sufficient references in St Paul's epistles to show

---

[1] Cf. for example E. Best, *One Body in Christ*, 1955, p. 135.
[2] II Cor. 1.5. [3] Eph. 1,23. [4] Cf. also II Thess. 1.4 and Eph. 3.13.

K

that this has a central place in his thought: 'I take pleasure in . . . necessities (ἀνάγκαις) . . . for Christ's sake' (II Cor. 12.10).[1]

Quite a number of the attributes which are associated with the Christian life in II Cor. 6.4–10 are referred in such a way as to suggest that St Paul regarded them as necessary constituents of the *imitatio Christi*:

στενοχωρία. 'I take pleasure in . . . στενοχωρίαις ὑπὲρ Χριστοῦ' (II Cor. 12.10).

πληγή. ἐν πληγαῖς ὑπερβαλλόντως (II Cor. 11.23).

κόποι. In II Cor. 11.23 κόποι are put first in a list of the essential marks of those who are διάκονοι Χριστοῦ, and in II Thess. 3.8 κόπος is a necessary part of the Christian life as an imitable example.[2]

μακροθυμία. I Tim. 1.16, whether actually St Paul's or not, is an excellent summary of whole doctrine of the *imitatio Christi*:

> I received mercy for this reason, that in me, as the foremost, Jesus Christ might display his perfect patience (τὴν ἅπασαν μακροθυμίαν) for an example (πρὸς ὑποτύπωσιν) to those who were to believe in him for eternal life.

Here we have clearly articulated the belief that the life of the Christian is a donation to his Lord to be used by him for the fulfilment of his purposes. The μακροθυμία of the Christian is not merely a personal quality, great and noble as that is; it confronts men with the Gospel of Christ, and they are thereby faced with the same kind of decision of faith as those who were confronted with the historical Jesus.

χρηστότης. This is one of the indispensable constants of the authentically Christian life, for St Paul, and is discussed in full below.[3]

ἀγάπη. Again, St Paul sees the ἀγάπη of the Christian as a process of imitating Christ; the ἀγάπη of the Christian points away from itself to the Lord Christ who is its origin and sustainer (through the Spirit):

> Who shall separate us from the ἀγάπη of Christ? (Rom. 8.35).

> The ἀγάπη of Christ controls (συνέχει) us (II Cor. 5.14).

> . . . to know the ἀγάπη of Christ which surpasses knowledge (Eph. 3.19).

Finally Christians are poor (πτωχοί) but enrich many (πολλοὺς δὲ πλουτίζοντες). This again is a facet of the lives of Christians as *imitatores Christi*. It points to him who, though he was rich, became poor (ἐπτώχευσεν) so that he might enrich men (II Cor. 8.9). Their very financial generosity is a kind of *mimesis* whereby the pouring out of their wealth points afresh

---

[1] Cf. I Thess. 3.7.　　[2] Cf. II Thess. 3.7; I Thess. 2.9.　　[3] Cf. p. 150 below.

to the unique and supreme libation of oneself which is found in the Incarnation.

This passage from II Corinthians has been analysed at length in order to show that behind the description of the Christian life as there presented by St Paul he intended the life of the Lord Christ himself to be discerned. This aim, probably more unconscious than conscious as far as the actual writing was concerned, sprang from his paramount conviction that his Lord lives and reigns, and that evident signs of this great fact are to be discerned, through the eyes of faith, in his activity in the lives of those who are 'following' him. It has been pointed out many times[1] that the new and better 'Way' ($\kappa\alpha\theta$' $\dot{\upsilon}\pi\epsilon\rho\beta o\lambda\dot{\eta}\nu$ $\dot{o}\delta\dot{o}\nu$) described in I Corinthians 13 is a life of Christ stressing in one glorious acclaim just those features which are picked out for emphasis in single passages throughout the epistles. The 'Way' of the Christian is the Way of Christ himself in a profound sense. The life of the Christian must have this essential form, because the intention of God is that behind it men may discern the figure of the Lord as $\delta\iota\dot{\alpha}\kappa o\nu os$ and in their relationship to the Christian, particularly to the apostolic minister, may know the Lord in a contemporary, living and personal way. In the life of the Christian the risen glorified Lord projects his incarnate proclamation and activity. The Gospel of the incarnate Lord can only be appropriately and meaningfully expressed in a life which points to him. Through the Spirit the Lord is at work in the life of the Christian in a way sufficiently analogous to the process of the Incarnation itself for it to be taken as a *mimesis* of the Exemplar. Christ is the Christian life for St Paul in a fundamentally realistic sense:

$\dot{o}$ $X\rho\iota\sigma\tau\dot{o}s$ $\dot{\eta}$ $\zeta\omega\dot{\eta}$ $\dot{\upsilon}\mu\hat{\omega}\nu$ (Col. 3.4).

$\dot{\epsilon}\mu o\grave{\iota}$ $\gamma\grave{\alpha}\rho$ $\tau\grave{o}$ $\zeta\hat{\eta}\nu$ $X\rho\iota\sigma\tau\acute{o}s$ (Phil. 1.21).

$X\rho\iota\sigma\tau\hat{\omega}$ $\sigma\upsilon\nu\epsilon\sigma\tau\alpha\acute{\upsilon}\rho\omega\mu\alpha\iota$ . . $\zeta\hat{\omega}$ $\delta\grave{\epsilon}$, $o\dot{\upsilon}\kappa\acute{\epsilon}\tau\iota$ $\dot{\epsilon}\gamma\acute{\omega}$, $\zeta\hat{\eta}$ $\delta\grave{\epsilon}$ $\dot{\epsilon}\nu$ $\dot{\epsilon}\mu o\grave{\iota}$ $X\rho\iota\sigma\tau\acute{o}s$ (Gal. 2.20).

This latter passage shows how St Paul is driven to coin verbs compounded with $\sigma\upsilon\nu$ to express the sense that his own life is part of his Lord's.[2] The life of the Christian is therefore, for St Paul, not ultimately his own individual private possession. Basically it is Christ's, purchased by him for his own use:

---

[1] Cf. recently W. D. Davies, *Paul and Rabbinic Judaism*, p. 147 n. 5: 'Only from the life of the historic Christ could such a picture of $\dot{\alpha}\gamma\dot{\alpha}\pi\eta$ as is found in I Cor. 13 have arisen.' Note the verbs $\mu\alpha\kappa\rho o\theta\upsilon\mu\epsilon\hat{\iota}$, $\chi\rho\eta\sigma\tau\epsilon\acute{\upsilon}\epsilon\tau\alpha\iota$, $\dot{\upsilon}\pi o\mu\acute{\epsilon}\nu\epsilon\iota$. Cf. also H. Riesenfeld, 'La voie de charité', *ST* 1, 1948, pp. 146–57.

[2] Cf. $\sigma\upsilon\mu\mu\iota\mu\eta\tau\alpha\iota$, etc.

οὐκ ἐστε ἑαυτῶν
ἠγοράσθητε γὰρ τιμῆς (I Cor. 6.19).
οὐδεὶς γὰρ ἡμῶν ἑαυτῷ ζῇ,
καὶοὐ δεὶς ἑαυτῷ ἀποθνῄσκει
. . . τοῦ Κυρίου ἐσμέν (Rom. 14.7).

The point is most strongly made in the passage already quoted from I Tim. 1.16, and the same thought is reflected in both the longer and shorter endings of St Mark's Gospel noted also above.

The influence of the *imitatio Christi* motif in St Paul is also evident in the way the *teaching* of Jesus has been woven by him into a description of the Christian life. On a first reading one might get the impression that St Paul makes very little reference to the teaching of Jesus. Certainly there is very little in the way of direct quotation or overt reference. It appears that St Paul could not detach the words of Jesus from the life of Jesus, as a kind of independent 'ethic', and it is the life of Jesus which he was anxious should be discerned behind that of the Christian. The way in which the *imitatio Christi* motif has influenced his way of thinking in this respect can be illustrated from those passages where St Paul is engaged in general *paraenesis*. It will be convenient to set beside St Paul's words the teaching of Jesus in the Gospel tradition which they recall:[1]

ST PAUL	JESUS
Abasing myself (ταπεινῶν) so that you might be exalted (ὑψωθῆτε) (II Cor. 11.7). (Cf. Phil. 2.8 [of Christ]: He humbled himself [ἐταπείνωσεν ἑαυτόν] . . . God exalted him [ὑπερύψωσεν].) Do not be haughty (μὴ τὰ ὑψηλὰ φρονοῦντες) but associate with the lowly (τοῖς ταπεινοῖς) (Rom. 12.16).	Everyone who exalts himself (ὁ ὑψῶν ἑαυτόν) will be humbled, and he who humbles himself (ὁ ταπεινῶν ἑαυτόν) will be exalted (Luke 14.11; cf. 18.14; Matt. 23.12).
Bless those who persecute you (εὐλογεῖτε τοὺς διώκοντας ὑμᾶς), bless and do not curse εὐλογεῖτε (καὶ μὴ καταρᾶσθε) (Rom. 12.14; cf. v. 17). When reviled we bless (λοιδορούμενοι εὐλογοῦμεν), when persecuted we endure (I Cor. 4.12 f.).	Bless those who curse you (εὐλογεῖτε τοὺς καταρωμένους) (Luke 6.27).

[1] Cf. W. D. Davies, *Paul and Rabbinic Judaism*, pp. 136 ff.

ST PAUL	JESUS
Be at peace (εἰρηνεύετε) among yourselves (I Thess. 5.13). Live peaceably (εἰρηνεύοντες) with all (Rom. 12.18).	Be at peace with one another (εἰρηνεύετε ἐν ἀλλήλοις) (Mark 9.50).
Rejoice always (πάντοτε χαίρετε) (I Thess. 5.16). Rejoice in your hope (τῇ ἐλπίδι χαίροντες) (Rom. 12.12). Rejoice in the Lord (χαίρετε) (Phil. 3.1; 4.4).	Rejoice in that day (χάρητε) (Luke 6.23).
Forbearing one another and, if one has a complaint against another, forgiving each other (χαριζόμενοι ἑαυτοῖς); as the Lord has forgiven you (ἐχαρίσατο), so you also must forgive (Col. 3.13).	Forgive (ἀπολύετε) and you will be forgiven (ἀπολυθήσεσθε) (Luke 6.37). If you forgive (ἀφῆτε) men their trespasses, your heavenly Father also will forgive you (Matt. 6.14).
Why do you pass judgment (κρίνεις) on your brother . . . Then let us no more pass judgment (κρίνωμεν) on one another (Rom. 14.10, 13).	Judge not (μὴ κρίνετε), that you be not judged (Matt. 7.1).
Let us decide never to put a hindrance or stumbling block (σκάνδαλον) in the way of a brother. I know and am persuaded in the Lord Jesus that nothing is unclean in itself (Rom. 14.13 f.).	There is nothing outside a man which by going into him can defile him (Mark 7.15). Whoever causes one of these little ones who believe in me to stumble (σκανδαλίσῃ) it would be better for him if a great millstone were hung round his neck and he were thrown into the sea (Mark 9.42).
Brethren, do not be children in your thinking; be babes in evil, but in thinking be mature (I Cor. 14.20).	Behold, I send you out as sheep in the midst of wolves; so be wise as serpents and innocent as doves (Matt. 10.16).

These are only a few of the passages in St Paul where there are clear reminiscences of the Lord's teaching. The interesting thing is that, as

Schweitzer pointed out,[1] St Paul nearly always paraphrased the sayings of Jesus instead of quoting them directly. The reason would seem to be that the teaching of Jesus was not for St Paul an objective ethical corpus to be quoted juridically. It was alive in his own day, discernible to a greater or lesser extent in Christian lives, and he referred to the teaching of the Lord in the context of a style of living which he knew. The *imitatio Christi* for St Paul (and for the New Testament writers in general) was not the attempt to copy a wholly external object; it was not the drawing of a 'still-life'. It was an active dynamic process, imitated, sustained and directed by the Spirit, involving a mutual personal and reciprocal relationship between the μιμητής and the εἰκών. Through the Spirit the Lord Christ is a living active Paradigm.

4. The constants in the Christian life as imitatio Christi

This analysis of St Paul's descriptions of the Christian life shows that he believed there were certain main qualities which unmistakably marked out the imitator of Christ, and they could be unhesitatingly seized upon, by anyone who willed to take them that way, as *semeia* of the Lord Christ. These were gentleness, patience, humility, charity, compassion, obedience, and suffering. We must now discuss these in turn.

Gentleness (πραΰτης, χρηστότης, ἐπιείκεια). 'I, Paul, myself entreat you by the meekness (πραΰτης) and gentleness (ἐπιείκεια) of Christ' (II Cor. 10.1). It would appear from this that the 'meekness and gentleness' of the Lord Christ was already a well-known formula in the Christian tradition of which St Paul could remind the Corinthians. Some relics of this may perhaps be found in the Matthaean tradition. It is St Matthew who particularly emphasizes this aspect of the character of Jesus in the entry into Jerusalem (21.5), in the sayings πραΰς εἰμι καὶ ταπεινός (11.29), and μακάριοι οἱ πραεῖς (5.5). St Paul's readers were to remember that their πραΰτης or ἐπιείκεια, to whatever extent it might appear in them, was a *mimesis* of the Lord and fundamentally a reminder of his presence: 'Let all men know your forbearance (τὸ ἐπιεικὲς ὑμῶν)' (Phil. 4.5). It is one of the attitudes which commends the apostles as διάκονοι Θεοῦ.[2] In the Pastorals the δοῦλος Κυρίου is to correct his opponents ἐν πραΰτητι (II Tim. 2.25), to be gentle (ἐπιεικής) and to show courtesy (πραΰτητα) to all men (Titus 3.2). It is, in fine, one of the 'fruits of the Spirit' (Gal. 5.23; 6.1).

Patience (ὑπομονή, μακροθυμία). This has already been discussed.[3]

---

[1] *Paul and his Interpreters*, p. 43.
[2] II Cor. 6.6 (ἐν χρηστότητι); cf. Eph. 4.2; Col. 3.12.   [3] Cf. p. 144 above.

The 'patience of Christ' is again a recognized formula for St Paul: 'May the Lord direct your hearts to the love of God and to the steadfastness (εἰς τὴν ὑπομονὴν) of Christ' (II Thess. 3.5). In the Christian's *mimesis* of this characteristic of Jesus the Lord is making evident for those with eyes to see his person and his work: ἵνα ἐν ἐμοὶ πρώτῳ ἐνδείξηται Ἰησοῦς Χριστὸς τὴν ἅπασαν μακροθυμίαν (I Tim. 1.16).

Humility (ταπεινοφροσύνη). The exemplar of this is the Incarnation itself and the humility of the Christian is a reproduction in miniature of that great mystery. The Incarnation is the great testimony to the fact that Christ did not please himself (Rom. 15.3); and Christians must imitate this perfect self-abnegation: 'We who are strong ought to bear with the failings of the weak, and not to please ourselves (μὴ ἑαυτοῖς ἀρέσκειν)' (Rom. 15.1).

Charity (ἀγάπη) *and compassion* (σπλαγχνή). This again is one of the necessary insignia of the *imitator Christi*.[1] 'Therefore be μιμηταί of God as beloved children. And walk in love, as Christ loved us and gave himself up for us' (Eph. 5.1 f.). The 'love of Christ' would seem to have been a Christian formula;[2] I Cor. 13 is, as we have seen, intended to indicate Christ as the 'Way' (ὁδός) of love.

Obedience (ὑπακοή, ὑπήκοος, ὑπακούω). This is the characteristic of Christ's ministry which is specially emphasized, and obedience is one of the conspicuous hallmarks of the Christian disciple. The process of the Incarnation itself involved an act of obedience; in it Christ 'humbled himself and became obedient (γενόμενος ὑπήκοος) unto death' (Phil. 2.8). This picture of Christ the obedient New Adam being contrasted with the disobedient first Adam is used again in Rom. 5.19: 'For as by one man's disobedience many were made sinners, so by one man's obedience (ὑπακοῆς) many will be made righteous.' The righteousness of the Christians will be an imitation of the sinlessness of Jesus (II Cor. 5.21).

Suffering. The Christian life of obedience will issue in suffering. This is most often the form which obedience will in fact take, and it is in suffering pre-eminently that the *imitatio Christi* is wrought. The sufferings of the Christian are not simply his own personal individual private sufferings. They are that of course in one aspect, and cannot cease to be that. St Paul would have been the last person to deny it. But, fundamentally, they are the sufferings of Christ in his Body and thereby the Gospel of the Crucified One is proclaimed, were we but willing to recognize it. God is staging his apostles' lives as a spectacle (θέατρον) wherein men can identify, according to their faith and insight, the μίμησις Χριστοῦ:

---

[1] II Cor. 6.6.   [2] Eph. 3.18, cf. Phil. 1.8 (σπλάγχνοι Χριστοῦ).

We are fools for Christ's sake,
But you are wise in Christ.
We are weak (ἀσθενεῖς) but you are strong.
You are held in honour, but we in disrepute.
To the present hour we hunger (πεινῶμεν) and
thirst (διψῶμεν), we are naked (γυμνητεύομεν)
and buffeted (κολαφιζόμεθα) and homeless, and we
labour, working with our own hands.
When reviled, we bless;
when persecuted, we endure;
when slandered, we try to conciliate (I Cor. 4.10–13).

Behind this description of the apostolic life there is the life in humiliation of the suffering Son of Man. If we are μωροί for Christ's sake, we may well be content to let that be the form which our obedience takes to the Son of Man who was held to be 'beside himself', and if we are weak we are weak 'in him who was crucified in weakness (ἐξ ἀσθενείας) but lives by the power of God' (II Cor. 13.4). There are interesting echoes in this passage of the influence of the 'parable' of the Sheep and the Goats on the early Christian conception of the life of the apostle:

For I was hungry (ἐπείνασα) and you gave me food,
I was thirsty (ἐδίψησα) and you gave me drink,
I was naked (γυμνός) and you clothed me,
I was weak (ἠσθένησα) and you visited me,
I was in prison and you came to me (Matt. 25.35 f.).

κολαφιζόμεθα in I Cor. 4.11 is interesting in this respect. As K. L. Schmidt has said:

In the enumeration of his sufferings in I Cor. 4.11 Paul speaks of being buffeted and homeless (κολαφιζόμεθα καὶ ἀστατοῦμεν). It is clear that Paul has interpreted the sufferings which have been inflicted on him in his apostolic mission as sufferings in Christ, as Christ's sufferings. When, therefore, he uses the word κολαφίζειν he may have had the Gospel tradition of Mark 14.65[2] in mind and appropriately remembered it. His being reviled and ill-treated like a martyr is something which takes place in and with Ἰησοῦς Χριστὸς κολαφιζόμενος.[1]

For as we share abundantly in Christ's sufferings, so through Christ we share abundantly in comfort too. If we are afflicted (θλιβόμεθα) it is for your comfort and salvation; and if we are comforted, it is for your comfort, which you experience when you patiently endure (ἐν ὑπομονῇ) the same sufferings that we suffer (II Cor. 1.5–7).

[1] 'Ἰησοῦς Χριστὸς κολαφιζόμενος und die "colaphisation" der Juden' in *Aux sources de la tradition chrétienne* (Mélanges Goguel), p. 221.
[2] καὶ κολαφίζειν αὐτόν.

This is a good illustration of the mutual interchange of life in complete reciprocity which St Paul sees as the distinctive feature of the *koinonia* of the Body of Christ. As L. S. Thornton puts it: 'The double fountain [of suffering and comfort] is reproduced in some sense in his [the Lord's] servant, and from him passes on to comfort the flock.'[1] As with the Lord Christ himself the humiliations and sufferings of the life of the Christian cannot completely obscure the glory to come. The coming of the Son of Man in humiliation and then in glory is reflected in the oscillations of the life of the Christian also. Present humiliations can be a basis of comfort! As with the Lord, there is glory to come, I Cor. 15.44, etc.

> On behalf of Christ (ὑπὲρ Χριστοῦ), then, I am content with weakness (ἀσθένεια), insults, hardships (ἀνάγκαι), persecutions (διωγμοί) and calamities (στενοχωρίαι) (II Cor. 12.10).

Here St Paul rejoices in those sufferings which, as we have seen, are for him pre-eminently the marks of his Lord.

> I rejoice in my sufferings for your sake, and in my flesh I complete what is lacking in Christ's afflictions for the sake of his body, that is, the church (Col. 1.24).

This great fact about the sufferings of St Paul comes about because the Gospel is still being preached, the End is not yet. 'Paul is convinced that God is making use of the sufferings of the apostle to the Gentiles to bring the church to its definite stature.'[2] Here again St Paul is really concerned with the complete mutuality and reciprocity of life in the Body of Christ. He will make up the Corinthians' share (ἀνταναπληρόω)[3] of the sufferings which are due.

> It has been granted to you that for the sake of Christ you should not only believe in him but also suffer on his behalf, engaged in the same conflict which you saw and now hear to be mine (Phil. 1.29 f.).

Once again one of the necessary data for the Christian life is suffering on behalf of Christ as part of the proclamation of his gospel. The same idea lies behind a later passage in Philippians:

> Whatever gain I had, I counted as loss for the sake of Christ. Indeed I count everything as loss because of the surpassing worth of knowing Christ Jesus my Lord. For his sake I have suffered the loss of all things,

---

[1] *The Common Life in the Body of Christ*, p. 35.
[2] C. Masson, *L'Épître de S. Paul aux Colossiens* (Commentaire du Nouveau Testament 10), p. 111.
[3] Cf. J. A. T. Robinson, *The Body*, p. 70.

and count them as refuse in order that I may gain Christ and be found in him . . . and may share his sufferings, becoming like him in his death, that if possible I may attain the resurrection from the dead (3.7–11).

These are the indispensable features of the Christian life as *imitatio Christi*, and they appear in the lists of virtues given, for example, in Gal. 5.22 f. and Col. 3.12–15:[1]

GALATIANS	COLOSSIANS
(The fruits of the Spirit are:)	(Christians are to 'put on':)
love (ἀγάπη)	compassion (σπλάγχνα)
joy (χαρά)	kindness (χρηστότης)
peace (εἰρήνη)	lowliness (ταπεινοφροσύνη)
patience (μακροθυμία)	meekness (πραότης)
kindness (χρηστότης)	patience (μακροθυμία)
goodness (ἀγαθωσύνη)	love (ἀγάπη)
faithfulness (πίστις)	peace (εἰρήνη)
gentleness (πραότης)	
self-control (ἐγκράτεια)	

Commenting on the close correspondence of these lists of virtues in St Paul's epistles, Lindsey Dewar writes: 'In view of the shortness of these lists, this is especially significant, and we may, therefore, legitimately assume that these virtues were of outstanding importance in the Apostle's mind.'[2] The reason is indicated in the fact that both these passages culminate in an exhortation to the *imitatio Christi* or words to that effect.[3] The features of the Christian life in the Pauline lists fall into two main groupings. There are, first, those which suggest a life of humiliation, trial, suffering, and, second, those associated with joy (because there is glory to come). Behind this alternating rhythm of the Christian life there is to be discerned the Son of Man who came in shame and was raised in glory.

5. *The* imitatio Christi *and the sacraments*

If the necessary form of the Christian life for St Paul is the *imitatio Christi*, its essential context is the Church as the Body of Christ. We have seen that he could speak of imitation of the 'churches of God . . . in Judea' (I Thess. 2.14), and it seems likely that he thought of the corporate life and activity of the Church as a whole taking the form of the imitation

[1] Cf. Eph. 4.32.   [2] *An Outline of New Testament Ethics*, 1949, p. 144.
[3] Gal. 5.25; Col. 3.15–17.

of Christ, and thereby constantly setting the pattern for the life of the individual believer. The life of the Church has one overall pattern, that of *mimesis* of her Lord, and the Christian life therefore begins with initiation into the one life of the Body of Christ: 'By one Spirit we were all baptized into one body—Jews or Greeks, slaves or free—and all were made to drink of one Spirit' (I Cor. 12.13). It is in the Church that the life of the individual Christian is kept in a unique living and active relationship with the indispensable Model whose likeness is, through the Spirit, being given new but recognizable expression in that individual. The *imitatio Christi* for St Paul was not a mere mental recollection or vague sentiment. It took quite concrete and realistic form in worship and in personal relationships. Nor, of course, was it some kind of endeavour initiated and carried through by the Christian. It was not a yogic copying of Christ. The Christian life for St Paul was only possible because of the redemptive action of God in Christ; it was the first-fruits of that. The Christian life itself had for St Paul an eschatological character. If Christ himself is the first-fruits (I Cor. 15.23), the life of the Christian now is a first-fruits of the life of perfect conformity to Christ which is to come (Rom. 8.23).

Further, the role played by the *imitatio Christi* motif in St Paul is important, as we shall see later, in assessing his 'mysticism'. It is linked with his ability to experience, particularly in worship, past events as present realities, and it is in the sacraments that, in an Old Testament way, he experienced through the miming of these events their contemporaneity. But this *mimesis* of paradigmatic events of the past brought with it also an experience, by anticipation, of their consummation in the future. For St Paul, if one may adapt some words of Mr T. S. Eliot, time past and time future were both contained in time present. There does seem to be that in St Paul, and other New Testament writers, which can properly be called, to use Schweitzer's term, eschatological mysticism. This fluidity of reference between what was, what is now, and what is to come is characteristic of mystical perception. The mystic has a profound sense of the successiveness of man and time being englobed in the simultaneity of God.[1] Time and history can take on a 'sacramental' character. It is difficult, in spite of his strong assertions to the contrary,[2] to determine what is the real difference between what Bultmann calls the eschatological 'now' and the eternal 'now' of the mystics. In fact by his exclusive concentration on

---

[1] Cf. Baron von Hügel, article on 'Gospel of St John' in *Encyclopaedia Britannica*, eleventh edition, Vol. 15, 1911, p. 454.

[2] *Kerygma and Myth*, ET 1953, pp. 115 f.

the *present*, by-passing the history of Jesus in the past (this is no longer available for Bultmann), and demythologizing the future, Bultmann comes very near to the kind of non-historical non-eschatological mysticism which he has renounced. Corell is right in suggesting that Bultmann's 'existential' eschatology is really a mysticism.[1] The sacraments of Baptism and the Lord's Supper in St Paul are 'mysteries' in the early Christian sense,[2] although he does not actually speak of them as such. To those with powers of discernment (I Cor. 11.29) (and these are morally rather than intellectually determined), the mysteries of Baptism and the Eucharist cannot be separated from the realities which they symbolize. There is in St Paul what can legitimately be named 'sacramental mysticism'.

The sacraments for St Paul were the means whereby the Christian in the Church made formal and normative rehearsal of his way of life as *imitatio Christi*. Both Baptism and Eucharist contained a mimetic element, and through this the Christian was being conformed to Christ and having reproduced in him, in miniature scale and imperfectly, the 'Way' of his Lord in life and death. There was a real *kenosis* involved in the process of the Christian life wherein the Spirit engaged in conforming believers to Christ. This time it was not finitude which obscured the reality, but unbelief, sloth, and sin. Nevertheless, here also something of the true lineaments of the Christian's life were discernible.

The whole Christian life is enacted in Baptism and Eucharist. St Paul saw it as the march to the Promised Land of the true Israel. The journey of the Old Israel was an anticipation of the journey which had been taken by Jesus himself in a new, unique and salvific way:[3]

> I want you to know, brethren, that our fathers were all under the cloud, and all passed through the sea, and all were baptized into Moses in the cloud and in the sea, and all ate the same spiritual food, and all drank the same spiritual Rock which followed them, and the Rock was Christ. Nevertheless with most of them God was not pleased; for they were overthrown in the wilderness (I Cor. 10.1–5).

The interesting thing here is that the journey of Israel from the Exodus and the Wanderings are taken not only typologically, as an anticipation of the 'Way' of the Christian, but there is also the suggestion that in some sense Christians are contemporaneous with these events. How such a thing can become possible is indicated by the allusion in v. 2 to Baptism and in vv. 3 f. to the Eucharist. In the two sacraments the basic pattern of the

---

[1] *Consummatum Est*, p. 2.   [2] Cf. p. 21 above.

[3] 'The position in which the believers find themselves corresponds to that of the Israelites in their journeyings', A. Schweitzer, *Mysticism of Paul the Apostle*, p. 259.

Christian life is constantly being re-enacted. The life of the Christian is the life of itinerant Israel over again, with the same trials and temptations (vv. 5–13), but the Christian now knows that what was being rehearsed in a preliminary way in the history of Israel was the life of Christ with his faithful followers. Because in Christ the Christians are the New Israel, their life is bound to be a series of variations on the theme of the 'Way' of the Old Israel as it has been summed up for them in Christ. We shall notice later how the same stretch of the history of Israel is used to delineate the life of the Christians in the Epistle to the Hebrews.

The Christian life for St Paul began, then, with a *mimesis* of the death and resurrection of Christ in Baptism:

> Do you not know that all of us who have been baptized into Christ Jesus were baptized into his death? We were buried therefore with him by baptism into his death, so that as Christ was raised from the dead by the glory of the Father, we too might walk in newness of life (Rom. 6.3 f.).

Baptism is the Christian's primary imitation of the Lord's redemptive death and glorious resurrection, and this is to be given extended mime in the dying to self and sin throughout life, and the resurrection is to be imitated by the 'walk' in newness of life;[1] the life of the Christian is thus a continuing variation on the basic pattern enacted once and for all in Baptism.

> You have died, and your life is hid with Christ in God (Col. 3.3).

> For as many of you as were baptized into Christ have put on Christ (Gal. 3.27).

> You were buried with him in baptism (Col. 2.12).

Among other things, St Paul saw in the death of Christ the perfect act of self-giving in obedience; that to which all men are called was here, and only here, perfectly done. Baptism he saw as the action whereby the Spirit takes the partial commitment which any human act of faith is bound to be, and transforms it into the perfect conformity to the will of God which was in Christ, the Cross being the focus of this:

> We know that our old man was concrucified with him, so that the sinful body might be destroyed, and we might no longer be enslaved to sin (Rom. 6.6).

> I have been concrucified with Christ (Gal. 2.20).

---

[1] Note the 'we too' (οὕτως καὶ ἡμεῖς) in Rom. 6.4.

Those who belong to Christ Jesus have crucified the flesh with its passions and desires (Gal. 5.24).

With Christ you died to the elemental spirits of the universe (Col. 2.20).

Clearly the dying and rising with Christ in Baptism was much more for St Paul than a commemorative or pedagogical gesture. Like the act of prophetic symbolism in the Old Testament, Baptism was no mere illustration of a great truth, it was the God-given means whereby the real existence of that truth was brought about. Some scholars in Germany, in spite of a general tendency amongst the Germans to deny the existence of a 'mystical' element in St Paul, have been ready to speak of his 'faith-mysticism'. But, as Wikenhauser points out,[1] while faith is the necessary presupposition of and preliminary to union with Christ, this latter is brought about by Baptism. Baptism, for St Paul, brought the Christian into such an intimate and unique relation with Christ that, as we shall see, it is difficult to deny the legitimacy of the term mystical union for it.

In I Cor. 5.6–8 St Paul speaks of the Christian life as a Passover festival:

Do you not know that a little leaven ferments the whole lump of dough? Cleanse out the old leaven that you may be fresh dough, as you really are unleavened. For Christ, our paschal lamb, has been sacrificed. Let us, therefore, celebrate the festival, not with the old leaven, the leaven of malice and evil, but with the unleavened bread of sincerity and truth.

This would imply that the manner of life of the Christian as a whole was meant to be an *anamnesis* of the 'Way' of Israel which had been traced by Jesus himself, the Christians' true Passover. As we have seen,[2] there is some suggestion in the mission charge of Jesus to the Twelve that he himself saw their enterprise as a festal Passover journey. There is also the possibility that this passage in I Corinthians may contain an allusion to the Eucharist.[3] If this is so, then the Eucharist was the normative means whereby the Israel 'Way' of the Christians 'in Christ' was constantly being re-enacted. Unfortunately we know very little of early Christian eucharistic practice. No doubt it was the occasion for the recital of the 'Way' of Jesus. This was probably confined to recounting verbally the mission of Jesus. The rite certainly included at least the miming of Christ's acts with bread and cup. This was the way the Lord was 'remembered'.

According to I Cor. 10.16 the Eucharist is a κοινωνία in the blood and

---

[1] On this particular issue see his *Die Christusmystik des Apostels Paulus*, Munster, 1928, pp. 70–86.

[2] Cf. p. 104 above.

[3] J. Héring, *La première Epître de S. Paul aux Corinthiens* (Commentaire du Nouveau Testament 7), 1949, *ad loc.*, thinks this possible.

body of Christ. It seems likely, following J. Héring,[1] that the reference here is to participation in the redemptive death of Christ (and its consequences) and in the new life of the risen body of the Lord. Through the Eucharist Christians are in the process of becoming in actuality what they are in virtue of Baptism: dead with Christ to self and sin, and risen with Christ to sit with him 'in the heavenlies'.

St Paul did not conceive of the Eucharist as a memorial service to the Lord; it was the place and the time when the Lord took shape[2] in the Christian assembly, when the mysterious reality of the Body of Christ could be perceived by a sensitive faith: 'Any one who eats and drinks without discerning the body (μὴ διακρίνων τὸ σῶμα) eats and drinks judgment (κρῖμα) upon himself' (I Cor. 11.29). The Eucharist has therefore the character of a 'sign'; it is, so to speak, the 'sign' of him who is *the* 'Sign', and a man is accountable for his decision (which will be revealed in his behaviour) as to whether this is just another meal, or the real presence, ἐν μυστηρίῳ, of Christ with his own. Through this mimetic action in worship the Last Supper in Jerusalem no longer belongs simply to the past but is contained in the experience, through faith, of the present Eucharist.

Furthermore, it is a *mimesis* which brings the future into the present: 'As often as you eat this bread and drink this cup, you proclaim (καταγγέλλετε) the Lord's death until he comes' (I Cor. 11.26). In this way it is, among other things, a significant form of Christian predication of the Gospel. Elsewhere St Paul uses the verb καταγγέλλω of proclaiming the Gospel.[3] The form of the Eucharist has then a missionary character. This *mimesis* of the Passover mystery in the past and of the Messianic banquet to come has a kerygmatic character for the present. It is a way of preaching Christ and him crucified.

6. *The* imitatio Christi *and personal relationships*

The Christian life as *imitatio Christi* was then rehearsed, at different levels of intensity, in the sacraments of Baptism and the Eucharist. But the Christian life was a μυστήριον, 'hid with Christ in God' not only in sacramental worship, but in the ordinary personal relationships of day to day life. The motif of the *imitatio Christi* has been at work not only in the Pauline view of the sacraments but also in what we call his 'ethical' teaching. Behind the Christian's free and truly personal relations with others there was to be discerned, by the eyes of faith again, his relation

---

[1] *Op. cit., ad loc.*   [2] Cf. Gal. 4.19.
[3] I Cor. 2.1; 9.14; Phil. 1.17.

with his Lord.[1] We have already referred to the Christian's relations with
the apostolic minister, as a means whereby the man of faith can realize
his imitation of Christ in a living concrete and personal way. As a further
example, we can take first the relation between man and woman in
marriage. The intimate relationship of man and woman in marriage is the
means whereby the relation between Christ and the Church is mimed,
and thereby known as a living personal reality:

> Wives, be subject to your husbands, as to the Lord. For the husband is
> the head of the wife as Christ is the head of the church, his body, and
> is himself its Saviour. As the church is subject to Christ, so let wives
> also be subject in everything to their husbands. Husbands, love your
> wives, as Christ loved the church, and gave himself up for her, that he
> might sanctify her, having cleansed her by the washing of water with
> the word, that the church might be presented before him in splendour,
> without spot or wrinkle or any such thing, that she might be holy and
> without blemish. Even so husbands should love their wives as their
> own bodies. He who loves his wife loves himself. For no man ever hates
> his own flesh, but nourishes and cherishes it, as Christ does the church,
> because we are members of his body. 'For this reason a man shall leave
> his father and mother and be joined to his wife, and the two shall
> become one.' This is a great mystery (μυστήριον) and I take it to mean
> Christ and the church (Eph. 5.22–32).

L. S. Thornton comments on this passage: 'Christian marriage is not
only to be modelled upon the mystical union of Christ and the Church.
It is actually to partake of its quality. It is not only to exemplify and
symbolize it, but also to embody it.'[2] The relationship between man and
woman in marriage is seen by St Paul as the means whereby the *imitatio
Christi* is most closely wrought. Other facilities are provided in the relationship between parents and children (Eph. 6.1–4), and between master
and slave (Eph. 6.5–9). This particular significance of all three relationships is given too in Col. 3.18–4.1:

> Wives, be subject to your husbands, as is fitting in the Lord (ἐν Κυρίῳ).
> Husbands, love your wives, and do not be harsh with them. Children,
> obey your parents in everything, for this pleases the Lord. Fathers, do
> not provoke your children, lest they become discouraged. Slaves, obey
> in everything those who are your earthly masters, not with eye-service,
> as men-pleasers, but in singleness of heart, fearing the Lord. Whatever

---

[1] A. R. George, in *Communion with God in the New Testament* (1953), writes (p. 195):
'Personal relationships were to him [Paul] important, but rather as the fruit or outwork-
ing, or indeed the illustration, of our dealings with God or his with us.' But they were
more than this for St Paul, approximating to having a sacramental character, as the use
of μυστήριον in Eph. 5.32 would suggest.
[2] *The Common Life in the Body of Christ*, p. 225.

your task, work heartily, as serving the Lord and not men, knowing that from the Lord you will receive the inheritance as your reward; you are serving the Lord Christ. For the wrongdoer will be paid back for the wrong he has done, and there is no partiality. Masters, treat your slaves justly and fairly, knowing that you also have a Master in heaven.

'All of you be subject one to another', as a summary of Christian personal relations, only makes sense because all of 'you' are both partly Christ and partly not. Here too 'you are serving the Lord Christ'.

7. The 'transfiguration' of the Christian

The *imitation of Christ* was not conceived by St Paul as a kind of yoga of endeavour, nor was it an attempted literal mimicry of Christ such as developed later in the Church. The life of the Christian was for St Paul a symbolic *mimesis* of the life of his Lord, and this not through an attempt to copy an external objective exemplar, but through a process of being *conformed* to the Lord as the true εἰκών of God, the true Adam.[1] This was the work of the Spirit, and St Paul's conception of the 'Christification' of the Christian is closely similar to the paraclete functions of the Spirit in St John's Gospel. The Spirit helps us in our weakness to achieve our destiny, which is to be conformed to the image of the Son of God (συμμόρφους τῆς εἰκόνος τοῦ υἱοῦ αὐτοῦ, Rom. 8.26–30):

> Just as we have borne the image (εἰκών) of the man of dust, we shall also bear the image (εἰκών) of the man of heaven (I Cor. 15.49).

> The Lord Jesus Christ . . . will change our lowly body to be like his glorious body, by the power which enables him even to subject all things to himself (Phil. 3.21).

> You have put on the new nature which is being renewed in knowledge after the image (εἰκών) of its creator (Col. 3.10).

In this connection it is significant that in St Paul's mind εἰκών and δόξα were in very close association. Important passages are I Cor. 11.7, where man is the εἰκών καὶ δόξα Θεοῦ; II Cor. 3.18, where εἰκών, δόξα and the theme of the Transfiguration are linked together; and II Cor. 4.4, where St Paul speaks of the 'light of the gospel of the glory of Christ who is the εἰκών of God'. It is interesting, further, to note in passing that in St Luke's account of the Transfiguration δόξα is used of the figures of Moses and Elijah.[2]

The evidence therefore suggests that St Paul was greatly influenced by

---

[1] Col. 1.15.
[2] Luke 9.31 f. This is one of many links between St Paul's epistles and the Gospel of St Luke.

the tradition about the Lord's Transfiguration. It seems to have been in his mind when he reflected on his own experiences of the Damascus road, and also when he was thinking of the process whereby the Christian engages in the imitation of his Lord. The *imitatio Christi* is a process of being conformed by transfiguration into some real likeness to him who is the object of our imitative life. In II Cor. 3, the 'glory' of the Christian apostle is compared with the transfiguration of Moses, and it is accomplished by the Lord the Spirit. In this passage the words εἰκών, δόξα and μεταμορφούμεθα all occur in the sentence which is the climax to the chapter and describes what is happening in the life of the Christian:

> We all with unveiled face, beholding the glory (δόξα) of the Lord, are being changed (μεταμορφούμεθα) into his likeness (εἰκών) from one degree of glory to another; for this comes from the Lord who is the Spirit.[1]

And it is evident that the Transfiguration lies behind such passages as II Cor. 4.1–6 ('veiling', 'glory', 'image') and Eph. 5.8–14.

The *imitatio Christi* in St Paul, therefore, is not some kind of human endeavour, a striving to emulate the life of Christ. It is a part of the mysterious hidden work of the Risen Lord through the Holy Spirit. It is a life lived in and through the Christian, moulding him to the shape of the Image of God which his Lord is.

8. The imitatio Christi *and Pauline mysticism*

There has been a long debate as to whether St Paul qualifies for the description 'mystic'.[2] If we adopt the concept of mysticism as 'mystery' outlined in the first chapter, then there would seem to be no difficulty about the propriety of using the term 'mysticism' for what we find in St Paul.

'Mystery' is, in fact, very much a Pauline term. He uses it in the following connections. The Gospel is spoken of as the 'mystery' or 'mystery of God': 'to proclaim the mystery of the Gospel' (Eph. 6.19):

> When I came to you I did not come proclaiming to you the mystery of God in lofty words or wisdom. For I decided to know nothing among you except Jesus Christ and him crucified (I Cor. 2.1).[3]

---

[1] II Cor. 3.18; cf. Rom. 12.2 (μεταμορφοῦσθε).

[2] For details of recent discussion see A. Wikenhauser, *Die Christusmystik des Apostels Paulus*.

[3] Vaticanus, Beza, the Latin versions and the Sahidic Coptic read here μαρτύριον (which Kilpatrick adopts in the British and Foreign Bible Society's 1958 edition of the Greek New Testament), but Pauline usage elsewhere inclines me to prefer the reading μυστήριον.

We speak God's wisdom in a mystery (ἐν μυστηρίῳ) (I Cor. 2.7).

. . . that they may know the mystery of God, Christ, in whom are all the treasures of wisdom and knowledge hidden (Col. 2.2 f.).

The mystery of God here is the Gospel of Christ and the phrase 'Jesus Christ and him crucified' suggests that what constitutes the Gospel the 'mystery' is not only the contents of it, but the *manner* of it: the Gospel of God in humiliation and crucifixion. The 'mystery of God' is coterminous for St Paul with the 'mystery of Christ'. Christ is the 'secret' of God, still very much an undiscovered secret to the eyes of unbelief, but for the eyes of faith he is the open secret:

Now to him who is able to strengthen you according to my gospel and the preaching of Jesus Christ, according to the revelation of the mystery which was kept secret for long ages but is now disclosed and through the prophetic writings is made known to all nations (Rom. 16.25).

For he has made known to us in all wisdom and insight the mystery of his will, according to his purpose which he set forth in Christ as a plan for the fulness of time (Eph. 1.9 f.).

. . . the mystery was made known to me by revelation, as I have written briefly. When you read this you can perceive my insight into the mystery of Christ (Eph. 3.3 f.).

. . . this grace was given, to preach to the Gentiles the unsearchable riches of Christ, and to make all men see what is the plan of the mystery hidden for ages in God (Eph. 3.8 f.).

. . . to make the word of God fully known, the mystery hidden for ages and generations but now made manifest to his saints. To them God chose to make known how great among the Gentiles are the riches of the glory of this mystery, which is Christ in you, the hope of glory (Col. 1.25–27).

. . . pray for us also, that God may open to us a door for the word, to declare the mystery of Christ (Col. 4.3).

In Eph. 5.31 f., speaking of the relation of man and woman in marriage, the fact that this relationship can be the means whereby the union of Christ and his Church is mimed is described as a μυστήριον:

'For this reason a man shall leave his father and mother and be joined to his wife, and the two shall become one.' This is a great mystery: and I take it to mean Christ and the church.

Putting these passages together we can say that μυστήριον for St Paul is an event, or series of events, or a relationship wherein the eternal purposes of God may be discerned. The 'mystery' is not superficially perceived and, because insight into it is morally conditioned (St Paul would have said by repentance), it can easily be missed. The mystery is at one and the same time the 'sign' and the reality which the 'sign' signifies, and, as we have seen, the perception which cannot divorce the 'sign' from the reality which underlies it the early Fathers spoke of as 'mystical'. St Paul's is certainly an example of 'mystery-minded mysticism',[1] and we have tried to illustrate how closely he sticks to the given 'mysteries' of Christ, the Church, the ministry, the sacraments, and relations in marriage, the family, and society. In St Paul's writings there is evidence of liturgical or sacramental mysticism. In the Eucharist there was for St Paul a profound realization that in this action the distinction between past, present, and future was transcended; here was a wonderful intermingling of the basic dimensions of time: 'As often as you eat [present, $\dot{\epsilon}\sigma\theta\dot{\iota}\eta\tau\epsilon$] this bread and drink [present, $\pi\dot{\iota}\nu\eta\tau\epsilon$] the cup, you proclaim the Lord's death [past] until he comes [future]' (I Cor. 11.26).

The relationship which exists between the Lord and the believer as a result of initiation in Baptism and growth through the Eucharist is described by St Paul in terms of Christ being 'in' the believer, and the believer 'in' Christ or 'with' Christ (particularly of the future state). It has become the fashion when discussing this feature of St Paul's vocabulary to emphasize right at the beginning that this is not mystical language, because St Paul at no point confuses the distinction between the believer and his Lord in the way which is thought to be the necessary feature of all mysticism. But the common feature of all types of mysticism is a profound perception and experience of union and oneness with the object of one's devotion, and not a particular theory as to the nature and manner of this union. St Paul's awareness of union with Christ was of this mystical kind. Union with Christ was not simply heightened awareness of a subjective kind. The believer's life in Christ had objective ontological reality; it was a relationship inseparable and indissoluble.

Pauline mysticism is prevented from moving in the direction of Neoplatonism because it is firmly rooted in the historical revelation in Jesus which exercises a controlling influence through the motif of the *imitatio Christi*. 'Like a light-house,' says Schweitzer, 'that throws its beam upon the ocean of the eternal, the Pauline mysticism stands firm, based upon the firm foundation of the historical manifestation of Jesus Christ.'[2] Some

---

[1] This is the phrase used by the translator for 'mystique des mystères' in the translation of Fr A. Plé's essay in *Mystery and Mysticism*.
[2] *The Mysticism of Paul the Apostle*, p. 379.

poets and artists can be unusually aware of the process of inspiration, so that while the words, ideas, composition are, of course, their own, that is not the thing they are much conscious of or would think worth mentioning. They would wish to emphasize that although, of course, they were seeing with their own eyes, they were most aware not that they were seeing but that they were being shown. In something of the same way St Paul is most aware not of his separate self, words, thoughts and so on (although he was the last person in the world to deny this aspect of things; in fact his temptation was to isolate them and overemphasize them in καύχησις), but of a life and an activity which is working in and through him moulding him into the shape of the vision of the Image of God which he has seen. This life and activity was the action of the Spirit bringing about the birth of Christ in the Christian,[1] and sustaining the growth of Christ in the believer to maturity.[2] In the Christian *imitatio Christi* the Lord Christ is at one and the same time the object of the *mimesis* and, through the Spirit, the means of it.

[1] Gal. 4.19.   [2] Eph. 4.13.

The First Epistle of St Peter and the Epistle to the Hebrews

IF ONE HAD TO CHOOSE a single book from the New Testament to illustrate the Christian conception of the imitation of God, none could be better than the First Epistle of St Peter. The author is avowedly concerned with the basis and character of Christian holiness which he defines as an imitation of the holiness of God: 'But as he who called you is holy, be holy yourselves in all your conduct; since it is written, "You shall be holy, for I am holy"' (I Peter 1.15 f.). He is concerned to show, however, that this must assume the form, for the Christian, of the imitation of Christ. It is the costly redemptive work of Christ which alone has made possible the life of the Christian as an imitator of Christ. The First Epistle of St Peter is perhaps one of the most instructive writings in the whole of the New Testament on the interrelationship of Christology, Atonement, and ethics, and more particularly for a study of the influence of the motif of the imitation of Christ on Christian spirituality.

The author seems to have had in mind a similar picture to that of the author of the Epistle to the Hebrews. He sees the Christian life as a journey to Christ who is at one and the same time the end of the journey, the guide and companion along the road, and the road itself. Christians are new Israelites following a path which Christ has made available by being Israel himself. They are introduced at the opening of the Epistle as exiled wanderers of the Diaspora waiting to be gathered together in their homeland (παρεπιδήμοι, 1.1). In 2.9 ff. they are further described in terms which remind them that they are a new Israel called out of darkness to journey to Zion (2.4, 6), as nomadic wanderers (παροίκους καὶ παρεπιδήμους, 2.11). This means following Jesus who has made the journey for them before them, having gone into heaven (πορευθεὶς εἰς οὐρανόν, 3.22). Jesus has re-enacted himself the Passover journey and is the Christian's Passover himself (1.19).

The Christian life is therefore a vocation to the *imitatio Christi*. The well-known injunction in 2.18–24 occurs in an admonition to servants to bear wrongs patiently (ὑπομενεῖτε). It is precisely to this kind of life that Christians are called (εἰς τοῦτο γὰρ ἐκλήθητε), because Christ did this very thing, leaving them an example (ὑπογραμμόν) that they should follow in his steps (ἵνα ἐπακολουθήσητε τοῖς ἴχνεσιν αὐτοῦ). The writer then goes on to give a description of the ὑπομονή of Jesus in such a way as to show that he has a definite tradition about the bearing of Jesus during the Passion in mind. It is interesting to note that he uses the term κολαφιζόμενοι (2.20) and, as indicated previously,[1] this may be due to a reminiscence of the tradition expressed in Mark 14.65. The bearing of Jesus is described in terms reminiscent of the fourth Isaianic Servant-song. 'The whole verse [24] is such', says E. G. Selwyn, 'as we might have expected to be written by an eye witness who had also in mind Is. liii. 7, 9.'[2]

The *imitatio Christi* motif lies behind the general exhortations of 3.8 f. The Christian vocation (εἰς τοῦτο ἐκλήθητε) is to follow Christ in compassion, love and humility: 'not rendering evil for evil, or reviling for reviling; but contrariwise blessing'. This is evidently a reminiscence of the teaching of Jesus such as is given in Luke 6.28 f. 'It is better to suffer for doing right, if that should be God's will, than for doing wrong. Because Christ also (ὅτι καὶ Χριστός) died for sins once for all, the righteous for the unrighteous' (3.17 f.). Here again the motive for putting up with injustice is not primarily because that is noble and right. That is of course assumed by the writer. The feature of this conduct, as it appears in the Christian, which he wishes to emphasize is that it is a *mimesis* of the behaviour of Christ.

> Since therefore Christ suffered in the flesh, arm yourselves with the same thought (4.1).

> Rejoice in so far as you share Christ's sufferings . . . If you are reproached for the name of Christ, you are blessed, because the Spirit of glory and of God rests upon you (4.13 f.).

> If one suffers as a Christian, let him not be ashamed, but under that name let him glorify God (4.16).

If, as Dr F. L. Cross[3] has suggested, I Peter is really a Paschal liturgy, much light would be thrown on these references to the *imitatio Christi* in sufferings. Baptism, as we have seen for St Paul, was the means whereby the Christian died with Christ and began the new life of going over the way he had pioneered. The use of κοινωνεῖτε here, and the emphasis on

---

[1] Cf. p. 152 above. [2] *The First Epistle of St Peter*, 1946, p. 180.
[3] In *I Peter: a Paschal Liturgy*, 1954.

seeing the sufferings of the Christian as a *mimesis* of those of Christ's, shows that I Peter is not far from the teaching of St Paul in this matter. The Epistle ends in a typical Pauline phrase: 'Peace to all of you who are in Christ (ἐν Χριστῷ)' (5.14). There is in St Paul and in I Peter a New Testament basis for the later passion-mysticism of, say, a St Ignatius of Antioch.

The concept of the Christian life as the *imitatio Christi* means, as we have seen previously, a lively awareness of its significant form. It is a *semeion* pointing those who encounter it to Christ himself. There is evidence of this view in I Peter:

> Maintain good conduct among the Gentiles, so that in case they speak against you as wrongdoers, they may see your good deeds and glorify God on the day of visitation (2.12).

> Keep your conscience clear, so that, when you are abused, those who revile your good behaviour in Christ may be put to shame (3.16).

The Epistle to the Hebrews is a very instructive example of 'liturgical mysticism'. The author clearly has the atmosphere and movement of worship in mind[1] and he has blended together the three themes of the 'Way' of Israel, the 'Way' of Jesus, and the 'Way' of the Christian in an intricate and illuminating fashion. The theme of the Epistle might well be called 'Following Jesus, the Way'.

The imagery of the 'Way' dominates the Epistle. The Christian life is presented as a pilgrimage along the Way of the Old Israel from the Exodus (ch. 3) through temptation to Mount Zion (12.1, 22 f.). This is possible because the road has been finally opened up by Jesus the 'pioneer' (ἀρχηγός) and 'forerunner' (πρόδρομος). He is the architect of Israel (3.3.) because he is himself pre-eminently and uniquely 'Son' (3.6). *Mimesis* of this journey, which is undertaken in worship, is not a mere historical commemoration of the past, but is a veritable journey to heaven, because the Lord of heaven gave the historical journey for just this purpose. And so the author can say to his readers:

> You have come to Mount Zion and to the city of the living God, the heavenly Jerusalem, and to innumerable angels in festal gathering, and to the assembly of the first-born who are enrolled in heaven, and to a judge who is God of all, and to the spirits of just men made perfect, and to Jesus, the mediator of a new covenant (12.22–24).

---

[1] 'The whole pattern of the Christian life is conceived in terms of worship', W. Manson, *The Epistle to the Hebrews*, 1951, p. 67.

The mission of Jesus is seen by this writer as a final and perfect liturgical action. Jesus as High Priest has walked in the 'Way of the Lord' and reached the goal which is the presence of the Father. In this he is our precursor (6.20). He has not only by his life and teaching marked out the 'Way'; as the first along it he has opened and dedicated it. This he has done by fulfilling the Way of Israel himself:

The call of Israel. He was faithful to him who appointed him, just as Moses also was faithful in God's house (3.2).

Perfect Sonship. Every high priest chosen from among men is appointed to act on behalf of men in relation to God . . . So Christ did not exalt himself to be made a high priest, but was appointed by him who said to him:
'Thou art my Son,
    today I have begotten thee' (5.1, 5).

The temptation of Israel. We have not a high priest who is unable to sympathize with our weakness, but one who in every respect has been tempted as we are, yet without sinning (4.15).

Israel's vocation to obedience. Although he was a Son, he learned obedience through what he suffered; and being made perfect he became the source of eternal salvation to all who obey him (5.9).

Suffering and vindication. We see Jesus, who for a little while was made lower than the angels, crowned with glory and honour because of the suffering of death, so that by the grace of God he might taste death for every one (2.9).

Jesus also suffered outside the gate in order to sanctify the people through his own blood (13.12).

Jesus, . . . who for the joy that was set before him endured the cross, despising the shame, and is seated at the right hand of . . . God (12.2). When Christ had offered for all time a single sacrifice for sins, he sat down at the right hand of God (10.12).

Christians then are true Israelites embarked on the Way which Jesus has constructed for them. Their Way is a *mimesis* of this:

The Call. Therefore, holy brethren, who share in a heavenly call, consider Jesus, the apostle and high priest of our confession (3.1).

Temptation. Take care, brethren, lest there be in any of you an evil, unbelieving heart, leading you to fall away from the living God. But exhort one another every day, so long as it is called 'today', that none of you may be hardened by the deceitfulness of sin. For we share in Christ, if only we hold our first confidence firm to the end, while it is said,

'Today, when you hear his voice, do not
  harden your hearts as in the rebellion' (3.12–15).

Obedience. Let us therefore strive to enter that rest, that no one fall by
the same sort of disobedience (4.11; cf. 6.1–7).

Patience in suffering. You endured a hard struggle with sufferings
(10.32).

And they look forward in hope to the glory to come (13.14). A passage
which is both a good illustration of this theme and characteristic of the
Epistle as a whole is 10.19–22:

> Therefore, brethren, since we have confidence to enter the sanctuary by
> the blood of Jesus, by the new and living way which he opened for us
> through the curtain, that is, through his flesh, and since we have a
> great high priest over the house of God, let us draw near with a true
> heart in full assurance of faith, with our hearts spinkled clean from an
> evil conscience and our bodies washed with pure water.

Christ has parted the veil into the Father's presence, but he does not
simply let it fall together again after he has gone through. The particular
pattern of the Christian life is only possible as the fruit of his redemptive
act. Jesus has penetrated to heaven, but only so that we should follow. He
has preceded us only to make our 'introductions', as it were. He beckons
over his shoulder to the long line of the pilgrims of the 'Way' who now
begin to make the journey after him. Both the Son and the 'sons' walk
together on this 'Way',[1] closely associated in a unique solidarity in the
same pilgrimage. This union with the ἀρχηγός, this solidarity, is such
that the author identified the way into the holy place (9.8) with Jesus
himself. The Way is 'dedicated' because it leads to God; it is 'new' because it has just been opened by Jesus, and it is 'living' because it is
Christ himself. *Vita tua, via nostra.* The Way not only leads to beatitude;
it is living and active in guiding and carrying those who are on it. This
unique and intimate relation to Christ the author thinks of in a way
similar to St Paul. Christians are 'partakers' of Christ (μέτοχοι τοῦ
Χριστοῦ, 3.14). As with both St Paul and St John, this relationship is
brought into being and sustained by the Spirit (6.4).

The life of the Christian as *imitatio Christi* is grounded, for the author
of the Epistle to the Hebrews, in the liturgy. Here the basic motions of
the *mimesis* of Christ are gone through in significant fashion, because
therein the Spirit is at work making subject and object truly μέτοχοι.
This writer, like St John, writes of the Christ he has contemplated and

---

[1] Here come the Shepherd and the sheep, 13.20.

known in the liturgy. He is the one writer in the New Testament who gives explicit instructions to contemplate Christ: 'Therefore, holy brethren, who share in a heavenly call, consider the apostle and high priest of our confession' (3.1); '. . . looking to Jesus the pioneer and perfecter of our faith. . . . Consider him who endured from sinners such hostility' (12.2 f.).

There is also a suggestion in the Epistle that the author shared St Paul's conception of the *imitatio Christi* through *mimesis* of apostolic ministers and fellow-Christians:

> . . . so that you may not be sluggish, but imitators of those who through faith and patience inherit the promises (6.12).

> Remember your leaders, who spoke to you the word of God; consider the outcome of their life, and imitate their faith (13.7).

> Let us consider how to stir one another up to love and good works (10.24).

The fact that the significance of the person and work of Christ are presented by this writer in terms of liturgical action suggests that worship occupied a central and indispensable place in the thought of the author, and the Epistle is in fact a good example of liturgical mysticism. It would seem that it was in the Christian assembly that this author was most deeply aware of the presentness of Jesus Christ, the same yesterday, today and forever. It is there that the key moments of the history of Israel become contemporaneous for the Christian; they are 'today' for him.[1] The Way of the historical Israel and the Way of the historical Jesus are blended in a profound awareness of the eternal Son in Godhead.

But the liturgical pattern needs to be filled out in personal life, and here the marks of the Christian life as *imitatio Christi* are similar to those we have noticed in St Paul: ἀγάπη, particularly towards the stranger (13.2) and the slave, and reverence for the marriage relationship (13.4).

---

[1] Cf. Heb. 3, especially vv. 13–15.

EPILOGUE

The vision claims nothing but worship; and worship
is a surrender to the claim for assimilation, urged with
the motive force of mutual love. The vision never
overrules.

A. N. WHITEHEAD

I I

The Imitation of Christ in Christian Doctrine, Devotion and Evangelism

The gist of religion is imitation of him who is worshipped.[1]
God is comprehended not by investigation but by imitation.[2]

SOME YEARS AGO Professor C. H. Dodd wrote: 'It is probable that the idea of the *imitatio Christi* had more to say than is commonly recognized by critics in the selection of incidents from the life of Jesus for record in the gospels.'[3] I think it likely that further study will show that Dodd was right, and that this motif has in fact determined many of the features of the Gospel tradition as it has been handled by all four evangelists. The consistently enigmatical character of St Mark's Gospel[4] (particularly if one holds that it ended at 16.8) may well reflect the conviction of the evangelist that the manner of writing the Gospel of Christ was inseparable from the duty of being faithful to the methods of Jesus himself as the 'sign of the Son of Man'. For St Mark, it would seem, the manner of Christian evangelism was indicated by the very character of the mission of Jesus. In St Luke's Gospel and the Acts, as we have seen, the influence of the idea of the imitation of Christ is clearly evident in the way in which discipleship and apostleship are there presented. The influence of the same motif on St Matthew's Gospel has been conveniently summarized by Professor Otto Weber. He writes: 'Matthew tells us more about the disciples than Mark. In the discourse relating to their mission (a conflation of several sources) he desires to show how in their activity the mighty works of Jesus are continued. The mission springs from the Lord's compassion with the harassed and helpless people (9.36). Just as He himself—before the cross—confined His ministry to the "lost sheep of the house of Israel" (15.24) so the disciples too are enjoined to keep within these limits (10.5 ff.). As His own teaching brings about a discrimination between

---

[1] '*Religionis summa imitari quem colis*', St Augustine, *De Civitate Dei*, VIII, 17.
[2] *Deus non comprehenditur per investigationem sed per imitationem,* Hugh of St Cher.
[3] *The Johannine Epistles,* p. 85. [4] Cf. p. 88 above.

men, so does theirs (10.11 ff.). As in His own works of healing He identifies Himself with the cause of the sick and proves His authority by the
casting out of demons, so must they do (10.8). As He found nothing but
opposition, they too must reckon with it (10.16 ff.). Just as the Master
"has nowhere to lay his head" (8.20) so the disciples are to be poor
(10.9, 10), wholly abandoned to God, and for that very reason fearless
(10.26 ff.). They belong utterly to Him, His honour is their honour
(10.32 ff.), but also His cross is their cross (10.34 ff., especially 10.38 ff.).
We see how all this forms the prototype for the coming Christian community. If the early believers are called "Christians" (Acts 11.26), this
means that they participate fully and unreservedly in what Christ is and
does.'[1] In St John's Gospel we can easily detect the deliberate parallelism
between the Father-Son relationship and that of Jesus and the disciple,
and there is also a tendency in this Gospel, as we have noted, to give concrete exemplars of the imitation of Christ.

If the motif of the *imitatio Christi* arose *ab initio* in the primitive Christian communities, then we have advanced no further than the form-critics
in our study of Christian origins. The shape and content of the Gospel
tradition would then be the result entirely of the demands of the mission
of the early Church. It is more probable, however, that the idea of the
imitation of God held a central place in the mind and purpose of Jesus
himself along the lines which we have indicated in this book, and if that
is the case history has exercised an important control over the creative
features of primitive Christian evangelism and teaching. It is true, as the
form-critics pointed out, that behind the whole of the New Testament
literature there were the Christian communities engaged in the three
activities which, it was alleged, were notorious for modifying or even dis-
torting the facts: preaching, teaching and liturgy. But if the concept of
imitation held the important place in the mind of Jesus which we have
suggested, both in relation to himself and his disciples, then we can go
further than form-criticism and point to an influence which controlled
the preaching, teaching and liturgy of the early Church, and prevented
them from being the instruments of elaboration and fabrication to the
extent that used to be supposed. The early Christians did not believe that
the *kerygma* was something which they possessed and were free to modify
according to their own fancy. On the contrary, the *kerygma* was something
which possessed them: the *kerygma* of the Lord himself who proclaimed
the Gospel through them (II Cor. 5.20) by the Spirit. Behind the *didache*
of the early Church there stood the Lord himself who, through the Spirit,

[1] *Ground Plan of the Bible*, ET 1959, pp. 122 f.

instructed them in the things pertaining to himself. And in the early Christian assembly for the Breaking of the Bread the Lord shaped his Body, so that therein his death was proclaimed till he should come. These three activities have been 'historified' because of the powerful attraction towards the original events exercised by the *imitatio Christi* motif, which involved the Christian in a going over the sacred 'Way' of Christ, particularly his passion, crucifixion and resurrection.

It has sometimes been objected that the idea that Jesus mimed certain features of Old Testament history introduces a note of artificiality into his mission, and suggests a lack of spontaneity. 'There is an essential weakness', writes Professor J. K. S. Reid, 'in thinking that either our Lord or the evangelists understood the Old Testament as no more than an earlier model which requires to be copied by the Saviour of the world when he comes.'[1] As we have seen, however, the *mimesis* in the ministry of Jesus is not of this external and artificial kind. The mission of Jesus, as he himself conceived it, was not simply to *repeat* (and copy in that sense) the history of Israel in some mimetic way, but to realize it afresh in terms of his own life, obedience and work. Further, the *mimesis* of Jesus looked not only to the past, but to the future. The *mimesis* of Jesus contained both historical and eschatological elements. The Israel realized before men's eyes in the ministry of Jesus was not only the Israel of the past, but also the Israel to come (and this would include the Gentiles). The imitation which is creative is always selective, and it is in the selection made by Jesus from the life of the Old Israel for personal embodiment in his own ministry that we must look for his uniqueness. Jesus was not simply a copyist, but a creative artist, in relation to his nation's history.

The New Testament treatment of the idea of the imitation of Christ has important bearings on the study of Christian doctrine and mysticism. This is a large subject to which I hope to return in a subsequent work, and it is only appropriate now to make some brief comment.

A good deal has been written in denigration of the 'exemplarist' interpretation of the Atonement, and the effect of this has been to create suspicion about the legitimacy of the idea of the imitation of Christ in the Christian life. Of course a bare exemplarism is inadequate as an expression of the redeeming work of Christ, and the defects of it have often been pointed out, perhaps never more succinctly than by St Bernard of Clairvaux:

Three principal things I perceive in this work of our salvation: the pattern of humility, in which God emptied himself; the measure of

[1] *The Authority of Scripture*, 1957, p. 265.

M

love, which he stretched even unto death, and that the death of the cross; the mystery of redemption in which he bore that death which he underwent. The two former of these without the last are as if you were to paint on the air. A very great and most necessary example of humility, a great example of charity and one worthy of all acceptation he has set us; but they have no foundation and, therefore, no stability, if redemption be wanting. I wish to follow with my strength the lowly Jesus; I wish him who loved me and gave himself for me to embrace me with the arms of his love, which suffered in my stead: but I must also feed on the Paschal Lamb, for unless I eat his flesh and drink his blood I have no life in me. It is one thing to follow Jesus, another to hold him, another to feed on him—neither the example of humility, nor the proofs of charity are anything without the mystery (*sacramentum*) of our redemption.[1]

Here the imitation of Christ is safeguarded from the excesses of 'exemplarism' by the insistence upon the prior fact of redemption upon which it all depends, and the emphasis upon the Eucharist ensures that this will not be forgotten or neglected. Set in this context, the imitation of Christ is not only compatible with essential Christian atonement doctrine but is an indispensable consequence of it. As Professor H. E. W. Turner has put it:

Even the most rigidly objective doctrine of the Cross must leave room for the *Imitatio Christi* at least as a corollary or a consequent.[2]

This insistence that the Christian's imitation of Christ is only a possibility because of the redemptive work of Christ we have seen to be one of the main features of the New Testament presentation of this theme.

The concept of the imitation of Christ also focuses attention on the reality of the Incarnation, and takes the consequences of that great fact with the utmost seriousness. A docetic or monophysite Christology obscures the central place which the historical Incarnation and the historical ministry of Jesus have in the thought and devotion of the Christian. The imitation of Christ in the New Testament is no amorphous spirituality, but gladly accepts the form of the Church and the lives of fellow-Christians as the means whereby the *mimesis* of the Lord's paradigmatic life is wrought in actuality.

The imitative life of the Christian does not injure his individuality or his creativity. Through the work of the Holy Spirit the relationship between the historical paradigm of the Lord's life and the Christian imitator is active and reciprocal. The Lord who shaped the form of his historical

[1] *Treatise against the Errors of Abelard* (=*Epistle* 190), ch. 9, *PL* 182, 1072.
[2] *The Patristic Doctrine of Redemption*, 1952, p. 117.

ministry shapes the form of his follower's through the personal and creative work of the Holy Spirit. This aspect of the Christian life as imitation of Christ has been well described by Dr E. L. Mascall:

> The Christian life does not consist of an external imitation of the character and actions of Jesus of Nazareth or of an external obedience to his commands; those are its fruits, not its roots. In its essence, it is the reproduction of Christ in us, or, viewing it from the opposite aspect, it is our continual and progressive fashioning into him. The Christian virtues are nothing less than the manifestation of Christ in his members, and because their incorporation into him is their incorporation into the Church which is his body and his bride, there can be no contradiction between life in Christ and life in the Church. Personal sanctification is an intensely corporate and churchly act; being built up in Christ is being built up in the Church.[1]

A similar insistence that the Christian imitation of Christ is not a slavish literal mimicry is made by Dr T. W. Manson:

> The teaching of Jesus in the fullest and deepest sense is Jesus himself, and the best Christian living has always been in some sort an imitation of Christ; not a slavish copying of his acts but the working of his mind and spirit in new contexts of life and circumstance.[2]

It is just because the New Testament idea of the imitation of Christ is grounded in the historical Incarnation and Atonement that it is safeguarded from any tendency to become a doctrine of works or a denial of grace in a way which is not true when men have been summoned to the imitation of God. Dean Inge has spoken of the dangers inherent in the latter idea:

> The error comes in . . . when we set before ourselves the idea of God the Father, or of the Absolute, instead of Christ, as the object of imitation . . . Mystics of all times would have done well to keep in their minds a very happy phrase which Irenaeus quotes from some unknown author: 'He spoke well who said that the infinite (*immensum*) Father is measured (*mensuratum*) in the Son, *mensura enim Patris Filius*.' It is to this measure, not to the immeasurable, that we are bidden to aspire.[3]

In this connection it is not without significance that, as we have seen, the whole tendency in the history of the idea of the imitation of God is towards the individual concrete exemplar. It looks as if the need for a visible model is a basic feature of human growth and development, and the Christian sees this need, among others, perfectly and uniquely fulfilled in his Lord Christ.

---

[1] *Christ, the Christian and the Church*, 1946, p. 205.
[2] *The Sayings of Jesus*, p. 9.   [3] W. R. Inge, *Christian Mysticism*, 1899, p. 193.

Further, the imitation of Christ as presented in the New Testament is not an isolated devotion to Jesus as the believer's model hero. It is the central part of the Christian's Trinitarian devotion. Through the imitation of Christ he realizes his union with the Son and shares with him the adoration of the Father through the Spirit in Godhead itself, in a proleptic way, even while still *in via*. It is this imitation of Christ which has always been distinctive of the mysticism which is uniquely and authentically Christian.

Finally, the Christian life as imitation of Christ commits the believer to obedience to the 'method' of Jesus. The Incarnation is seen by the Christian as the way God would have his truth taught, and this same manner must be reflected in any presentation of the Gospel of the Incarnation. The form of the presentation of the Gospel is part of its content, and therefore any manner of evangelism which is in fundamental contradiction to the mode of revelation given us in the Incarnation would constitute a *skandalon* of the wrong kind. The distinctive and normative method of evangelism laid upon the Church is that of the *semeion*, and the nearest analogy is the method of the artist.[1] God chose the method of the 'sign' because that way alone preserves human freedom and responsibility intact, and the Church and the Christian may not use any procedure which is incompatible with the revealed manner of God. Not all the methods at the disposal of the modern propagandist may be used legitimately by the Church or the Christian. Evangelism is distinct from the type of propaganda which will go to any lengths to secure its point. The naked and unscrupulous use by the latter of the method of the *teras* is prohibited to the Christian who seeks to walk in the 'Way' of his Lord. In so far as the Church follows this 'Way' in faith and obedience, she can be certain that this faithful imitation will be taken by her Lord and, through the Spirit, transformed by him into a *semeion* of himself, and than this there can be no greater contentment either for the Church or for the Christian.

[1] I have developed this point in an essay, 'The Incarnation, Art and Evangelism', in *The Church and the Arts* (SCM Press, 1960).

INDEXES

INDEX OF NAMES

INDEX OF BIBLICAL REFERENCES

OLD TESTAMENT

NEW TESTAMENT